Home and Community for Queer Men of Color

Home and Community for Queer Men of Color

The Intersection of Race and Sexuality

Edited by
Jesús Gregorio Smith and C. Winter Han

LEXINGTON BOOKS
Lanham • Boulder • New York • London

Published by Lexington Books
An imprint of The Rowman & Littlefield Publishing Group, Inc.
4501 Forbes Boulevard, Suite 200, Lanham, Maryland 20706
www.rowman.com

6 Tinworth Street, London SE11 5AL, United Kingdom

British Library Cataloguing in Publication Information Available

Library of Congress Cataloging-in-Publication Data Available

ISBN 978-1-4985-8229-2 (cloth)
ISBN 978-1-4985-8231-5 (pbk)
ISBN 978-1-4985-8230-8 (electronic)

Contents

Introduction

Home Is Where the Heart Is: Invisibility and Marginalization for Queer Men of Color

Jesús Gregorio Smith

A house is much more than a home. It's family.

—Pray Tell in *Pose*,
Season 1: "Mother of the Year"

This quote comes from the FX series *Pose* (2018), a series about queer Black and Latino gay and trans people living in New York during the 1980s ball scene. Here, the character Pray Tell, a queer, HIV positive, Black man, grapples with the reality of what makes a home for the people so often rejected from their families. The reality is that for queer men of color, finding a home is no easy feat. If family is meant to be home, what does it mean when your home, filled with people of color, doesn't recognize you as its own? If family is meant to be home, what does it mean when your home of sexual minorities rejects you based on your gender performance, race, or class status? Pray Tell, who is also the master of ceremonies during the Balls, loses his Latino lover to AIDS early on in the series. He becomes close friends with the series protagonist Blanca as well as with her "children" in the house of Evangelista, as racism, poverty, and death help them make a home for themselves and create family among each other, healing many of Pray Tell's wounds. Pray Tell's story arch signifies how queer people of color find home and make family in a world that rejects them for either their race or sexuality, or both. The fictional world of *Pose* provides some relief to its viewers that despite the struggle of poverty, the pain of racism and the hatred of homophobia, there is hope. This hope is necessary because outside of the fantasy of television, racism and homophobia have prospered. An example of this can be found in the contrasting stories of two famous Black men, Kevin Hart and Michael Sam.

A TALE OF TWO BLACK MEN

Comedian Kevin Hart pulled himself out of the running to be the host for the 2019 Academy Awards after the academy requested that he apologize for homophobic jokes he made in the past. The jokes in question ranged from him saying, "As a heterosexual male, if I can prevent my son from being gay, I will," to how if he saw his son playing with a dollhouse, he would tell him to "stop, that's gay" and break the toy over his head (Owens 2019). Hart argued he already apologized several times for the incident and felt like the bringing up of old tweets was a staged attack on the comedian's career. Black musician and actor Nick Cannon came to Hart's aid by bringing up past homophobic tweets made by White comedians who didn't receive a backlash such as Amy Schumer, Sarah Silverman, and Chelsea Handler (Owens 2019). While the conversation around the issue accurately revealed the double standard placed on Black actors and comedians for their homophobic behavior that is not imposed on White performers, and while highlighted the flaws in the stereotype of the homophobic Black man, left out of much of the conversation was the way sexual minorities, such as Black lesbian, gay, bisexual, trans (LGBT), and queer people feel marginalized in different mainstream Black communities.

An investigation by Vulture could not find any actual apologies from Hart (Wright 2019). Even though Cannon does come to Hart's defense, he does not in fact come to the aid of the many LGBT people who were ostracized and stigmatized by the jokes. In fact, jokes made about Black people by non-black people are appropriately seen as highly inappropriate at the very least if not downright racist. Unfortunately, this same compassion is not extended to queer people for homophobic or transphobic jokes. The lack of compassion for sexual and gendered minorities, despite the similarities between the communities, is troubling precisely because LGBT people of color who experience racism in the gay community and society at large might look for acceptance from their larger racial community, only to find it lacking and their identities made invisible. This is not to suggest that homophobia or transphobia in racial communities is a greater issue than in society at large, but that the addition of other forms of marginalization only increases the vulnerability of already stigmatized communities.

While the case of Kevin Hart illuminates the way that LGBT people are marginalized, stigmatized, and erased in heterosexual spaces, the story of Michael Sam presents a different case entirely. Michael Sam is a Black athlete and the first openly gay player to be drafted by the National Football League (NFL) (Greenberg 2014). Many anticipated that Sam would be drafted within the first three rounds. He was eventually drafted in the seventh. Once he was drafted, he embraced his White boyfriend at the time and kissed him, solidifying a historical moment in LGBT progress. It didn't take much time for things to change. Not much after his initial drafting in the NFL, Sam was eventually cut from the league with many people feeling underline issues of homophobia as the main reason (Ziegler 2014). Still, many in the LGBT community celebrated this historical moment of having a gay man in the heterosexual bastion: the NFL.

Despite Sam's cut from the league and embrace by the LGBT community as an icon of progress, Sam did express feeling like racism was a bigger issue in the LGBT community than homophobia in the straight Black community. In an interview with *Attitude* magazine, Sam touched on the topic of racism in the gay community, stating:

> It's terrible. People have told me I'm not gay enough, people have told me I'm not black enough. I don't know what that means. You want to be accepted by other people but you don't even accept someone just because of the colour of their skin? I just don't understand that at all. How are you saying that, "oh, I want people to accept me because I'm gay but I don't accept you because you're black, or because you're white or because you're Asian." (Sam 2016)

For Sam, the language around preference in terms of racial partners and the idea of acceptance in the gay community contradict each other (Smith 2017; Callander, Holt, and Newman 2012). In this sense, he cannot see how the LGBT community, which frames itself as a place where people can "come out" and "be their authentic selves" can also use race to reject other people. Like the Hart scenario, people of color are erased in the gay community as well.

Both the Hart and the Sam cases present complicated scenarios regarding race and sexuality. While Hart's homophobia marginalized LGBT people, White lesbian comic and television star, Ellen DeGeneres, came to Hart's aid, accepting his apology and legitimizing it. While Sam disparaged the racism in gay communities, LGBT people celebrated him as a gay icon while arguably it was the homophobia in the NFL that resulted in him being cut. Both these stories show how imminent issues of race and sexuality are today, how intimately tied to one another they are, and how, as a result of racism in one community and homophobia in another, gay men of color lack a space for themselves, one that they can call home.

The issues presented in both Hart's homophobia and Sam's experiences with racism have been well documented. Scholars of color have detailed the way homophobia in communities of color has left queer men of color to feel unaccepted and less "ethnic" while racism in gay communities has left them feeling rejected because of their race or only desired for their race (Loiacano 1989; Han 2007). In recent decades, queer scholarship and scholarship on race have begun to examine what it means to be raced and/or sexed in the United States. Yet despite this movement, both queer studies and ethnic studies have often overlooked the existence of gay men of color. In a quest for "legitimacy," both movements have looked for ways to legitimize their existence against the backdrop of White, heterosexual America, one group through a shared race, the other through a shared sexuality. As such, "gay" has come to mean "white" while "people of color" has come to mean "straight" and the existence of gay men of color has simply been footnoted (Teunis 2007). Not surprising then, writings by gay men and women of color have pointed to this invisibility in both sexual and ethnic communities (Smith and Morales 2018; Callander, Holt, and Newman 2016; Ibañez et al. 2009; Liu 2015). Reflecting on being Black and gay in San Francisco, Marlon Riggs noted in *Tongues Untied*:

> I pretend not to notice the absence of black images in this new gay life, in book-stores, poster shops, film festivals, even my own fantasies. . . . In this great, gay mecca, I was an invisible man. (Riggs 1989)

Likewise, in ethnic communities, gay men and women are also invisible as Russell Leong wrote in *Asian American Sexualities*:

> In the United States, the myth of Asian Americans as a homogeneous, het-erosexual "model minority" population since the 1960s has worked against exploration into the varied nature of our sexual drives and gendered diversity. (Leong 1996)

Not surprising then, in looking for a gay Asian identity, Eric Reyes asks exactly where it is that we should be searching, "The Eurocentric and het-erosexual male-dominated America, the white gay male-centered Queer America, the marginalized People of Color (POC) America, or our often-romanticized Asian America?" (Reyes 1996). This collection of works attempts to answer the questions, where do gay men of color find a "home" and what kind of home do they find? If home is where the heart is, and our racial and sexual communities lack the heart for queer men of color, then where is and what is our home? In answering these questions, our desire is to examine how gay men of color come to make sense of race and sexuality and how their experiences reflect what it means to be raced and sexed in North America.

Of course, in discussing "gay men of color" it is important to point out that this group includes people with vastly different backgrounds along every imaginable social delineation. Care should be taken when referencing the experiences of this "group." At the same time, it is important to point out that as both racially and sexually marginalized groups, they all confront levels of racism and heterosexism that is practiced by the larger ethnic and sexual communities that use White heterosexuality as the "norm" to which all others are compared. Our interest in this book is to point out that, despite different constructions of race and ethnicity, there are similar themes for racialized groups that need to be explored.

CHAPTER BREAK DOWN

In what follows, each scholar or group of scholars examines the way race and sexuality impact the life of queer people of color. As such, the chapters are grouped around different themes that all attempt to answer these questions. To grapple with how race and sexuality reflect what it means to be raced and sexed in society, each section of chapters explores how "home" is represented in each context. Therefore, the anthology is sectioned into four groups: racialized and sexualized desires to capture what it means when your home is your body and your body is either desired or rejected; queer of color and education to make sense of race and sexuality in what many people consider their home away from home, schools, and universities; queer location to explore the way that home is created or transformed through space and geography; and last, how race and sexuality impact one's identity, and what home houses such an identity.

Our bodies and our intimate desires frame the first set of chapters. If one makes a home within himself, what does it mean when he is rejected based on the race of his body? In other words, how does the experience of racial rejection in sexual preferences and racial sexual desire shape the lives of queer men. Jason Crockett tackles this topic in his chapter. Crockett examines the development and expression of what he calls racial sexual orientation or erotic attractions and responsiveness based on race. He finds that race, like gender, plays a fundamental role in social classification and power suggesting that race, in terms of social classification and power, should not be ignored. C. Winter Han and Scott E. Rutledge continue the theme in their chapter as well. Here, both scholars accept that there is recognition of racism in the gay community but point out that less work has been done to explore the *nature* of that racism for gay men of color. Unlike other scholars, they emphasize White gay men as the perpetuators of this racism and maintainers of racial inequality in the gay community.

Schools and universities are home for many people as they spend a considerable amount of time there. Yet, what does it mean if your school and its curriculum don't include you? In Michael Bartone's chapter, he addresses just that. Bartone understands that one's intersecting racial and sexual identity is something Black queer youth must face that their White queer peers do not confront. As such, his chapter focuses on the schooling narratives of five Black gay youth growing up in metro-Atlanta, often considered the Black Gay Mecca, in a time where the Black gay community was becoming much more visible in society, particularly through representations on television. Building on research examining fraternities, Manuel Del Real's chapter attempts to fill in the gap within research that looks at how sexuality shapes and is shaped by these organizations. His chapter explores how five gay/queer members of Sigma Lambda Beta International Fraternity Inc., the largest Latino-based fraternity in the United States, find a home within an ethnic, cis, and heteronormative brotherhood.

The phrase "home is where the heart is" implies that wherever one finds comfort and love, regardless of space and location, that is their home. In the next section of chapters, space, geography, and location take center stage. Jason Orne tracks the transformation of a sexual minority enclave due to rising social acceptance, acculturation, and assimilation, and the sexual and racial consequences of that transformation. Drawing on an in-depth ethnography of Chicago's Boystown gay neighborhood, he is able to see how this transformation has radically changed the sexual culture of Boystown, replacing queer sexual culture (e.g., acceptance of multiple partners, casual sex, and public sexuality) with hegemonic straight sexual norms. This assimilation has had racial consequences: hardening racial divisions, positioning the neighborhood as White, and queer men of color as outsiders. Shinsuke Eguchi's chapter exemplifies how their relocation to the southwest for their academic job offers them an additional opportunity to question, struggle with, and renegotiate the performative rhetoric of gay and Asian/American. By situating their chapter in the genealogy of queerness and queer autoethnography, they critique the rhetoric around being Asian and American through feeling suffocated by the present; missing the past; and bringing the past into the future. Sulaimon Giwa, Kofi Norsah, and Ferzana Chaze, using qualitative thematic analysis, interview six English-speaking Black gay men in Montréal, Canada, who had emigrated from sub-Saharan African and Caribbean countries. Applying the theory of intersectionality to their data, they examine racism and homophobia and the impact of immigration on the health and well-being of racialized LGB immigrants. Their findings highlighted how participants negotiated the confluence of social discriminatory experiences and emphasized the importance of health and social service providers meeting clients where they are in their lives.

In the last section of chapters, how race and sexuality impact identity and how that then influences what is considered home is explored. Jesús Smith looks at the criminal case of gay, Black, HIV-positive wrestler Michael "Tiger Mandingo" Johnson, who was charged with recklessly infecting other gay men with HIV. By embracing a pro-Black male identity in the stereotype of the Mandingo and making a home with other Black gay men in the House of Mizrahi, Smith argues that Johnson inadvertently made himself more vulnerable to anti-Black misandry from the state. Using the man-not thesis and a queer of color critique as a framework, Smith illuminates how the trial reified heteronormativity by stereotyping Johnson as a threat not only to gay White men but straight White people who perceive pro-Black men as threats to the social order. Last, Mario Suarez explores how transitioning from a Latina lesbian into a cisgender transgender man of color has shaped the way he navigates queer spaces and how he feels he is perceived in these spaces. Informed by Gloria Anzaldúa's (2015) notion of shape-shifting as a means to better explain the spaces he comes in and out of as a means of survival, Suarez answers the questions, how is it that I am perceived now as co-opting the very space that made me feel safe as a young adult and why is it that I do not feel welcome anymore in the community I am a part of? The answers to such questions call us to think beyond the binaries of Black and White and male and female but to instead reconsider how we fit in places we once called "home."

A PLACE TO CALL HOME

While this collection is not exhaustive, it presents a unique look into race and sexuality in the lives of queer people. Much like the case of Kevin Hart and Michael Sam, the fusion of race and sexuality does not create clearly defined boundaries but leaves them messy and incomplete. Hart's rejection of his son if he were gay might have been a joke to him but is the reality of many queer people who feel rejected from their racial communities. Yet, even then, a White lesbian woman came to his aid, blurring the boundaries of homophobia and acceptance. Michael Sam could have been that little boy Kevin Hart rejected but instead it was the gay community he felt rejection from and the Black community where he got acceptance. Nonetheless, homophobia cut him from the NFL while queer people made him a gay icon, once again blurring the boundaries between race and sexuality. With both cases, we see how queer people of color can be embraced and rejected simultaneously. More importantly, like Pray Tell in *Pose* (2018), we see how on the margins of race and sexuality, queers of color make a space for themselves to call home.

REFERENCES

Callander, Denton, Martin Holt and Christy E. Newman. 2016. "'Not Everyone's Gonna like Me': Accounting for Race and Racism in Sex and Dating Web Services for Gay and Bisexual Men." *Ethnicities* 16 (1): 3–21. https://doi.org/10.1177/1 468796815581428.

Callander, Denton, Martin Holt and Christy E. Newman. 2012. "Just a Preference: Racialised Language in the Sex-Seeking Profiles of Gay and Bisexual Men." *Culture, Health & Sexuality* 14 (9): 1049–63. https://doi.org/10.1080/13691058.20 12.714799.

Greenberg, Chris. 2014. "Michael Sam is the First Openly Gay Football Player Drafted into the NFL." *Huffington Post*, May 10, 2014. https://www.huffpost.com/entry/michael-sam-drafted-rams_n_5298968.

Han, C. Winter. 2007. "They Don't Want To Cruise Your Type: Gay Men of Color and the Racial Politics of Exclusion." *Social Identities* 13 (1): 51–67. https://do i.org/10.1080/13504630601163379.

Horder-Payton, Gwyneth, dir. 2018. *Pose.*, Season 1, Episode 8, "Mother of the Year." Aired July 22, 2018 on FX.

Ibañez, Gladys E., Barbara Van Oss Marin, Stephen A. Flores, Gregorio Millett and Rafael M. Diaz. 2009. "General and Gay-Related Racism Experienced by Latino Gay Men." *Cultural Diversity & Ethnic Minority Psychology* 15 (3): 215–22. https://doi.org/10.1037/a0014613.

Leong, Russell. 1996. "Home Bodies and the Body Politic." *Asian American Sexualities: Dimensions of the Gay and Lesbian Experience*: 1–20. New York: Routledge.

Liu, Xiaofei. 2015. "No Fats, Femmes, or Asians." *Moral Philosophy and Politics* 2 (2): 255–76. https://doi.org/10.1515/mopp-2014-0023.

Loiacano, Darryl K. 1989. "Gay Identity Issues among Black Americans: Racism, Homophobia, and the Need for Validation." *Journal of Counseling Psychology* 68 (1): 21–24.

Owens, Ernest. 2019. "Kevin Hart's Oscars Controversy Feeds the Stereotype of the Black Homophobe." *Vox Online*, January 7, 2019. https://www.vox.com/first-pers on/2018/12/11/18134366/kevin-hart-resigns-homophobic-tweet-oscars-2018-elle n-degeneres.

Reyes, Eric Estuar. 1996. "Strategies for Queer Asian and Pacific Islander Spaces." *Asian American Sexualities: Dimensions of the Gay and Lesbian Experience*: 85–90. New York: Routledge.

Riggs, Marion. 2008. *Tongues Untied*. Motion Picture. Directed by Marion Riggs. USA: Strand Releasing.

Sam, Michael. 2016. "Michael Sam Opens Up About 'Terrible Racism in the Gay Community'." *Attitude* magazine, March 31, 2016. https://attitude.co.uk/article/michael-sam-opens-up-about-terrible-racism-in-the-gay-community/10219/.

Smith, Jesús Gregorio. 2017. "Two-Faced Racism in Gay Online Sex: Preferences in the Frontstage or Racism in the Backstage." *Sex in the Digital Age* 1: 134–46. New York: Routledge.

Smith, Jesús Gregorio and Maria Cristina Morales. 2018. "Racial Constructions among Men Who Have Sex with Men: The Utility of the Latin Americanization Thesis and Colorblind Racism on Sexual Partner Selection." *Issues in Race and Society: An Interdisciplinary Global Journal* 6 (1): 25–44.

Teunis, Niels. 2007. "Sexual Objectification and the Construction of Whiteness in the Gay Male Community." *Culture, Health & Sexuality* 9 (3): 263–75. https://doi.org /10.1080/13691050601035597.

Wright, Megh. 2019. "Where Are Kevin Hart's Past Apologies? An Investigation." *Vulture*, January 4, 2019. https://www.vulture.com/2019/01/kevin-hart-homopho bic-tweets-apologies-ellen-degeneres.html.

Zeigler, Cyd. 2014. "Michael Sam's NFL Snub Already at Historic Level." Out-Sports.com. November 4, 2014. https://www.outsports.com/2014/11/4/7152717/m ichael-sam-nfl-draft-snub-gay.

Chapter 1

"Damn, I'm Dating a Lot of White Guys"

Gay Men's Individual Narratives of Racial Sexual Orientation Development

Jason Crockett

Although the literature devoted to understanding sexuality has grown significantly in the past twenty years, it has focused almost exclusively on the development and expression of erotic attractions and responsiveness based on gender. Although there is acknowledgment in the literature of diverse erotic and romantic preferences, less attention has been paid to other ways sexuality is organized. This research examines the development and expression of racial sexual orientation (that is, erotic attractions and responsiveness based on race). Race presents an interesting case because, like gender, it plays a fundamental, if notorious, role in social classification and power. While there are arguably good reasons to afford gender a special status in regard to sexuality, the role of race in social classification and power suggests that preferences in regard to it should not be ignored.

BACKGROUND AND PREVIOUS RESEARCH

The existence of sexual and romantic partner preferences that take race into account is itself established. In analogy to a predominant focus on explaining same-gender rather than opposite-gender attractions, preferences for a different race are more likely to be noticed and accounted for because they fall outside of social norms (Cutrone 2000). Therefore I focus my attention on cross-race attractions and interracial relationships as an initial approach to investigation of development of racial sexual orientation. Although interracial relationships do not necessarily imply racial sexual orientation, studies

1

of interracial relationships sometimes touch on the existence of race-based preferences as one reason for their existence. In addition, studies of gay male subculture have noted existence of terms referring to racial sexual partner preferences as well as historical existence of a handful of organizations for men who prefer interracial relationships. Finally, while the literature on sexual development does not directly deal with racial sexual orientation, its treatment of gendered sexual orientation provides theoretical insights and a methodological model to aid in their investigation.

Interracial Relationships and Racial Sexual Orientation

Research on interracial committed relationships has tended to focus on how racial and gender inequalities and prejudices affect mate choice. Interracial relationships make up only 6 to 12 percent of all married and cohabiting couples, in part because a "unitary system of heterosexual same-race marriage [has] been assiduously maintained since colonial times" and has only recently begun to "fray" (Rosenfeld and Kim 2005, 559). Law, custom and "traditional" beliefs, residential segregation and suburbanization, and direct interventions by communities and families have all historically supported this system.

A popular explanation for the phenomenon of interracial relationships (usually focusing on the case of black-white relationships) has been based on exchange theory, in which whites of low socioeconomic status marry blacks of higher socioeconomic status in exchange for an improvement in racial caste position. However, Rosenfeld's (2005) recent critique of this theory uses demographic data to demonstrate that status homogamy is the norm among interracial couples. His conclusion resonates not only with what we know about relationships in general, but also with a long history of ethnographic findings (Du Bois 1899; Porterfield 1978; Root 2001; Spickard 1989) that interracial relationships are based in "solidarity and affection and personal choice, not . . . exchanges" (Rosenfeld 2005, 1320).

Long before Rosenfeld, Freeman (1955) interviewed University of Hawaii students who expressed preferences for dating and marriage partners outside of their own race or ethnicity. More recent studies of interracial relationships also frequently acknowledge that such relationships are not always simply "happenstance" but often the result of racial preferences (Chow 2000; Cutrone 2000; Lockman 1984; McDermit 1980; Scott 1994; Twine 1996b). While racial partner preferences in interracial relationship studies are only sometimes explicitly about sexual desires, at least one study confirms that racial sexual preferences do factor into interracial dating. Kaplan (2004) found that high ratings of "typical" physical attractiveness for another racial category predicted an interracial dating history.

What is considered attractive is influenced by the racial hierarchy. At best, minorities (and particularly blacks) may be seen as "inappropriate" dating and marital partners; at worst, they may be seen as dangerous and deviant (Frankenberg 1993; Grant 2018; Smith, Morales, and Han 2018; Twine 1996a; Yancey 2003). The "natural" superiority of white characteristics is so culturally dominant that standards of physical beauty in the United States tend to be Eurocentric even within minority communities (Han and Choi 2018; Rafalow, Feliciano, and Robnett 2017). The association of light skin with attractiveness within the African American community is well documented (Esmail and Sullivan 2006; Hill 2002; Ross 1997). Chow (2000) found that physical characteristics more common to whites were favored even among those who preferred relationships with other Asians, while those expressing a preference for white spouses felt more identification with European American culture and were more likely to overtly racialize personality characteristics of the opposite gender. An example of such racialization is characterizing white men as "confident" and "giving," (versus Asian men as "insecure" and "self-ish"), or white women as "outspoken" and "vivacious" (versus Asian women as "submissive" and "shy").

These gendered interactions with racial beliefs may be evocative of ways in which gendered sexual orientation in turn affects experiences and beliefs around interracial dating and racial sexual orientation. For example, whereas a cultural belief about gender "inversion" exists around same-sex attraction (e.g., the stereotyped feminine gay male "queen" or masculine "butch" lesbian), gay Asian men may also be particularly seen as "overly" feminine and exotic in part due to racialized beliefs (Han 2006, 2015). However, although there are several studies which address the experience of lesbian, gay, bisexual, transgender, and queer (LGBTQ) racial and ethnic minorities more generally, and some may briefly address interracial relationships, McDermit's (1980) small study of five white men and Lockman's (1984) exploratory survey of twenty-seven black and white men involved in black-white relationships appear to be the only social science research that explicitly focuses on interracial same-sex relationships. Therefore, whether persons of different gendered sexual orientations have different experiences and beliefs around interracial dating, as well as how they experience racial sexual orientation, are questions that remain largely unaddressed.

There is also little data on the prominence of race-based attractions. There is no clear way to measure cross-race sexual preferences in the general population, but using interracial relationships as a proxy (although those with a cross-race orientation may not necessarily have interracial relationships, and those in interracial relationships may not necessarily have a cross-race orientation) demonstrates the likelihood that this is a small population of interest. The rate in the United States in 2010 was almost 7 percent for married couples, and 14 percent for unmarried partner households including opposite and same-sex couples. For the West region, however, numbers jump to approximately 11 percent and 21 percent (Lofquist et al. 2012). In one of the few studies that examine same-sex dating patterns alongside opposite-sex dating patterns, Phua and Kaufman (2003) found that men seeking men through online personal ads were more likely to request a particular race than men seeking women, supporting the possibility that gay men may be particularly likely to express racial preferences in romantic and sexual relationships. Additional studies of online dating apps (Callander, Holt, and Newman 2016; Paul, Ayala, and Choi 2009; Rafalow, Feliciano, and Robnett 2017; White et al. 2014) support the finding that race is a key influential criteria in selection of dating partners among men who have sex with men. This suggests that a strategic area to explore development of racial preferences may be among gay men and gay male communities.

Gay Male Subculture and Racial Sexual Orientation

There are additional reasons to believe there is a noteworthy link between gendered sexual orientation and racial sexual orientation. Scholars of linguistics, folklore, and sociology have documented the development of terminology based on racial sexual and romantic partner preferences since at least the 1970s, largely originating in gay male subculture (Goodwin 1989; Hom and Ma 1993; Lockman 1984; Long 1996; Newall 1986; Stanley 1970).[1] Examples of such terminology can be seen in table 1.1. No specific explanations are offered for the appearance of these terms, but the appearance of a wide variety of sexual slang terms as well as an elaborate "handkerchief code" (symbolically indicating a variety of sexual interests) during that same period reflects development of a complex sexual taxonomy within gay male subculture.

The terms reflecting racial partner preferences are more commonly used and critiqued in cultural studies literature since the mid-1990s, reflecting an increasing interest in intersections between categories of race and sexuality. Although the earliest documented terminology has clearly derogatory overtones ("dinge queen" for white men who prefer black men), and later terminology plays on stereotypes and notions of exoticism (e.g., "rice queen" for non-Asian—especially white—men who prefer Asian men), there are also connotations of irony and (self-)parody (Hayes 2000). These labels not only imply stable patterns of attraction but also raise the possibility of identities (or at least proto-identities) around racial sexual orientation; and, if it is not merely a linguistic accident, the development of terminology within gay male subculture suggests that understandings of racial sexual orientation may be inflected by gendered sexual orientation. In other words, the experiences

Table 1.1   Gay Slang Terms for Racial Preferences

	Preferred Race			
	Asian	*Black*	*Latino*	*White*
Cross-Race Preference	⁻ Rice Queen ⁻ Yellow Fever	⁻ Chocolate Queen ⁻ Coal Queen ⁻ Dinge Queen	⁻ Bean Queen ⁻ Salsa Queen*	⁻ Dairy Queen ⁻ Potato Queen ⁻ Snow Queen
Same-Race Preference	⁻ Sticky Rice	⁻ Double Chocolate	⁻ Refried Beans	⁻ Mashed Potatoes

* denotes terms that may be used less frequently in reference to gay Latino men.

of gendered sexual development by gay men and/or community interactions among gay men appear to be a contributing factor in the unique attention paid within this gendered sexual orientation group to racial sexual orientation.

Another demonstration of gay male subculture's unique attention to racial sexual orientation is the formation and sustained existence of the social movement organization Black and White Men Together (BWMT). Michael J. Smith, a white man who preferred interracial relationships with black men, founded BWMT in 1980 as a way to meet other gay men already in or interested in pursuing interracial relationships. The organization currently lists fourteen active local and regional chapters across the United States, and at the height of its activity had as many as forty. Although not the first gay organization founded around interest in interracial relationships (short-lived support groups popped up in Chicago, Los Angeles, and Milwaukee), it was the first to be more than a local or transient phenomenon. The group defines itself as a "gay multiracial, multicultural organization committed to fostering supportive environments wherein racial and cultural barriers can be overcome and the goal of human equality realized" (National Association of Black and White Men Together [NABWMT] 2010). However, a major impetus for membership in the organization is "interracial orientation" and/or the desire to "find that 'someone' of a different race" (NABWMT 1993). This and similar terminology make comparable implications to the "queen" terminology while moving away from stereotype and closer to language used around gendered attractions. Concurrently, BWMT itself evokes the possibility of community around the idea of racial sexual orientation.

Narratives of Gendered Sexual Orientation and Sexual Development

Studies of narratives of gendered sexual orientation only rarely address race directly. Instead, I draw upon them as a model for understanding sexual development of racial sexual orientation. Studies of sexual development now generally agree on a set of common components that make up the process of sexual development for same-sex attracted individuals. These typically include feelings of "differentness" that may be associated with sexual feelings or gender-atypical behavior, appearance, or interests; preoccupation with or sexual attraction toward one or more members of the same sex; realization of a predisposition toward sexual and/or affectional feelings toward the same sex; experimentation or initiation of sexual behavior; conscious questioning of sexual identity; seeking information about others with similar attractions; adoption of a sexual identity; disclosure of sexual identity to others; and involvement in a same-sex romantic relationship. Although at one time conceptualized as linear stages, it is now recognized that there is diversity in terms of the presence, timing, and order of these components in individual experiences of sexual development (Diamond 1998; Dubé 2000; Rosario, Schrimshaw, and Hunter 2008; Rosario et al. 2009; Russell, Clarke, and Clary 2009; Savin-Williams 1998; Savin-Williams and Diamond 2000).

Although there is recognition of diverse pathways, males are more likely to experience feelings of "difference" in early childhood compared to women and, on average, experience most other milestones at an earlier age than females (Diamond 2000; Savin-Williams and Diamond 2000). Males also typically experience stability of attractions by late adolescence or early adulthood, while women are somewhat more likely to experience fluidity in their attractions as adults (Diamond 2000, 2008). This basic set of concepts and patterns is useful as a reference point for investigation of the presence or absence of similar milestones in the case of racial sexual orientation. The acknowledgment of diversity also indicates a need to examine to what degree development of racial sexual orientation follows a similar or different track to gendered sexual orientation for individuals, and to what degree milestones of racial sexual orientation development tend to vary in their presence, timing, and order across individuals.

As well as describing the trajectories of experience of sexual orientation and identities, sexual development literature also theorizes regarding the nature or origins of sexual desires (and, in particular, gender-based desires). One such theory which may bear particular relevance to study of cross-race attractions is Bem's (1996) "Exotic Becomes Erotic" (EBE) theory of sexuality. Bem suggests that generalized arousal in childhood toward peers who are dissimilar or exoticized (but not too exotic) becomes associated with eroticization of that same group of dissimilar peers. While this theory was created as a way of dealing with the question of gendered sexual orientation, I argue that the theory can be generalized to existence of sexual desires based on perceived difference in the form of race. Themes of difference or exoticism in the context of race, then, should be of particular interest in attempting to understand development of racial sexual orientation.

Narratives of Sexual Development
as a Methodological Approach

Research on gendered sexual orientation analyzes narratives in the form of retrospective questionnaires and interviews asking about childhood, adolescent, and earlier adult experiences. This is a core methodological approach of sexual development literature (Bell, Weinberg, and Hammersmith 1981; Diamond 1998; Dunne et al. 2000; Isay 1989; McDonald 1982; Phillips and Over 1992, 1995; Savin-Williams 1996, 1998; Savin-Williams and Diamond 2000). Most of these studies take the approach of asking discrete, closed-ended questions about developmental milestones and related beliefs and behaviors (e.g., "When did you first experience sexual attraction?" or "When did you have your first homosexual relationship?") and reconstructing a generalized developmental path from the answers. Several of these developmental milestones can be usefully translated into a study of racial sexual orientation.

However, Horowitz and Newcomb level a relevant criticism of such studies for focusing too much on identity as "the only legitimate and valued outcome" or endpoint in a way that essentializes sexual identities. Because "identity can only arise in those societies in which [a categorization] is acknowledged" and because "there is no necessary relationship between a particular pattern of sexual behavior and taking a sexual identity," they recommend separating out models of desire, behavior, and identity (Horwitz and Newcomb 2001, 15–16). They also note that because sexual development is an "ongoing process" there is "no true endpoint" (Horwitz and Newcomb 2001, 4). This is a valuable perspective from the point of view of investigating racial sexual orientation because identities regarding such preferences may be rare. In a culture that does not commonly recognize the existence of racial sexual orientation and is disapproving of racial preferences in general there would seem to be little cultural space for the creation of (at least a positive) identity around race-based desires (Barnard 2004; Moran 2001). Also, in a society that continues to be socially segregated along lines of race, particularly in the realms of romantic love and sexuality, desires and behaviors may also not necessarily align.

In contrast with the closed-ended questionnaire approach, some have employed a more open-ended narrative approach in which the respondent is asked to reconstruct their own history in a qualitative, elaborated, integrated, process-oriented way. Although some early qualitative work is based on psychological or psychoanalytic patient studies (Isay 1989), most modern research from the qualitative, integrative narrative approach utilizes one-time face-to-face semi-structured interviews focused around personal histories of sexual attractions, behaviors, and experiences of identity (Diamond 1998; Savin-Williams 1996, 1998). Whereas more quantitative research tends to focus on generalizable stage theories leading to identity, as a general rule qualitative research has tended to give more attention to differential developmental trajectories across subgroups. In other words, rather than assuming a set of milestones and the ability to construct a singular sequencing of those milestones, the open-ended narrative approach allows for the possibility that not all milestones are shared, and it gives attention to variability in both presence and sequencing of the milestones.

That said, like the quantitative studies, these studies also tend to focus on identity as an ultimate outcome. However, in her longitudinal study of women's sexual development, Diamond (1998, 2003b, 2005) has notably challenged this assumption by including those not adopting a sexual identity label, as well as by studying the phenomenon of relinquishing identity labels. Like Horowitz and Newcomb, her approach recognizes that because sexual development is an ongoing process, there is not one set "endpoint." Therefore, Diamond's work provides a particularly relevant model to borrow from for study of racial sexual orientation.

Given that most studies of sexual development are based on retrospective reporting, another critique has been that the data represents a "reconstructed past" (Boxer and Cohler 1989; Phillips and Over 1992, 1995). In response to these critiques a few prospective studies have been conducted, while other researchers have responded to the concerns by selecting younger cohorts of teens and young adults, thus narrowing the window of time in which events can be distorted or forgotten. However, while supporting the need for more prospective studies, Diamond (2006) cautions that neither prospective data nor the approach of selecting younger cohorts escapes the problem of the "reconstructed past." A closely related concern is that longitudinal research may itself influence or create developmental processes, as asking individuals to regularly account for their attractions, behaviors, and identities may itself influence said attractions, behaviors, and identities.

Instead of trying to determine "true" accounts, Diamond (2006) suggests asking: "What is it about this particular scenario or memory that has given it such prominence as a core feature of this individual's narrative sense of self?" (478) and "How do individuals craft developmentally specific, goal-relevant interpretations of their own erotic subjectivity in the service of maintaining a comfortable, coherent, and socially meaningful sense of self?" (482). To help answer these questions, she references four types of self-event relations: "explain/illustrate relations, in which an event is described as exemplifying an existing trait or characteristic; dismiss relations, in which an uncharacteristic event is discounted; cause relations, in which an event is portrayed as instigating change in the self; and reveal relations, in which an event prompts discovery of a hidden truth about the self" (Diamond 2006, 483).[2]

THE CURRENT STUDY

As demonstrated in the previous section, what is known about the phenomenon of sexual and romantic partner preferences based on race suggests that such preferences influence who a person falls in love with or has close emotional attachments to, has sexual desires for or fantasizes about, actually has sex with, has romantic or sexual relationships with, how a person identifies, and/or in which communities a person spends time or feels most comfortable. Race-based desires, if paid attention to at all, are often explained as fetishism (that is, an objectifying desire focused solely on sexual behavior and gratification). Yet the description offered of racial sexual preferences seems more analogous to the meanings usually ascribed to the concept of "sexual orientation" (Diamond 2003a; Klein, Sepekoff, and Wolf 1985; Sandfort 2005). However, the concept of "sexual orientation" is limited to an understanding of sexuality that is gender-centered. While it is acknowledged that a person may have multiple sexual preferences (in the broadest sense of the word), they are generally understood to have only one sexual orientation, and that is in regards to *gender*.

A significant body of academic literature addresses the interactions between gender and (gendered) sexual orientation. Research and theory work on sexual development has indicated a link between childhood gender nonconformity and adult same-sex sexual orientation (Bailey 1996; Bem 1996, 2000; Dunne et al. 2000), although it is also clear that some gender-typical children grow up to be homosexual and some gender-atypical children grow up to be heterosexual (Bailey 1996; Fausto-Sterling 2007; Sandfort 2005). There is also empirical evidence that sexual development trajectories differ for men and women (Diamond 1998; Savin-Williams and Diamond 2000).

No doubt the discourse positing a special (and perhaps unique) link between gender and orientation is related to beliefs and supporting research indicating that at least some aspects of gendered sexual orientation develop early in the life course and tend to be consistent over time (especially if these findings are seen as indicative of essential difference). A focus on orientation in the context of monosexual exclusivity may also be a factor, since "preference" suggests more choice or at least "middle ground" in attractions. However, it is unclear that these factors do not apply to any other sexual preferences, including those in regards to race.

Therefore, this study questions the assumption that orientation equals gender by examining to what extent the lens of sexual orientation is useful to examine racial sexual preference. While there are arguably good reasons to afford gender a special status in regard to sexuality, race's role in social classification and power suggests that preferences in regard to it should not be ignored. For that reason, this research seeks to shed light on the sexual development of racial sexual preference by using a sexual orientation development perspective.

This narrative study of racial sexual orientation brings new perspective to the sexual development literature in several ways. First, unlike gendered sexual orientation, categories around race-based sexual attractions are not as commonly recognized in our society, and so while the possibility of individuals creating identities or proto-identities should not be ignored, it presents an interesting case for applying Horowitz and Newcomb's critique of focusing on identity as an endpoint. Second, it may shed some light on the extent to which gender differences in gendered sexual orientation trajectories are generalizable to other sexual development processes. In other words, can similarities be found between development of racial orientation and gendered orientation, and are differences in racial sexual orientation development related to differential patterns of gendered sexual orientation development? Finally, in relation to Diamond's observations around consistency and authenticity, an examination can be made of how narratives of sexual development are (re)constructed in a case where there are few guiding identities and cultural narratives. If existing identities and cultural narratives are not themselves prominent or necessarily consistent, this might shift how individuals produce consistency and a sense of self in relation to their sexual preferences.

Thus, this research addresses the following questions:

1. What are the narratives of cross-race sexual orientation? What experiences and beliefs are held by people who prefer to date and have relationships with persons of a different race? How consistent are narratives across cases?
2. Does the narrative structure (e.g., the presence and sequencing of milestones) of one's development of cross-race sexual orientation correspond in any way to that of gendered sexual orientation?

DATA AND METHODS

Participants

Participants include thirteen gay men who have a sexual or romantic preference for a different race. This study focused on gay men because

Table 1.2   Interview Participant Demographics

Participant (by Pseudonym)	Racial Identity	Primary Racial Preference	Location (State/Country)	Age	Education
P1 (Paul)	White	Asian	Korea	23	Bachelor's
P2 (David)	White	Black	Arizona	20	Some college
P3 (Jerome)	Black	Latino	Arizona	33	Graduate degree
P4 (Craig)	White	Latino	California	30	Graduate degree
P5 (Edward)	White	Latino	Arizona	50	Some graduate
P6 (Alex)	Mixed	White/Latino	Arizona	25	Some college
P7 (Terell)	Black	White	Wisconsin	38	Bachelor's
P8 (Jeff)	Latino	White	Arizona	27	Some college
P9 (Lavon)*	Black	White	Arkansas	47	Some college
P10 (Kenton)*	Black	White	Florida	51	Graduate degree
P11 (Michael)*	White	Black	Florida	64	Graduate degree
P12 (Bill)*	White	Black	Pennsylvania	49	Some college
P13 (Kenneth)	Multi	White	Arizona	44	Graduate Degree

* denotes Black and White Men Together members.

of the apparently unique awareness, terminology, and community building around racial sexual orientation in the gay male subculture, including slang terminology and the development of the BWMT organization. Because the project focuses on comparison of narratives and includes investigation of identities of racial sexual orientation, identity was the key component of gendered sexual orientation that was used to determine what category a person fell within. Therefore, men had to self-identify as gay in order to participate in the study. A list of the participants along with basic information on their racial sexual orientations and demographics is presented in table 1.2.

I sought to locate individuals who were diverse in terms of racial identity, primary race preference, and geographic location. A primary goal in this regard was to select equal numbers of white men and men of color; my sample is 54 percent men of color. Previous similar studies that have intentionally recruited with an eye to racial diversity had difficulty in reaching levels of participation at even 20–30 percent of the overall sample (Diamond 1998; Savin-Williams 1998). Higher participation by racial minorities could reflect the fact that the research explicitly focuses on race. It is also possible that this ratio reflects a lower likelihood for white men to express a cross-race preference. I did not actively recruit with an eye to social class diversity, and as with similar studies the sample is largely middle-class and relatively highly educated.

Recruitment methods included posting flyers on university campuses and at nonprofit agencies and businesses targeting the LGBTQ community. Advertisements were also posted on online bulletin boards, forums, and advertising sites such as craigslist.com. I also recruited directly by presenting flyers at the BWMT organization's 2009 annual conference in Philadelphia, PA.

Procedures

I conducted semi-structured interviews face to face and via the internet. Interviews ranged from one to four hours in length. Face-to-face interviews were conducted in a university office or a location of the participant's choosing. Five interviews were conducted via instant message system with a verbatim transcript, four interviews utilized a typed real-time transcription using a notebook computer during the interview, and three interviews utilized written notes that were transcribed into an electronic format immediately after the interview. Transcribed data were edited to remove all personal identifying and contact information and pseudonyms were used for participants.

Semi-structured interviews were selected both because individual narratives are a conceptual focus of the study and because interviews have the potential to elicit rich, thick descriptions. In addition, this type of interview gave me the opportunity to ask for clarification and to probe for additional information. Because of the sensitive nature of the study, discretion as to question wording and timing helped to keep interviews informal and unthreatening to respondents, while also allowing exploration of unanticipated statements relevant to this relatively unexplored area of study (Singleton and Straights 1999).

Qualitative interviews are used to attempt to elicit the participants' points of view, the meaning of their experiences, and understandings of their lived world (Kvale and Brinkmann 2009). This provides a good fit with the intent of gathering personal narratives, because these are stories that make meaning from a person's life and point of view. This is also consistent with the goal of giving voice. Borrowing from the structure of interviews designed to elicit narratives of gendered sexual orientation development (Diamond 1998; Savin-Williams 1996, 1998), my research questions grounded the development of my framework of interview questions. The schedule worked well with initial interviews; as themes emerged, in subsequent interviews they were incorporated into the structure of the instrument.

As a mode of data collection, interviews do have limitations. First, they depend upon the cooperation, motivation, perception, truthfulness, and articulateness of the interviewee. Second, they depend upon the knowledge and interviewing skills of the researcher, including knowledge of the topic, structure of the interview, clarity of questions, and sensitivity in speaking and listening.

RESULTS AND DISCUSSION

Comparing Gendered and Racial Sexual Orientation

Like gendered sexual orientation, racial sexual orientation appears to develop early in the life course. Almost all participants experienced cross-race attractions very early in their lives—often at the same time they started noticing same-sex attractions. Typically this started with crushes or infatuations on classmates. David,[3] a white man, explained that he "had a nebulous attraction" to a black classmate in his mostly white school which he described as "a little bit of a crush, a big desire to be his friend." This experience of cross-race attraction occurred in fifth grade and predated his awareness of sexual attraction to boys more generally a year later. Similarly, Jerome, a black man, first experienced same-sex attractions at the age of thirteen through crushes on other boys in his classes. Although he attended a racially blended high school, the two boys he remembers liking "in particular" were white. Edward (white) explicitly connected the two budding attractions himself: "My attractions to Hispanic men were simultaneous with my attractions to men—I certainly remember from junior high school." The most striking example of this early onset of a pattern of racial preference may be from Craig (white), who not only established a pattern of attraction remarkably early, but also acted on this attraction:

> Well I first started to realize I liked boys very, very young. I was about 5 years old when I kissed a boy at school, we were both shepherds in the school play. . . . [His] race was . . . half Argentinian. I know that one thing I notice looking back and also seeing my tastes now in men, Latin men have always been my preference.

Craig's quote also demonstrates a related similarity—the language used to describe this early onset of cross-race attraction is reminiscent of that used in gay narratives. Just as gay men commonly report they were "always" attracted to men when describing their memories of childhood and adolescence, it was common for those interviewed to state that race had "always" been a factor in their preferences. Even one interviewee (Paul, white) who did not establish a firm racial orientation until late high school reported that he was "always aware of [his] sexuality in terms of race" because the racial diversity of his hometown gave him cause to think of men of different races as "different sexual 'types.'" This similarity in language is perhaps unsurprising given how intertwined the two experiences were for many of these men. However, it is remarkable that among these interviewees they were more likely to use this "always" language explicitly in regard to their racial attractions than their gendered attractions. Bill (white) takes this similarity one step closer by explicitly connecting his beliefs about his racial preferences with the common belief that same-sex attractions are inborn:

> It does seem to be bred into me from the get-go, much like I feel homosexuality was always a part of me, as opposed to a specific incident or relationship that set me on that path of attraction. It just feels right to me, like breathing.

Bill does not quite make a genetic argument, suggesting that there is a spiritual element, and that he is even tempted to believe a friend's argument that "it has something to do with a past life." Nevertheless, he clearly uses the language of innateness used to discuss gendered sexual orientation, indicating it has influenced his thoughts and language use around his racial sexual orientation.

Three of the five oldest interviewees (late forties and older) had somewhat differing experiences. These men spent most of their time as children and teens in segregated, relatively racially isolated communities. The youngest of the five (Lavon, black) reported growing up in a somewhat segregated environment, but moved to an integrated neighborhood at the age of twelve. Edward (white) is in this age range as well, but the primary racial/ethnic line in the community he was raised in was not black/white but rather Latino/white and was not subject to residential and educational segregation. However, the three other participants, who experienced the strongest levels of racial isolation, nevertheless recalled childhood and adolescent experiences of attraction for persons who were racially or ethnically distinct from themselves:

> My first attraction may have happened in 1st or 2nd grade. My best friend was black because of the one drop rule but "high yellow" or mulatto—he could pass for white. We had a very close bond. (Kenton, black)

> Where I grew up was very segregated, there were no blacks in town or at the university. . . . A friend in high school would talk to me about the Italians in town, an ethnic minority. There was an exoticness to it growing up in an all-white area. (Michael, white)

Although these men lived in communities that were understood to be racially uniform, they nevertheless perceived racial differences that translated into attraction. So, even these men see an early development of their racial orientation in their life story.

As with gendered sexual orientation, attractions are not only reported to develop early on, but to be relatively consistent or stable over time by the onset of early adulthood. Craig, as noted above, had stable racial attractions since the age of five, Edward and Kenneth since junior high school, and David since early high school. Five of the men's narratives indicated attractions had not varied since at least the age of seventeen to eighteen. Four men reported a steady pattern of attractions since at least their early twenties. Those whose narratives indicated relatively later consistency seem to reflect later sexual experiences with persons of their preferred race and/or later sexual experiences with men in general.

Sexual behavior in general is also generally consistent with stated preferences. All but two of the participants reported that a majority of their sexual partners were of their preferred race. Both of the exceptions were white men whose largest number of sexual partners was other white men, and both explained the discrepancy in terms of relative availability or access to partners of their preferred race. It seems unlikely to be coincidence that these exceptions were the oldest and youngest members of the sample. In the case of Michael, segregation was a factor, while David had had relatively few sexual partners and was raised and went to college in a mostly white environment in an area with a small black population.

Despite this consistency of attraction, participants most often reported that they were not conscious of this pattern of attractions even well after this consistency had emerged. For example, while Craig reported very early attractions to Latinos, he also reported that "it was something that I didn't even really take full note of as a full on preference till about the age of 22." In his case, he noticed that his pornography collection consisted almost entirely of Latino men. "I had known I found them sexy but that really confirmed it for me . . . when I'd go to purchase a video or something I'd notice I always picked that up first." More commonly this awareness grew out of the interviewees' dating histories:

I just never really thought about it. I have had Hispanic boyfriends, but it was always just a boyfriend as far as everybody was concerned. (Edward, white)

I think my process began when I realized that, even though I was growing up and coming out in large cities, each with a small universe of queers of all ethnicities, I had to stop and think, "Damn, I'm dating a lot of white guys." (Terell, black)

I had eight relationships—it was significant that only one of eight was a black guy. (Kenton, black)

Here, then, is a marked difference from themes commonly found in gendered sexual orientation narratives. Unlike this apparent gradual consciousness of a confirming racial pattern of dating, dating or even just showing interest in dating the same sex is typically found to be immediately remarkable both to the persons involved and those around them. It would perhaps be more common in gay narratives to have reports of *disconfirming* long-term dating patterns (e.g., consistently dating women and becoming conscious of preferences for men because they found those relationships unfulfilling).

One possible explanation for this difference is that racial sexual orientations among the men I interviewed are less exclusive than their gendered sexual orientations. Nine of thirteen men interviewed reported exclusive day-to-day physical attractions to men (range: 90–100%), whereas only one of thirteen reported exclusive day-to-day physical attractions to other races (range: 50–100%). Similarly, six of thirteen men reported exclusive same-sex sexual behavior (range: 87.5–100%), whereas only one of thirteen men reported exclusive sexual behavior with other races (range: 45–100%). Emotional attractions of romantic love or attraction were the least exclusive in respect to both race and gender, but even here four of thirteen men indicated exclusive emotional attractions to men (range: 50–100%), versus only one of thirteen men indicating exclusive emotional attractions to other races (range: 50–100%). This relative lower level of exclusivity might make the experience more similar to a bisexual person becoming aware of their relative preference for men versus women. For example, as part of a person's initial awareness of their bisexual attractions, they might have some idea of whether they tend to be more typically attracted to men or women (or have an equal attraction to both), but they might also draw such a conclusion by reflecting upon their long-term dating history (e.g., Rust 2000).

However, I argue that non-exclusivity is not adequate as a stand-alone explanation. I believe this phenomenon is also related to another major difference between gendered sexual orientation and racial sexual orientation in the area of identities. Although all interviewees had firm gay and/ or queer identities (expected given the criteria for inclusion in the study), only two considered themselves to have an identity in terms of racial sexual orientation. Directly connecting this to the finding of non-exclusiveness, four (Edward, Lavon, Kenton, Michael) did not see an identity as relevant because their attractions were not exclusively for their preferred race. They emphasized that they were attracted to "many different types of men" or at least that their primary racial preference does not mean they are not ever attracted to men of other races. However, again, non-exclusiveness does not seem a fully adequate explanation given that people with bisexual or pansexual (non-exclusive) attractions may have a sexual identity, or even people who identify as gay or lesbian may in fact have non-exclusive attractions (as, in fact, some of the participants in this study themselves reported).

I assert an additional factor in the rarity of racial sexual orientation identities (which, in turn, delays consciousness of racial attractions) is normative beliefs about race and racism in the United States, and particularly "color-blind" ideology. Recognition of racial differences and preferences based on race are taboo topics. Several of the participants discussed trying to reconcile their experience of race-based attractions and their beliefs about race, and expressed feelings of being conflicted, embarrassed, and hypocritical. For minorities who were attracted to white men, in particular, they commonly expressed a belief that their attractions were based at least in part on white men being at the top of the racial hierarchy. Says Jeff, "White men symbolize success, beauty, popularity, good, and what to aspire to become." From that point of view, then, following those attractions equates to participating in one's own oppression. Terell (black) held strong beliefs about racial justice and stated, "I want to think that my views on race...would've led me away from interracial dating ever." He goes on to say that they didn't and at this point in his life stopping would be "ridiculous."

It was not only minority men who held this awareness and concern. David (white) sums up almost every conflict mentioned in one discussion:

> Those are loaded terms when directed around and directed at yourself. Higher tolerance or acceptance of different behaviors in different races. . . . I didn't want to like it because it was a little bit embarrassing—the whole thing about being attracted to other races is sort of an embarrassing thing. I think part of it for me, the bottom line, it is nicer to have the whole "you're colorblind" but not everyone is the same, there are these clear delineations and I notice them. Positive stereotypes are still stereotypes, are still views. I mean, there is also the . . . I don't know, I think there is some truth, I think I have had some conflicted notions.

Here David expresses an inclination toward colorblind ideology, but also explains how his race-based attractions do not conform to this ideology. Stereotyped notions of racial appearance and behavior are part of his attractions for other races. They are positive stereotypes in that he prefers a partner that displays those traits, but he nevertheless believes it is ideal not to stereotype based on race. Therefore, for David it would be difficult to build a racial sexual orientation identity given that he sees it as in conflict with his view of himself as a person who does not discriminate and believes in colorblindness.

Perhaps because of this dissonance around race-based attractions, there are few terms available to describe racial sexual orientation. Three participants (David, Edward, Alex) were not familiar with any labels for racial sexual orientation, while two others (Jerome, Jeff) were aware of terms but did not see them as relevant to their particular experiences of racial attraction. With no term to help articulate their experiences, it is arguably more difficult to build an identity. Says David, "If I were aware of terms I might use one. I'm not fundamentally opposed to the distinction [of a racial sexual orientation label]." This suggests that if David were aware of a term that had positive connotations (and could perhaps help him resolve the conflict between his attractions and ideology) he might adopt it as part of his identity. He simply does not know of any such term. Those terms that are most widely known carry negative connotations. Five participants (Craig, Terell, Lavon, Michael, Bill) were aware of terms such as those listed in table 5.1, but found the terms "mildly" to "strongly offensive," and thus did not identify with them. These participants described such terms as used to "incite," "deflate," "be deroga-tory," "belittle," and "put down." Michael compared them to names straight men call out to gay men on the street. The four interviewees who were mem-bers of BWMT further corroborated that use of such terms was discouraged within the group. Interestingly, while a separate line of archival research on BWMT (Crockett 2016) revealed that a number of terms have been proposed to describe the phenomenon of racial orientation, none of the interviewees from the organization were aware of or recalled any of these terms. That none of the terms took hold in a group formed around cross-race orientation is perhaps a strong indicator of the influence of colorblind ideology, since it suggests even a community with an interest in deliberately creating a label or identity may have been stymied in its efforts by the norms against racial preferences.

Not everyone in the sample rejected a racial sexual orientation identity. When asked if he had an identity, Bill responded, "Yes, although I do find some white men attractive, I identify myself as being primarily attracted to African American men." In a sense, he was not so different from the other participants. He affirmed a diversity of attractions in the same breath as he affirmed his particular preference, and he did not have a particular label for his identity. If a difference can be found, it may be in this statement:

> I think it would be great if more people had a "colorblind" ideology in general social terms, but when it comes to taste or preference in a partner, it really is as individual as taste in food, etc. People like what they like, often without reason.

Unlike other participants quoted above, Bill seems to have worked out a system of belief that reconciles his experience of race-based attractions with a broader ideology that calls for race-neutrality. Arguably, this is parallel to the solution represented by those holding both to a general social belief in gender-neutrality and an allowance for the experience of explicitly gendered sexual attractions.

Paul had both a racial sexual orientation identity and a label to go along with it ("rice queen"). In this case, he explained that he took on this label precisely because "it's not 'PC,' so to speak." He reveled in the "taboo-breaking fun" of his attractions, which he felt were just enhanced by "studying cultural studies and becoming sort of consciously antiracism." Another aspect of this, which also put him at odds with the other study participants, was his view of his attractions as a form of fetishism.

> My social/political affinities can be seen as at odds with my "fetish." But I definitely think I have more fun thinking of myself as a rice queen now. And the fun is a sort of taboo-breaking feeling of fun. (Paul)

His difference from the other members may stem from this view of his attractions as a fetish (although not only a fetish), or perhaps his particular educational background in postmodern cultural studies which emphasizes irony and play/disruption/subversion (Kellner 1995; Samuels 2009; Weinstock 2008), or perhaps both in that his view of attractions as a fetish may interact with and/or be a product of his postmodern studies. In any case, the difference appears to stem from a different relationship with colorblind ideology.

The Content of Racial Attractions

The predominant aspect reported as attractive was physical characteristics. Eight (Jerome, Craig, Edward, Jeff, Lavon, Kenton, Bill, and Kenneth) mentioned skin color or complexion. Six (Paul, David, Alex, Jeff, Lavon, and Michael) mentioned aspects of body size such as height or musculature, while five (Edward, Terell, Jeff, Lavon, and Kenton) mentioned hair color, and five (Jeff, Lavon, Kenton, Bill, and Kenneth) mentioned eye color. Other physical characteristics mentioned included body hair (David, Craig, Alex, and Bill), other facial features (Jerome, Edward, and Bill), and penis size (Paul). Some of these interests seem to be expressed in a relatively "deracialized" way. For example, while Terell found racial preference terms offensive, he did call himself a "redhead-seeking missile." This seems similar to the phenomenon that discussions of preferences for blonde, brunette, or redheaded women are relatively socially appropriate. Although there are clear correlations between race and hair color, hair color does not designate race per se so it is deemed more acceptable.

Other characteristics were also mentioned, including attitude/personality (Paul, Jerome, Craig, Lavon, Kenton, Kenneth), difference (Craig, Edward, Lavon, Kenton, Bill, Kenneth), gender roles (Paul, David, Alex, Jeff, Kenton), culture (Jerome, Craig, Edward, Lavon), intelligence (Terell, Lavon), friendship (David, Kenton, Kenneth), power (David), language/speech (Paul, Jerome), and smell (Kenton). Culture and culture-related factors are, unsurprisingly, particularly cited by those attracted to Latino and Asian men, groups where a difference in culture is arguably most salient.

Themes of difference or exoticism were common in the interviews, which would seem to fit with Bem's EBE theory of sexual attraction. However, some of these cases seem to conflict with Bem's theorizing about same-sex attracted individuals. Bem suggests that those who are same-sex attracted may be so because they feel alienated from their own assigned gender group and thus see them as exotic. David, Jerome, Terell, Jeff, and Kenneth all describe alienation from their racial/ethnic reference group as part of the reason for the development of cross-race attractions. David describes growing up hating the "rich, white, yuppie, clean-cut, all-American cliché." Jerome, Kenneth, and Terell described rejection from same-race peers, Jerome and Kenneth because of their mixed racial heritage and Terell because of his perceived femininity/homosexuality. Jeff did not identify with what he saw as the stereotypical gay Latino man. However, in all of these cases disidentification is part of their narrative of cross-race attractions rather than same-race attractions. This difference of alienation not resulting in eroticism may be due to differences between gender and racial dynamics or due to differences in life course timing of the experience of alienation (early childhood versus late childhood or adolescence).

Another aspect of racial attraction is the occurrence of attraction to multiple racial types among some of the interviewees. For example, Paul explains that he is generally attracted to dominant, masculine, physically large men of color, but in the case of Asian men (his primary attraction), he is additionally attracted to submissive, feminine, smaller men as well. He believes this is because "it's already an established 'type' for Asian men." David describes a similar set of types, preferring physically large, masculine, dominant black men, physically smaller, feminine, submissive Asian men, and either extreme for Latinos. Alex did not report any different personality preferences, but liked different physical types: hairy, muscular white men and smooth, "twinkish" (slender) Latino men. Most participants did not report typologies but this may nevertheless reveal that racial preferences more generally are shaped strongly by preestablished cultural stereotypes (which may vary across location, generation, etc.). Another way this may be revealed is in the way the participants talked about racial categories. One participant basically spoke of race in terms of black and white (with Latino individuals being treated as a particular ethnicity subsumed into or a combination of these categories), while all of the rest discussed Asian, black, Latino, and white. Some also added to these groupings: Eastern Indian, Middle Eastern, and Native American as additional categories. In addition, a few discussed finer gradations of categories, such as "Mediterranean" whites versus other whites.

A related observation in regard to the content of racial attractions is in terms of exclusions. Of the four major racial/ethnic groups focused on in this sample, Asians were most likely to be specifically mentioned as a group a respondent was "not very attracted" to and were rarely mentioned as sexual partners. A particularly striking example here is that one respondent reported having over 1,000 sexual partners and specifically reported only one of them being Asian. Given that Asian men and non-Asian men primarily attracted to Asians are under-represented in the sample, this may indicate that attraction to Asians tends to occur along a different dimension than attraction along a black-brown-white continuum. This may be due to stereotypical perceptions of Asians as a particularly "exotic" racial group, or may be due to more specific cultural beliefs that stereotypically ascribe femininity to Asian men more commonly than members of other racial groups (Han 2006, 2015). Black men were also less commonly mentioned as sexual partners among those who did not have a primary racial sexual orientation toward black men. This may be a reflection of the fact that blacks are more likely to prefer same-race partners and that blacks are perceived as being the lowest status in the U.S. race hierarchy (Phua and Kaufman 2003).

A final concern in terms of content of racial attractions is fetishism. As discussed earlier, most of the participants rejected the notion that their experience of racial preference constituted racial fetishism. However, this does not necessarily mean they rejected the notion of racial fetishism. For example, Kenton explains that he sees in the gay community that white men in particular are likely to view men of different races as sexual objects, and he calls this objectification fetishism. He then goes on to explain how his expression of racial preference is different:

> Something happens when there is a sincere attraction. The whole person goes with that, you get to know the person. There is a desire to know the person beyond the attraction. You are open to venues to get to know each other—understand their different culture and economic situation.

The distinction, then, is between treating the other person as an object versus a subject. Other respondents expressed their opinions on fetishism similarly. For example, David stated, "I don't call it a fetish because it is something that is not innately sexual . . . but [rather] I am still attracted to the individual." Craig likewise explains that he sees a fetish as "something more frivolous" while his attraction "has gotten much deeper . . . I think maybe through all the compounded experiences both sexual and just day to day life as partners." Craig's narrative suggests that his preference started out as "merely" a fetish, but over time developed into something else.

CONCLUSION

This study reveals some striking similarities between narratives of gendered sexual orientation and racial sexual orientation. As with their same-sex attractions, these men commonly experienced cross-race attractions at an early age and on a consistent basis over the life course. Even those men who grew up in segregated societies recalled being attracted to other boys who they perceived as racially distinct, although understood to be part of their racial "in-group." Several of the men described their racial attractions using a language of innateness similar to that commonly used for gendered sexual orientation. The similarities between the two narratives evoke the possibility that a variety of sexual preferences, not just gendered sexual orientation, can be profoundly influenced in early childhood and adolescence. This may be because the mechanisms that shape sexual desire allow for a diverse set of attractions to form during that period of the life course or because gendered sexual orientation development is open to association of gendered desires with other characteristics. Borrowing from Bem's EBE theory, which assumes the former view but could be consistent with the latter view, it may be that cultural factors and social interactions that emphasize racial difference create arousal to differently raced peers in a way that eroticizes them to some individuals.

Despite having some remarkable similarities with gendered sexual orientation, these narratives of racial sexual orientation also reveal some important differences. For one, "racial sexual preference" seems like an equally suitable term for these attractions for most of the men interviewed. Although it may be a product of the fact that this was a sample of gay men (and thus a sample of relatively strong, mono-gendered sexual orientations), most of these men reported their race-based attractions were less exclusive than their gender-based attractions. Presumably, then, gender was at least as strong (and generally stronger) a factor as race in dating and mating choices for most of the men.

Another difference is that the men were unlikely to have an identity related to their racial sexual orientation, in some cases including a distancing from the possibility of an identity by emphasizing the inclusiveness of their attractions. This emphasis on inclusiveness seems to be an intentional avoidance of the rhetoric of sexual racism (Callander, Holt, and Newman 2016; Smith 2017). This suggests that racial preferences are experienced differently not only because of differences in gender-based versus race-based interactions, but also specific ideological beliefs about race and racism. In particular, the configuration of beliefs about race makes it very difficult to establish identities based on racial sexual orientation because racial preferences *in general* are seen as unacceptable, even by those who see racial sexual preferences as distinct (Thai, Stainer, and Barlow 2019). An exception to this might be a racial solidarity ideology within minority groups, but cross-race attractions also violate this norm.

However, the exceptions to the pattern of nonidentity also suggest some ways identities might develop based on racial sexual orientation. One way is in drawing a parallel with gendered sexual orientation. Our culture does allow for gendered preferences in sexual desire while still holding to gender-neutrality in other areas, and a cultural exception for racial sexual prefer-ences could be acknowledged by analogy. Another is through a postmodern worldview that takes a pose of ironic contradiction, simultaneously affirming antiracism and reveling in racial preference in the form of sexual desires.

Race-based beliefs also shape the content of racial attractions, as well as particular configurations of racial preference. The content of racial attractions are primarily physical, although those interviewed express that other ele-ments of attraction are also important, particularly in moving beyond a "racial fetish" paradigm of racial preference that is only about sexual gratification. However, moving beyond a racial fetish paradigm does not necessarily mean moving beyond racial stereotypes. The interviews demonstrate evidence that cross-race attractions are influenced by cultural stereotypes based on race (examples include the stereotyped hypermasculine black man or feminine Asian man). These types also reveal that, at least among these gay men, racial desires are not independent of gendered beliefs. This may be additional evi-dence of the primacy of gender in attraction. On the other hand, these findings may simply serve to point toward the fact that gender-based beliefs are influ-enced by gender stereotypes and gendered desires may be inherently raced.

A clear set of potential future areas of research present themselves based on this research. First of all, collection of interviews about cross-race racial sexual orientation could expand to include other gender and gendered sexual orientation groups. For example, do heterosexual men (who commonly have had to reflect less on their sexual development and thus may have less structured gendered sexual orientation narratives) tell similar narratives of racial sexual orientation or are their narratives more variable without another structured narrative to borrow from? Do women's narratives vary in similar ways to the variation seen between men and women's gendered preferences? Do women experience more fluidity in their racial sexual preferences? Of particular theoretical interest may be bisexuals and pansexuals, who like other sexual minorities are likely to have a gendered sexual orientation nar-rative, but whose experience of sexual desire may be less centered on gender (if gender-based at all). A related area of inquiry may be whether a non-specificity of gendered attractions for bisexuals and pansexuals translates into a non-specificity of racial attractions. A second direction for future inquiry could be other forms of racial sexual orientation, particularly same-race attractions. Studying same-race orientation may be particularly difficult both because of their normalization and insofar as they may interact with racial nationalist ideologies. However, it could be a particularly important area for examination of interactions between gender and race since racial homogamy in romantic relationships does tend to be treated as customary and is generally unexamined for its racial content. Finally, a contribution of this research is that it demonstrates the potential usefulness of adopting the narrative methodological approach used in studies of gendered sexual orientation development to study other aspects of sexual desire and preference. Therefore, this research could in turn be used as a model for studying other sexual desires, preferences, and practices that are not directly related to gender.

NOTES

1. Exceptions where terminology has referred primarily to mainstream, heterosexual contexts include "jungle fever"—meaning white preference for black partners—used in Spike Lee's 1991 film *Jungle Fever*, and "rice king"—meaning a white man with a preference for Asian women (Holmlund and Wyatt 2004). It seems likely the latter was constructed as an analogue to the gay subcultural term "rice queen." "Nigger lover" is a long-standing derogatory term that bears a relationship with these other terms, but carries connotations much broader than sexual or romantic preferences.

2. Diamond derives these self-event relation types from Pasupathi, Mansour, and Brubaker's (2007) work.

3. All interviewees have been anonymized through the use of pseudonyms.

REFERENCES

Bailey, J. Michael. 1996. "Gender Identity." In *The Lives of Lesbians, Gays, and Bisexuals: Children to Adults*, edited by Ritch C. Savin-Williams and Kenneth M. Cohen, 71–93. Fort Worth, TX: Harcourt Brace.

Barnard, Ian. 2004. *Queer Race: Cultural Interventions in the Racial Politics of Queer Theory*. New York: Peter Lang Publishing.

Bell, Alan P., Martin S. Weinberg, and Sue K. Hammersmith. 1981. *Sexual Preference: Its Development in Men and Women*. Bloomington: Indiana University Press.

Bem, Daryl J. 1996. "Exotic Becomes Erotic: A Developmental Theory of Sexual Orientation." *Psychological Review* 103 (2): 320–35.

———. 2000. "Exotic Becomes Erotic: Interpreting the Biological Correlates of Sexual Orientation." *Archives of Sexual Behavior* 29 (6): 531–48.

Boxer, Andrew M. and Bertram J. Cohler. 1989. "The Life Course of Gay and Lesbian Youth: An Immodest Proposal for the Study of Lives." *Journal of Homosexuality* 17 (3–4): 315–55.

Callander, Denton, Martin Holt, and Christy E. Newman. 2016. "'Not Everyone's Gonna like Me': Accounting for Race and Racism in Sex and Dating Web Services for Gay and Bisexual Men." *Ethnicities* 16 (1): 3–21.

Chow, Sue. 2000. "The Significance of Race in the Private Sphere: Asian Americans and Spousal Preferences." *Sociological Inquiry* 70 (1): 1–29.

Crockett, Jason L. 2016. "Black and White Men Together: The Case of the Disappearing Organizational Narrative of Racial Sexual Orientation." *Making Connections: Interdisciplinary Approaches to Cultural Diversity* 16 (2): 88–116.

Cutrone, Chris. 2000. "The Child with a Lion: The Utopia of Interracial Intimacy." *GLQ: A Journal of Lesbian and Gay Studies* 6 (2): 249–285.

Diamond, Lisa M. 1998. "Development of Sexual Orientation among Adolescent and Young Adult Women." *Developmental Psychology* 34 (5): 1085–95.

———. 2000. "Sexual Identity, Attractions, and Behavior Among Young Sexual-Minority Women Over a 2-Year Period." *Developmental Psychology* 36 (2): 241–250.

———. 2003a. "What Does Sexual Orientation Orient? A Biobehavioral Model Distinguishing Romantic Love and Sexual Desire." *Psychological Review* 110 (1): 173–192.

———. 2003b. "Was It a Phase? Young Women's Relinquishment of Lesbian/Bisexual Identities Over a 5-Year Period." *Journal of Personality and Social Psychology* 84 (2): 352–64.

———. 2005. "A New View of Lesbian Subtypes: Stable Versus Fluid Identity Trajectories Over an 8-Year Period." *Psychology of Women Quarterly* 29 (2): 119–128.

———. 2006. "Careful What You Ask For: Reconsidering Feminist Epistemology and Autobiographical Narrative in Research on Sexual Identity Development." *Signs: Journal of Women in Culture and Society* 31 (2): 471–91.

———. 2008. *Sexual Fluidity: Understanding Women's Love and Desire*. Cambridge, Massachusetts: Harvard University Press.

Dubé, Eric M. 2000. "The Role of Sexual Behavior in the Identification Process of Gay and Bisexual Males." *Journal of Sex Research* 37 (2): 123–32.

Du Bois, W. E. B. 1899. *The Philadelphia Negro: A Social Study*. Philadelphia, Pennsylvania: University of Pennsylvania Press.

Dunne, Michael P., J. Michael Bailey, Katherine M. Kirk, and Nicholas G. Martin. 2000. "The Subtlety of Sex-Atypicality." *Archives of Sexual Behavior* 29 (6): 549–65.

Esmail, Ashraf and Jas M. Sullivan. 2006. "African American College Males and Females: A Look at Color Mating Preferences." *Race, Gender and Class* 13 (1–2): 201–20.

Fausto-Sterling, Anne. 2007. "Frameworks of Desire." *Daedalus* 136 (2): 47–57.

Frankenberg, Ruth. 1993. *White Women, Race Matters: The Social Construction of Whiteness*. Minneapolis: University of Minnesota Press.

Freeman, Linton. 1955. "Homogamy in Interethnic Mate Selection." *Sociology and Social Research* 39 (6): 369–77.

Goodwin, Joseph P. 1989. *More Man Than You'll Ever Be: Gay Folklore and Acculturation in Middle America*. Bloomington and Indianapolis: Indiana University Press.

Grant, Patrick. 2018. "Some 'Black Gay Fantasy': An Exploratory Study of Discrimination and Identity-Appraisal Among Black Same Gender Loving Men." *Journal of Black Sexuality and Relationships* 4 (3): 49–72.

Han, C. Winter. 2006. "Being an Oriental, I Could Never Be Completely a Man: Gay Asian Men and the Intersection of Race, Gender, Sexuality, and Class." *Race, Gender and Class* 13 (3–4): 82–97.

———. 2015. *Geisha of a Different Kind: Race and Sexuality in Gaysian America*. New York, New York: New York University Press.

Han, C. Winter and Kyung-Hee Choi. 2018. "Very Few People Say 'No Whites': Gay Men of Color and the Racial Politics of Desire." *Sociological Spectrum* 38 (3): 145–61.

Hayes, Jarrod. 2000. *Queer Nations: Marginal Sexualities in the Maghreb*. Chicago: Chicago University Press.

Hill, Mark E. 2002. "Skin Color and Perceptions of Attractiveness Among African Americans: Does Gender Make a Difference?" *Social Psychology Quarterly* 65 (1): 77–91.

Holmlund, Chris and Justin Wyatt. 2004. *Contemporary American Independent Film: From the Margins to the Mainstream*. New York: Routledge.

Hom, Alice Y. and Ming-Yuen S. Ma. 1993. "Premature Gestures: Speculative Dialogue on Asian Pacific Islander Lesbian and Gay Writing." *Critical Essays: Gay and Lesbian Writers of Color*: 21–51.

Horowitz, Janna L. and Michael D. Newcomb. 2001. "A Multidimensional Approach to Homosexual Identity." *Journal of Homosexuality* 42 (2): 1–19.

Isay, Richard A. 1989. *Being Homosexual: Gay Men and Their Development*. New York: Farrar, Straus, and Giroux.

Kaplan, Adam M. 2004. "Factors Predicting Whites' Involvement in Interracial Relationships." *Dissertation Abstracts International, B: Sciences and Engineering* 65 (12): 6656–B.

Kellner, Douglas. 1995. *Media Culture: Cultural Studies, Identity, and Politics Between the Modern and the Postmodern*. New York: Routledge.

Klein, Fritz, Barry Sepekoff, and Timothy J. Wolf. 1985. "Sexual Orientation: A Multivariate Dynamic Process." *Journal of Homosexuality* 11 (1–2): 35–49.

Kvale, Steinar and Svend Brinkmann. 2009. *Interviews: Learning the Craft of Qualitative Research Interviewing*. Thousand Oaks, CA: Sage.

Lockman, Paul T. 1984. "Ebony and Ivory: 'The Interracial Gay Male Couple'" *Lifestyles: A Journal of Changing Patterns* 7 (1): 44–55.

Lofquist, Daphne, Terry Lugaila, Martin O'Connell, and Sarah Feliz. 2012. *Households and Families: 2010*. Washington, DC: U.S. Census Bureau.

Long, Daniel 1996. "Formation Processes of Some Japanese Gay Argot Terms." *American Speech* 71 (2): 215–24.

McDermit, Craig W. 1980. "White Men Loving Black Men: An Explication of the Experience Within On-Going Erotic Relationships." *Dissertation Abstracts International, B: Sciences and Engineering* 41 (12): 4676–B.

McDonald, Gary J. 1982. "Individual Differences in the Coming Out Process of Gay Men: Implications for Theoretical Models." *Journal of Homosexuality* 8 (1): 47–60.

Moran, Rachel F. 2001. *Interracial Intimacy: The Regulation of Race and Romance.* Chicago: University of Chicago Press.

National Association of Black and White Men Together. 1993. *Chapter Development Manual: 1993 Revision.* GLBT Historical Society.

———. 2010. "About Us." Accessed May 25, 2010. http://www.nabwmt.org/aboutus.html.

Newall, Venetia. 1986. "Folklore and Male Homosexuality." *Folklore* 97 (2): 123–47.

Pasupathi, M., Emma Mansour, and Jed R. Brubaker. 2007. "Developing a Life Story: Constructing Relations Between Self and Experience in Autobiographical Narratives." *Human Development* 50: 85–100.

Paul, Jay P., George Ayala, and Kyung-Hee Choi. 2010. "Internet Sex Ads for MSM and Partner Selection Criteria: The Potency of Race/Ethnicity Online." *Journal of Sex Research* 47 (6): 528–38.

Phillips, Gabriel and Ray Over. 1992. "Adult Sexual Orientation in Relation to Memories of Childhood Gender Conforming and Gender Nonconforming Behaviors." *Archives of Sexual Behavior* 21 (6): 543–58.

———. 1995. "Differences between Heterosexual, Bisexual, and Lesbian Women in Recalled Childhood Experiences. *Archives of Sexual Behavior* 24 (1): 1–20.

Phua, Voon C. and Gayle Kaufman. 2003. "The Crossroads of Race and Sexuality: Date Selection among Men in Internet 'Personal' Ads." *Journal of Family Issues* 24 (8): 981–94.

Porterfield, Ernest. 1978. *Black and White Mixed Marriages.* Chicago: Nelson-Hall.

Rafalow, Matthew H., Cynthia Feliciano, and Belinda Robnett. 2017. "Racialized Femininity and Masculinity in the Preferences of Online Same-Sex Daters." *Social Currents* 4 (4): 306–21.

Root, Maria P.P. 2001. *Love's Revolution: Interracial Marriage.* Philadelphia, PA: Temple University Press.

Rosario, Margaret, Eric W. Schrimshaw, and Joyce Hunter. 2008. "Predicting Different Patterns of Sexual Identity Development over Time Among Lesbian, Gay, and Bisexual Youths: A Cluster Analytic Approach." *American Journal of Community Psychology* 42: 266–82.

Rosario, Margaret, Eric W. Schrimshaw, Joyce Hunter, and Anna Levy-Warren. 2009. "The Coming-Out Process of Young Lesbian and Bisexual Women: Are There Butch/Femme Differences in Sexual Identity." *Archives of Sexual Behavior* 38: 34–49.

Rosenfeld, Michael J. 2005. "A Critique of Exchange Theory in Mate Selection." *American Journal of Sociology* 110 (5): 1284–325.

Rosenfeld, Michael J. and Byung-Soo Kim. 2005. "The Independence of Young Adults and the Rise of Interracial and Same-Sex Unions." *American Sociological Review* 70 (4): 541–62.

Ross, Louie E. 1997. "Mate Selection Preferences among African American College Students." *Journal of Black Studies* 27 (4): 554–69.

Russell, Stephen T., Thomas J. Clarke, and Justin Clary. 2009. "Are Teens 'Post-Gay'? Contemporary Adolescents' Sexual Identity Labels." *Journal of Youth and Adolescence* 38: 884–90.

Rust, Paula C. 2000. "Two Many and Not Enough." *Journal of Bisexuality* 1 (1): 31–68.

Samuels, Robert. 2009. *New Media, Cultural Studies, and Critical Theory after Postmodernism: Automodernity from Zizek to Laclau.* New York: Palgrave MacMillan.

Sandfort, Theodorus G. M. 2005. "Sexual Orientation and Gender: Stereotypes and Beyond." *Archives of Sexual Behavior* 34 (6): 595–611.

Savin-Williams, Ritch C. 1996. "Memories of Childhood and Early Adolescent Sexual Feelings among Gay and Bisexual Boys: A Narrative Approach." In *The Lives of Lesbians, Gays, and Bisexuals: Children to Adults,* edited by Ritch C. Savin-Williams and Kenneth M. Cohen, 94–109. Fort Worth, TX: Harcourt Brace.

———. 1998. *And Then I Became Gay: Young Men's Stories.* New York: Routledge.

Savin-Williams, Ritch C. and Lisa Diamond. 2000. "Sexual Identity Trajectories Among Sexual-Minority Youths: Gender Comparisons." *Archives of Sexual Behavior* 29 (6): 607–27.

Scott, Darieck. 1994. "Jungle Fever? Black Gay Identity Politics, White Dick, and the Utopian Bedroom." *GLQ: A Journal of Lesbian and Gay Studies* 1: 299–321.

Singleton Jr., Royce A. and Bruce C. Straits. 1999. *Approaches to Social Research,* 3rd ed. New York: Oxford University Press.

Smith, Jesús G. 2017. "The White Racial Frame and Resistance to Sexual Racism." In *The Psychic Life of Racism in Gay Men's Communities,* edited by Damien W. Riggs, 105–22. Lanham, MD: Lexington Books.

Smith, Jesús G., Maria Cristina Morales, and C. Winter, Han. 2018. "The Influence of Sexual Racism on Erotic Capital: A Systemic Racism Perspective." In *Handbook of the Sociology of Racial and Ethnic Relations,* edited by Pinar Batur and Joe Feagin, 389–99. New York, New York: Springer.

Spickard, Paul. 1989. *Mixed Blood: Intermarriage and Ethnic Identity in Twentieth-Century America.* Madison: University of Wisconsin Press.

Stanley, Julia P. 1970. "Homosexual Slang." *American Speech* 45 (1–2): 45–59.

Thai, Michael, Matthew J. Stainer, and Fiona Kate Barlow. 2019. "The 'Preference' Paradox: Disclosing Racial Preferences in Attraction Is Considered Racist Even by People Who Overtly Claim It Is Not." *Journal of Experimental Social Psychology* 83: 70–77.

Twine, France Winddance. 1996a. "Brown Skinned White Girls: Class, Culture, and the Construction of White Identity in Suburban Communities." *Gender, Place and Culture* 3 (2): 205–24.

———. 1996b. "Heterosexual Alliances: The Romantic Management of Racial Identity." In *The Multiracial Experience: Racial Borders as the New Frontier*, edited by Maria P. P. Root, 291–304. Thousand Oaks, CA: Sage Publications.

Weinstock, Jeffery A. 2008. *Taking South Park Seriously*. Albany, New York: State University of New York Press.

White, Jaclyn M., Sari L. Reisner, Emilia Dunham, and Matthew J. Mimiaga. 2014. "Race-Based Sexual Preferences in a Sample of Online Profiles of Urban Men Seeking Sex with Men." *Journal of Urban Health* 91 (4): 768–75.

Yancey, George. 2003. *Who Is White? Latinos, Asians, and the New Black/Nonblack Divide*. Boulder, CO: Lynne Rienner Publishers.

Chapter 2

They Don't Date Any Dark People

The Queer Case of Gay Racism

C. Winter Han and Scott E. Rutledge

By now, it has been well documented in both the academic and mainstream literature that the social organization of contemporary gay life is largely based on racial exclusion and marginalization (Armstrong 2002; Bérubé 2001; Callander, Holt, and Newman 2016; Epstein 1996; Riggs 2018; Teunis 2007). Where racial integration takes place, it takes place only at venues where men of different races come together specifically for the purpose of seeking sexual partners of a given race while "the mainstream gay community and its political aspirations remain white in its orientation" (Teunis 2007, 263). In fact, even when gay spaces are integrated, there continues to be high levels of micro-segregation within those spaces (Orne 2017).

In addition, gay men of color report high and increasing levels of racism within the gay community (Ayala et al. 2012; Choi et al. 2013; Giwa and Greensmith 2012; Haile et al. 2014; Ruez 2017; Han 2008; Han 2015; Ibanez; Ichard 1985). In fact, existing evidence indicates that gay men of color may experience more racism from gay white men than from the larger society. Latino men, especially those with darker features, report high rates of racial discrimination from gay white men (Ibanez et al. 2009). Among gay African American men, many report high rates of discrimination at gay bars, night clubs, and other social settings, as well as report feeling marginalized and unaccepted in the gay community (Ichard 1985; Kraft et al. 2000). In a study of 911 gay Latino men in New York, Miami, and Los Angeles, Ibanez et al. found that 36 percent of their study participants reported experiences of general racism while 58 percent reported racism specifically from gay white men (Ibanez et al. 2009). Similarly, a more recent study found that 70 percent of 1,196 gay Asian, black, and Latino men in the greater Los Angeles area reported experiencing racism in the gay community while only 57 percent of the respondents reported experiencing racism within the general community

(Choi et al. 2013). Also, in a survey of gay, lesbian, bisexual, and transgender Asian and Pacific Islander Americans in New York City, 82 percent of the respondents reported personal experiences with racism specifically in the gay community (Dang and Hu 2005) and gay Asian men report that they felt racism more acutely from gay white men than from others (Ruez 2017). As high as these numbers are, the true percentage of gay men of color who experience racism may be even higher as stigmatized people may avoid attributing negative treatment to racism given the high negative costs of making such claims (Kaiser and Miller 2001; Kaiser and Miller 2003). In fact, Czopp and Monteith demonstrate that members of dominant groups often do respond negatively to claims of racism or sexism by members of minority groups, adding more credence to Kaiser and Miller's argument that experiences of racism may be higher than what is reported (Czopp and Moteith 2003; Kaiser and Miller 2001; Kaiser and Miller 2003).

Despite the recognition that racism is wide spread in the gay community, few scholars have attempted to explore the nature of racism experienced by gay men of color. Instead, most studies on the experiences of gay men of color use racism as a taken-for-granted social fact and focuses on the effects of racism rather than on racism itself. In this way, studies about gay men of color's experience with racism mirror studies of racism in general. As Bonilla-Silva noted, "Too many social analysts researching racism assume that the phenomenon is self-evident, and therefore either do not provide a definition or provide an elementary definition" (Bonilla-Silva 1997, 465). On the surface, it would seem self-evident what does and does not constitute "racism." Like pornography, we assume that we will know it when we see it.

Because academic inquires about racism use the taken-for-granted definition when examining the effects of racism on minority populations, they attempt to examine the impact of racism on minority populations by asking how racism impacts a number of different outcome variables without any attempt to define exactly what it is that is doing the impacting. Imagined this way, racism is always thought to be something that exerts an influence on something else, as if it is outside of the social processes that create it. The problem with this definition is that it is often treated as a given with little attempt to expand not only on what it is but on *how* it exerts an influence. Unfortunately, this type of use of racism erases the perpetrators of racism from the analysis (Feagin 2009; Feagin and Elias 2013). Rather than an action that certain people engage in, racism becomes a part of the social structure as if it is another unfortunate consequence of modern life that leaves "victims" but do not have "perpetrators."

Because of this tendency, the general questions about what counts as "racism" go largely unanswered leading to disagreements about who can even be "racist." All too often, racism is conflated with discrimination or bias, to which anyone can fall victim. Imagined this way, people of color can easily be racist if they hold negative views of whites. Yet Magnus Hirschfeld (1933) in his original conceptualizing of "racism" noted that racism involves far more than simply a bias against others. Instead, racism involves the development of racist ideology that creates a hierarchy of race which leads to institutionalized discriminatory practices. Racism is not simply a collection of individual biases or even individual acts of discrimination, but is deeply rooted in larger social beliefs about certain racial group. For racism to exist, it requires collective action from members of a dominant group, clearly identifiable social hierarchies based on race, and discriminatory practices that are instructional, not individual. Given this, racist discourse is often deployed to create the illusion of a biological difference between one group and another, between who belongs and who doesn't. In this exploratory chapter, we attempt to examine how racism manifests itself in the gay community and examine specifically how gay men of color experience racism from gay white men. In the spirit of inquiry rather than confirmation, we analyze comments made by gay men on various online websites that cater to a gay audience to find the nuances of how gay men of color talk about racism and the specific types of ways that racism operates within this arena.

EXPERIENCING GAY RACISM

The feeling that gay men of color experience more racism from gay white men than from the larger society is wide spread among members of these groups. For example, a gay black man calling himself Jay wrote on the website About.com in response to a story written by a gay black man:

> As a 22 year old gay black male, I've faced more racism in the gay community than anywhere else. Love has no color, the discrimination needs to stop in order for us gays to have equal rights.

Echoing his sentiment, another poster who called himself Shane wrote:

> I'm a gay black male and recently turned 33, and like Jay, I have experienced more racism in the GAY community than anywhere else. It seems to be a constant, almost to the point of being the NORM. And that really shouldn't be. I recently went to a pride event in New Orleans and STILL experienced it from other gays at the event. It was disheartening . . . but not discouraging as I still had a blast. But honestly, I have NO idea how to change it. The younger generation of gays seem to be even MORE racist than the gays I grew up with. Hopefully it something they will grow out of.

Likewise, a poster calling himself Trey wrote on the gay website Queerty in response to an article about racism in the gay community:

> Most displays of overt racism that have been directed at me have come from white gay men . . . usually in the form of a left-handed compliment. I've also been refused service and denied entry into clubs. As a gay black man, it can be depressing.

Yet another gay black man calling himself Greg noted:

> I use to think maybe I was overreacting, but after mingling and socializing with gay men since the mid 1990s and still experiencing rampant bigotry from most of them, I can say emphatically that gay racism is alive and well in the gay culture. And as a gay black man, this makes me feel angry, depress, and sad. If I could be straight, I would. Because at this stage of my life, I would have been happily married to a female, had children, and not had to put up with all the baggage being gay brings. Because for me and some other black men who I've spoken with, being gay and black is a depressing and sad experience. We tend to be looked at as ugly and not worthy to be friends with nor have a relationship with. It also seems we're not even worthy to be in most gay publications, tv shows, or films compared to our gay white male counterparts. Who would've thought my greatest disappoint and sadness would come from gay society and not straight society. I now know why most gay men suffer from depression and suicidal tendencies. It's because of the lack of emotional support one receives from the gay male culture and the utter shallowness it presents. If you're a gay man of color, the odds are you'll feel very isolated within the gay culture.

The sentiments expressed by gay men of color are not surprising given that gay white men behave in blatantly racist ways online. On March 7, 2014, *LGBTQ Nation* posted an Associated Press article about San Francisco 49ers cornerback Chris Culliver and his attempt to make amends with the gay community after making antigay comments during the Super Bowl media day in 2013. Specifically, the article shared how Culliver had been working with the Trevor Project, an organization that provides crisis intervention for LGBT youth and his future plans to work with Michael Sam, a University of Missouri defensive end who is widely expected to become the first openly gay professional football player. Because *LGBTQ Nation* requires commenters to log in to the account using their Facebook account, the race and gender of the commenters is visibly deducible. Many of the white posters expressed doubts about Culliver's "change of heart," while most black posters were likely to congratulate Culliver on his efforts to reach out to the gay community. Not surprisingly, there were a number of hurtful comments made toward Culliver, inciting many posters to comment on the "disheartening" nature of the comments, particularly the one made by Ricky Roberts who simply wrote, "Fuck him." Responding to those who were opposed to Ricky Roberts' comment, one poster named Sandro Em wrote in defense of Ricky Roberts by writing:

> Saying bad things for self defense is essential, every time you don't react to an injustice you character become weaker and you can no longer defend your self or loved once . . . so YES FUCK HIM??? Send him to AFRIKA!!! Filthy pig.

Of course, Chris Culliver never threatened Ricky Roberts, so Roberts' statement can hardly be counted as "self-defense." Also, it seems completely lost on Sandro Em that the need to react to injustice does not necessitate making racist comments about where members of certain racial groups should be sent.

Blatantly racist comments on gay forums are legion. When the website Queerty posted a short story on The Urban League of Atlanta presenting a Champions of Justice and Equality Award to Dan Cathy, the vocal and visible antigay CEO of the Christian fast food company Chick-fil-A, readers were understandably irate. Not surprisingly, many readers made blatantly racist comments such as "Dottie Johnson [head of The Urban League] has a lot o' 'splainin' to do!" and "Fried chicken? I guess this award might make sense if he Urban League also gave an award to a brewer of 40 oz. Malt liquor. Oh, and a heroin dealer while they're at it."

The blatant racism of gay white men was most evident following the passage of Proposition 8 in California that invalidated marriage rights for LGBT people. Following the passage of Prop 8, many gay commentators openly and explicitly blamed black Americans for the passage of the act, turning black Americans into easy scapegoats for their own failure. Rather than address the fact that opposition to Prop 8 was high only a few months before the election but slowly narrowed under the well-coordinated campaign launched by anti-marriage proponents and virtually evaporated following what most media analysts have agreed was a disastrous response by GLBTQ groups, GLBYQ leaders and organizations shifted the blame to black voters. But as if scapegoating blacks for their own failure were not enough, black Americans became targets of racist vitriol, some of which were collected by blogger Pam Spaulding. According to Geoffrey, a gay black student who shared his experience during a marriage equality rally held outside the Mormon temple in Los Angeles stated:

> It was like being at a klan rally except the klansmen were wearing Abercrombie polos and Birkenstocks. YOU N****R, one man shouted at me. If your people want to call me a FAGGOT, I will call you a n****r. Someone else said same

thing to me on the next block near the temple . . . me and my friend were walking, he is also gay but Korean, and a young WeHo clone said after last night the n****rs better not come to West Hollywood [the gay neighborhood in Los Angeles] if they knew what was BEST for them.

Another gay black man named Ronald wrote that he and his boyfriend, also black, were verbally accosted during the rally while holding NO ON PROP 8 signs:

> Three older men accosted my friend and shouted, "Black people did this, I hope you people are happy!" A young lesbian couple with mohawks and Obama buttons joined the shouting and said they were "very disappointed with black people" and "how could we" after the Obama victory. This was stupid for them to single us out because we were carrying those blue NO ON PROP 8 signs! I pointed that out and the one of the older men said it didn't matter because "most black people hated gays" and he was "wrong" to think we had compassion. That was the most insulting thing I had ever heard. I guess he never thought we were gay.

Ronald's comment demonstrates how the construction of "gay" as being equivalent to "white" has impacted the lives of gay men of color. As evident from the racist taunts of the gay white men, Ronald and his friend are not a part of a gay community but reduced to their race. The idea that, as a gay black man, Ronald's rights have also been denied is not fathomable to the white men. Rather than a victim, Ronald is a part of the alleged homophobic black community that is against the "gay" community and responsible for the alleged homophobia inflicted upon them.

Invisibility and Exclusion

As Allan Bérubé noted, the fight for social justice by gay men which focused on achieving visibility and individual equality within existing social and political institutions led to the emergence of "an exclusively gay rights agenda isolated from supposedly non-gay issues, such as homelessness, unemployment, welfare, universal health care, union organizing, affirmative action, and abortion rights" (Bérubé 2002, 235). Thus, gay acceptance came at the cost of presenting the "gay community" as upscale, mostly male, and mostly white consumer market. As Bérubé notes, "such a strategy derives its power from an unexamined investment in whiteness and middle-class identification" (Bérubé 2002, 235). Achieving acceptability for the "gay community" meant "reinforcing a racialized class divide." In essence, gays became heteronormalized as white and middle class.

The invisibility that gay men of color experience in the gay community was captured by Marlon Riggs in his film *Tongues Untied* when he noted:

I pretend not to notice the absence of black images in this new gay life, in bookstores, poster shops, film festivals, even my own fantasies. . . . In this great, gay Mecca, I was an invisible man. I had no shadow, no substance, no place, no history, no reflection (Riggs 1989).

The sense of exclusion is both sexual and communal. As one gay black man calling himself Anthony in Nashville noted on the website Queerty:

As a black gay male, I've experienced my share of racism in the gay community, from being excluded from certain bars to not feeling like my opinions were seriously considered in community organizations to the general sexual objectification that I think is a common experience for black gay men. I used to believe that gays were more progressive than straights, but there are plenty of examples that prove otherwise.

Exclusion and invisibility are hardly limited to black men. As Song Cho wrote:

The pain of being a gay Asian, however, is not just the pain of direct discrimination but the pain of being negated again and again by a culture that doesn't acknowledge my presence. . . . Not only did I have to deal with the question of sexual invisibility as a gay man, there was also the issue of racial invisibility. (Cho 1998, 2)

The absence of images of men of color doesn't simply erase them but reinforces the construction of a "gay community" as being homogeneously white. As Teunis (2007, 269) stated, "Whiteness in the gay community is visible, palpable, if for no other reason than that images of men of colour are absent."

The invisibility of gay men of color in the larger conception of what it means to be "gay" in the United States leads to the trivialization of their experiences as people who are both racialized and homosexualized. In an earlier chapter, the first author noted that gay white men view alternative ways of "being" gay as somehow lacking or illegitimate (Han 2007). Even well-meaning gay white men have a tendency to judge the lives of gay men of color from the white perspective. For example, one gay white man calling himself Alan down in Florida who was very sympathetic to issues of racism in the gay community wrote on Queerty:

The African-American branch of the GLBT community needs to do much more work at home. They need to change their own community's mind about homosexuality. They need to change an environment that is so hostile to gay men that the entire down low phenomenon flourishes. They need to stop the intentional blindness to the staggering number of blatantly, if not openly, gay men and women that they see in church every week. Kick out the queers and there will be no more choirs and music. These people need to be recognized and validated as useful, important members of the black community. They are people and not just stereotypes. And these people need to stand up and demand acknowledgment and acceptance, to do the bridge building between the two communities from within their neighborhoods. This cannot be done by outsiders.

There are multiple issues with Alan down in Florida's comments. First, he assumes that the black community is "hostile" to gay men and that the down low phenomenon is a reaction to black homophobia rather than gay racism. Yet as a number of scholars have found, the down low is a complex identity that black men adopt specifically in order to avoid being labeled as "gay" even when others are aware of his sexual orientation. Rather than a reaction to black homophobia or an attempt to hide their same sex attraction, it is a reaction to a gay community that many of the men who self identify as "down low" view as being overwhelmingly white and unwelcoming of blacks (Han et al. 2014). Alan down in Florida also assumes that blacks are "intentionally blind" to gay black men who are active in their churches, often as leaders in the church choir. Stereotyping of black choirs aside, Alan in Florida assume that not being blatantly and openly "out" with their sexuality is somehow means that they are not "acknowledged" or "accepted." However, many commentators have noted, gay men of color may avoid coming out of the closet or identifying as "gay" because they view "gay" as a white identity or see the gay community as hostile to men of color. Yet in Alan down in Florida's mind, any way of "being" gay that is different from the white way of being gay is somehow lacking. It is just taken as a given that the gay white experience is the legitimate gay experience and anyone who deviates from that experience is somehow not being fully truthful in their lives.

The tendency to make white gay experiences the only legitimate gay experience is evident in one of the only stories to feature gay men of color in *The Advocate*, the largest gay publication in the United States. Published online on May 17, 2013, the article titled "Rising above the Down Low" by Sunnivie Brydum, traces the coming-out process of two black men named Tarrodd and Marvin. As expected, the article sensationalizes the down low "phenomenon" popular in media discourse and blames black culture as the source of the phenomenon. Rather than make any attempt to discuss the social context of a "down low" which has been discussed by gay scholars and activist of color as both an "activity" and an "identity," or to explore the role that racism plays in the down low phenomenon and the adaptation of a down low identity, the article celebrates the two men for finally coming out of the closet and living an "openly" gay life endorsed by mainstream gay social norms. As if the endorsement of mainstream gay social norms was not enough, any attempt to create a gay existence or subjectivity outside of that norm, such as through developing a down low identity, is demonized as not being true to one's "authentic" self and being "trapped" by society.

In fact, even when gay men and women of color are celebrated by some media outlets, their legitimacy to be celebrated is also challenged by some gay white men. For example, Queerty ran a column titled "Seven LGBT African Americans Who Changed the Face of the Gay Community," during black history month in 2012. While many of the comments were thoughtful, with some listing others who did not make the list, a poster calling himself Isaac C wrote:

> All of these people are pretty much irrelevant in the grand scheme of things outside of racial/color representation, which I guess is important enough for some people. I certainly don't consider most of them a part of the GLBT rights movement.

Thus in multiple ways, gay men and women are color are not only marginalized but also actively erased from gay history, leading to the continuing belief that gay white people are central while others are marginal.

Sexual Rejection

Not only does racism perpetuate legal and economic inequality, it also promotes social inequality by creating racial hierarchies where members of some racial groups are believed to be superior while members of other racial groups are believed to be inferior. Among gay men, this is achieved by a hierarchy of attractiveness that is based on race. When coupled with race, the language of sexual preference reinforces the dominant racial systems of oppression. As Peter Jackson has noted:

> When desirability is linked with race, and when certain races are ascribed a greater erotic interest than others, then to be a member of an "unsexy" ethnic group is to be equated with an inferior form of existence. (Jackson 2000)

Sexual rejection comes in many forms, some subtle and some not so much. It can be both active and/or passive. I consider sexual rejection in the gay community as being "active" because it involves more than simply declining sexual advances from men of color or not seeking men of color as sexual partners. Rather, sexual rejection in the gay community involves active rejection of members of certain racial groups before initial contact. For example, Phua and Kaufman found that gay men are more likely to distinguish between potential partners based on race than heterosexual men (Phua and Kaufman 2003). Similarly, Callander, Holt, and Newman found that gay white men were the most likely to specifically exclude non-same race potential partners in their online dating profiles (Callander, Holt, and Newman 2012).

Rather than racial exclusion, gay white men attempt to discuss sexual rejection based on race as "sexual preference," a strategy that has been demonstrated to be used by individuals who hold racist views in order to avoid being label a "bad racist" (Bonilla-Silva 1997). For example, a man calling himself WhiteGuy wrote on the website About.com in response to an article on racism in the gay community:

> It's hard to call somebody a racist just because they don't date outside their race. It's like saying all gay men are sexist and/or chauvinistic cause they aren't attracted to women. Personally, I don't date blacks, Asians, middle easterners, Indians, or any dark people, period because I'm just not attracted. It's that simple. Do I hate them? No. Do I want to sleep with them or cuddle or share my most intimate moments? No!

What's interesting about the way they frame their preferences is the way that gay white men attempt to conflate racial preference with sexuality itself. As the above commenter noted, his disinterest in men of color is similar to his disinterest in women. This is a similar tactic, as a man using the non de plume Anonymous wrote on the website Thought Catalog:

> There's something I can't explain that just doesn't feel a sexual attraction to [black men]. You know, chemistry. It's as simple as that. I'm not attracted to black guys in the same way that I don't like girls. It's all a question of preference.

Arguments veiled in the language of biology are difficult to counter. Things that are too difficult, or too uncomfortable, to address come to adorn the mantle of "human nature," as if human behavior is guided by an invisible hand embedded in genetics rather than human agency. Not surprisingly, the tendency to view racial preference as deeply rooted in biology rather than based on socially constructed notions of desirability and the carefully choreographed hierarchies of race run rampantly unopposed in gay media productions. Not surprisingly, attempts to justify racial preferences use the language of biology and conflate racial preference with sexuality itself. Other attempts to equate racial preference with sexuality are legion. For example, a poster calling himself Cory123 wrote on Queerty:

You basically tell me I should force myself to sleep with everyone whether or not I'm attracted to them to re-arrange my brain or something. Why the fuck would I want to do that? So that obese, hairy, odorous, half black half Asian men everywhere can feel confident hitting on anyone they want? Really???? That's what you think people should do? I've always listed my preference to white guys only and always will. Just as I'll always go with guys not girls. Once again, remember what you're implying, that we CHOOSE who we're attracted to. Well, if that's the case, let's all be straight!

Yet another gay white man calling himself dleon84 wrote:

If sex and attraction are the same with everyone, then why are we gay? We then choose the aesthetic of same sex partners and refuse the opposite sex. By your definition, then there is no reason that we are gay/straight/bi/trans.

The problem, however, is that when gay white men let their "preference" for white partners publicly know, many go out of their way to make racist comments. The website Douchebags of Grindr collects various personal profiles from the mobile application Grindr, the most popular application used by gay men to find nearby sexual partners. Grindr includes a function called blocking which allows users to prevent other users from sending them messages. Some of the profiles written by gay white men include statements such as "I block more Asians than the great wall of China," "Squinty eye, no reply," "I don't speak Ebonics," and "I am thoroughly impressed with China in the Olympics. They are using the same person for every event." Similarly, on the dating websites OKCupid, Manhunt, and Adam4Adam, derogatory comments about racialized others such as "I don't like Asians, I like big cocks," or "How many times do I have to tell black guys that I don't like chocolate?" are common. Thus rather than a way of simply listing their preference for white men, online sites for seeking sexual partners have delved into venues for gay white men to vocalize their racist beliefs.

A gay man calling himself Matt Thomas made an excellent point in response to the FAB Magazine article by Alex Rowlson about the rampant racism on gay dating sites when he noted:

Usually when I want chicken not veal, I order chicken. I don't tell the whole restaurant that the veal is fucking gross and anyone who approaches me with veal is an idiot. Nor do I come up with some kind of vague insult or slur against it. (Rowlson 2011)

As Matt Thomas notes, what makes gay white male behavior surrounding racial preferences isn't that they have a racial preference, but that they use the ruse of preference to voice and publicize their racist beliefs.

Even when white men discuss the desirability or attractiveness of men of color, it is often couched in the language of exceptions. For example, a poster calling himself Pands commented on an article about the actor Shemar Moore on the gay website Adam4Adam that:

> I am not into black men BUT, he is one of the few I would do.

Another poster calling himself James also commented:

> I'm not normally attracted to black men, but Shemar Moore is so good looking, he transcends race or ethnicity.

In fact, even the author of the article, who called himself Dave wrote this about Shemar Moore:

> His face and look are so different than any other black guys out there because of his interesting mix. Moore's father is African American and his mother, who was born in Roxbury, Massachusetts, is of Irish and French-Canadian descent.

By marking Moore as "different than any other black guys," the author distances Moore from other black men. More interestingly, while Moore's father is simply noted as being "African American," his white mother, from whom we are to assume Moore gets his "different" look that makes him worthy of sexual praise from a white man is from somewhere, and has an identifiable white ethnic background.

Similarly, during the rare times that a man of color is included among the "sexiest something" lists that are legion in gay publications, they are again marked as exceptions. For example, on March 28, 2014, Queerty ran an article titled "Nine Pocket-sized Guys We'd Love to Pack Up and Carry Around With Us," about shorter but sexy men which included both gay and straight celebrities including Josh Hutcherson, Elijah Wood, and Ryan Seacrest. The list also includes singer Bruno Mars who is described rather unenthusiastically. While the white men on the list are described specifically using their physical traits that make them attractive or as sexually desirable, the description of Alec Mapa, the gay Filipino comedienne begins with "gay funny man Alec Mapa may not be traditional movie star handsome." One can only guess why the writers and editors at Adam4Adam felt the need to specifically point out that Alec Mapa was not attractive in order to justify his inclusion on the list.

Sadly, some gay men of color have become apologists for gay white men. As an Asian poster calling himself JonDorian noted on Queerty:

> We so strongly driven by our sexuality that I think that we voice our preferences frankly for the sake of, for the lack of a better word, efficiency. You can ask

any Latino, Black or Asian or even Caucasian person every now and then, that they have been turned down because of their ethnicity. It's not something to be offended by because we all have our preferences—race related or not.

Ironically, this defense of racial preferences came after JonDorian shared his own personal experiences being a gay Asian man. According to JonDorian:

> As an Asian when I was in my early teens I couldn't get a date anywhere. Asians weren't by any means attractive in the 90s and now I'm getting a lot of the (mildly offensive) "I'm not usually attracted to Asian guys but . . ."

What's interesting is that JonDorian completely ignores his own personal experiences of rejection based on race in order to argue that racial preferences are not racist by attempting to universalize these experiences.

Even more problematic is that gay men of color come to measure their desirability based on the criteria established by those who find them undesirable.

Objectification

In his essay "China doll," Tony Ayres notes:

> It is an attraction to me *because* of my Asianness, my otherness. Again, this has nothing to do with who I think I am, my individual qualities as a person, or even as an object of desire. It is the fact that I conveniently fit into someone else's fantasy. . . . And they expect me to be so flattered by the attention of a white man that I will automatically bend over and grab my ankles." (1999, 80; emphasis in the original)

This sense of being objectified is repeated by other gay men of color. As one gay black man calling himself Daniel K noted on Queerty:

> I can tell you as a GBM (gay black man) it's just as disturbing to me to have a guy not give me the time of day just because I'm black as it is to have white guys hound me just BECAUSE I'm black.

As the above quote demonstrates, gay men of color are in a racial bind when it comes to dating gay white men. On the one hand, they are sexually marginalized by gay white men yet the gay white men who seek out men of color for sex often reduce them to their race. As such, gay men of color report meeting racial expectations during their sexual encounters with gay white men or risk being rejected (Teunis 2007; Han 2008).

Sexual behaviors are also influenced by how gay men of color are objectified. Husbands et al. found that black men's sexual behaviors changed based
on the race of their sexual partner, with black men expected to meet the
stereotypical role of the dominant sexual top when with white partners as
opposed to black partners (Husbands et al. 2012). Similarly, Han found that
gay Asian men attempt to meet stereotypical expectations in order to please
white sexual partners (Han 2008).

Objectification implies that it is the racial characteristic that matters rather
than the person in finding someone attractive. During a lively discussion on
racism on the website Queerty, a gay white man calling himself Jaroslaw
began his post with, "JonDorian—I always thought Asians were hot and I
work in New Center. Any chance for a date?" before making his point about
Proposition 8 and African Americans. Given that Queerty does not use photos
of posters, Jaroslaw's romantic overture toward JonDorian was based only on
JonDorian's race as no other information such as age, height, weight, occupation, education, and so on were provided. What drew Jaroslaw to JonDorian
was simply that he was Asian. To Jaroslaw who "always thought Asians were
hot," no other information was necessary to ask JonDorian for a date.

The problem with objectification is that, when taken to the extreme, people
come to be seen purely in terms of stereotypical traits associated with the
body (Bartky 1990). It isn't simply that they come to be seen as objects for
consumption but as being a consumable good with predictable characteristics.
And when people come to be seen as a consumer product, they are judged
and valued in terms of the utility that they provide for the enjoyment of others
rather than on intrinsic characteristic that they may possess as human beings.
As Cornel West noted, the expected large penis of a black man is a metaphor
for hypersexuality that is both pleasurable and dangerous (West 1993). So
when black men are objectified by white men as being hypersexual or having
large penises, he becomes equated with the penis, an object to be used rather
than a subject to be known.

Gay men of color are only desirable precisely because they are different,
because they represent something outside of the social norm that defines the
gay community. As bell hooks has noted, "The commodification of otherness
has been so successful because it is offered as a new delight, more intense,
more satisfying than normal ways of doing and feeling" (hooks 1992, 21).
The language of sexual objectification of men of color by gay white men
clearly demonstrates this "otherness" that has come to define racialized
sexual desire. It isn't simply a sexual desire for something "different" but
rather something more tribal, traditional, authentic, or any number of other
adjectives that have come to be code words for someone that is outside of
any conceivable beliefs about who "we" are opposed to who "they" are. One
must ask then, how can we discuss sexual preferences that are dictated largely

by race and held-for-granted assumptions about race as anything other than being deeply and intimately rooted in racialized beliefs about the other?

As bell hooks has noted, this "commodification of otherness has been so successful because it is offered as a new delight, more intense, more satisfying than normal ways of doing and feeling" (hooks 1992, 21). If gay men of color are to be sexually consumed, they must be sexually consumed because of their otherness, because of the exotic experience that they provide. For example, in a recent article that appeared in *The Advocate*, Michael Lowenthal describes his trip to Nanjing, China, where he traveled across twelve time zones "to find a gay experience as foreign as the culinary delicacies his hosts won't stop serving." The article is teased as being about how the author engaged in a sexual experience that he would never even have thought to engage in "at home." At the end of the article, this "foreign" sexual experience is exposed as sex with an Asian drag queen. Given that the author resides in Boston, one must ask why it is that having sex with an Asian drag queen was something he could not even have imagined before traveling across the globe. For Lowenthal, Asian men, drag queen or not, are only acceptable as sexual partners if they are contextualized as a foreign experience that adds flavor to an exotic adventure. Stateside, they are simply others to be avoided at best and discarded at worst.

CONCLUSION

Recent studies on gay men of color have demonstrated that members of this group experience widespread racism in the gay community from gay white men. However, these studies have largely been limited to examining how racism impacts their lives rather than on how racism manifests itself in the gay community. A part of the reason for this may be the larger tendency in the social sciences to take racism as a given and examine the impacts of racism on racial minorities rather than to study racism itself. In this chapter, we attempted to examine the nature of racism experienced by gay men of color from gay white men. To do so, we examined the stories told by gay men of color about race and racism and the responses from gay white men.

In examining these narratives, we found that gay men of color experience racism in three different ways. First, the larger gay community, both its social spaces and media products, largely ignores gay men of color, rendering them invisible as gay men. Second, gay men of color also experience sexual rejection from gay white men based on their race. While gay white men argue that it is a "preference" and not racism, their actions betray racist beliefs about gay men of color that excludes the possibility of social encounters of a sexual nature. Finally, when gay men of color are seen as acceptable sexual partners, they objectified by gay white men and reduced to their race.

Clearly, observant readers will note that the racist comments made by gay white men on gay forums are not unique to the gay community. Straight people make equally racist comments on general websites. Certainly, gay men of color confront racist comments on numerous websites and in their everyday lives that have little to do with their sexuality. In many ways, the types of racism found in the gay community simply mirror those in the larger society. However, the goal of this chapter is not to argue that these types of behaviors are unique to the gay community or that they are contained by gay websites. Rather, the goal of this chapter was to explore how racism exerts itself in the gay community and how gay men of color experience racism from gay white men.

As an exploratory and narrative study, the findings from this chapter are not universal and readers should avoid making generalized conclusions from them. Nonetheless, this study offers a new insight into racism and how racism manifests itself in the gay community. In order to expand on these findings, future research should focus on examining the nature of racism in the gay community using a more representative sample of gay men of color.

REFERENCES

Armstrong, Elizabeth A. 2002. *Forging Gay Identities: Organizing Sexuality in San Francisco, 1950–1994*. Chicago: University of Chicago Press.

Ayala, George, Trista Bingham, Junyeop Kim, Darrell P. Wheeler, and Gregorio A. Millett. 2012. "Modeling the Impact of Social Discrimination and Financial Hardship on the Sexual Risk of HIV Among Latino and Black Men Who Have Sex with Men." *American Journal of Public Health* 102: 242–249.

Ayres, Tony. 1999. "China Doll: The Experience of Being a Gay Chinese Australian." *Journal of Homosexuality* 36: 87–97.

Bartky, Sandra L. 1990. *Femininity and Domination: Studies in the Phenomenology of Oppression*. New York: Routledge.

Bathhouse Diaries, "Racism or Preference (At the Baths)?". Accessed February 10, 2005. http://www.bathhouseblues.com/racism.html.

Bérubé, Allan. 2001. "How Gay Stays White and What Kind of White it Stays." *Making and Unmaking of Whiteness*, edited by Brigit Brander Rasmussen, Eric Klinenberg, Irene J. Nexica, and Matt Wray, 234–265. Durham, NC: Duke University Press.

Bonilla-Silva, Eduardo. 1997. "Rethinking Racism: Toward a Structural Interpretation." *American Sociological Review* 62: 465–480.

———. 2006. *Racism Without Racists: Color-Blind Racism and the Persistence of Racial Inequality in the United States*. New York: Rowman & Littlefield.

Brydum, Sunnivie. "Rising Above the Down Low." *The Advocate*. Accessed May 17, 2013. http://www.advocate.com/arts-entertainment/television/2013/05/17/two-stories-rising-above-down-low.

Callander, Denton, Martin Holt, and Christy E. Newman. 2012. "Just a Preference: Racialised Language in the Sex-seeking Profiles of Gay and Bisexual Men." *Culture, Health & Sexuality* 14: 1049–1063.

———. 2016. "'Not Everyone's Gonna Like Me': Accounting for Race and Racism in Sex and Dating Web Services for Gay and Bisexual Men." *Ethnicities* 16: 3–21.

Cho, Song. 1998. *Rice: Explorations into Asian Gay Culture & Politics*. Toronto, Canada: Queer Press Non-Profit Publishing.

Choi, Kyung-Hee, Jay Paul, George Ayala, Ross Boylan, and Steven E. Gregorich. 2013. "Experiences of Discrimination and Their Impact on the Mental Health Among African American, Asian and Pacific Islander, and Latino Men Who Have Sex with Men." *American Journal of Public Health* 103: 868–874.

Czopp, Alexander M. and Margo J. Monteith. 2003. "Confronting Prejudice (Literally): Reactions to Confrontations and Racial and Gender Bias." *Personality and Social Psychology Bulletin* 29: 532–544.

Dang, Alain and Mandy Hu. 2005. *Asian Pacific American Lesbian, Gay, Bisexual and Transgender People: A Community Portrait*. New York: National Gay and Lesbian Task Force Policy Institute.

Epstein, Steven. 1996. *Impure Science: AIDS, Activism, and the Sociology of Knowledge*. Berkeley, CA: University of California Press.

Feagin, Joe R. 2009. *The White Racial Frame: Centuries of Racial Framing and Counter-Framing*. New York: Routledge.

Feagin, Joe R. and Hernan Vera. 1995. *White Racism: The Basics*. New York: Routledge.

Feagin, Joe R. and Sean Elias. 2013. "Rethinking Racial Formation Theory: A Systemic Racism Critique." *Ethic and Racial Studies* 36: 931–960.

Haile, Rahwa, Tawandra L. Rowell-Cunsolo, Edith A. Parker, Mark B. Padilla, and Nathan B. Hansen. 2014. "An Empirical Test of Racial/Ethnic Differences in Perceived Racism and Affiliation with the Gay Community: Implications for HIV Risk. *Journal of Social Issues* 70: 342–359.

Han, C. Winter. 2007. "They Don't Want to Cruise Your Type: Gay Men of Color and the Racial Politics of Exclusion." *Social Identities* 13: 51–67.

———. 2008. "A Qualitative Exploration of the Relationship Between Racism and Unsafe Sex Among Asian Pacific Islander Gay Men." *Archives of Sexual Behavior* 37: 827–837.

Han, C. Winter, Scott E. Rutledge, Lisa Bond, Jennifer Lauby, and Archana B. LaPollo. 2014. "You're Better Respected When You Carry Yourself as a Man: Black Men's Personal Accounts of the Down Low 'Lifestyle.'" *Sexuality & Culture* 18: 89–102.

Han, C. Winter. 2015. *Geisha of a Different Kind: Race and Sexuality in Gaysian America*. New York: New York University Press.

hooks, bell. 1992. *Black Looks: Race and Representation*. Cambridge, MA: South End Press.

Husbands, Winston, Lydia Makoroka, Rinaldo Wolcott, Barry D. Adam, Clemon George, Robert S. Remis, and Sean B. Rourke. 2013. "Black Gay Men as Sexual Subjects: Race, Racialisation and the Social Relations of Sex Among Black Gay Men in Toronto." *Culture, Health & Sexuality* 15: 434–449.

Icard, Larry. 1986. "Black Gay Men and Conflicting Social Identities." *Journal of Social Work & Human Sexuality* 4: 180–190.

Jackson, Peter A. 2000. "'That's What Rice Queens Study!': White Gay Desire and Representing Asian Homosexualities." *Journal of Australian Studies* 24: 181–188.

Kaiser, Cheryl R. and Carol T. Miller. 2001. "Stop Complaining! The Social Costs of Making Attributions to Discrimination." *Personality and Social Psychology Bulletin* 27: 254–263.

———. 2003. "Derogating the Victim: The Interpersonal Consequences of Blaming Events on Discrimination." *Personality and Social Psychology Bulletin* 27: 254–263.

Kraft, Joan M., Carolyn Beeker, Joseph P. Stokes, and John L. Peterson. 2000. "Finding 'Community' in Community-Level HIV/AIDS Interventions: Formative Research with Young African American Men Who Have Sex with Men." *Health Education & Behavior* 27: 430–441.

Orne, Jason. 2017. *Boystown: Sex and Community in Chicago*. Chicago: University of Chicago Press.

Phua, Voon C. and Gayle Kaufman. 2003. "The Crossroads of Race and Sexuality: Date Selection Among Men in Internet 'Personal' Ads." *Journal of Family Issues* 24: 981–994.

Riggs, Damien W. (Ed.) 2018. *The Psychic Life of Racism in Gay Men's Communities*. New York, NY: Lexington Books.

Riggs, Marion. *Tongues Untied*. Motion Picture. Directed by Marion Riggs. USA: Strand Releasing. 2008.

Robinson, Brandon A. 2015. "'Personal Preference' as the New Racism: Gay Desire and Racial Cleansing in Cyberspace." *Sociology of Race and Ethnicity* 1: 317–330.

Ruez, Derek. 2017. "I Never Felt Targeted as an Asian… Until I Went to a Gay Pub': Sexual Racism and the Aesthetic Geographies of the Bad Encounter." *Environment and Planning* 49: 893–910.

Teunis, Niels. 2007. "Sexual Objectification and the Construction of Whiteness in the Gay Male Community." *Culture, Health & Sexuality* 9: 263–275.

Warner, Michale. 1993. *Fear of a Queer Planet: Queer Politics and Social Theory*. Minneapolis: University of Minnesota Press.

West, Cornell. 1993. *Race Matters*. New York: Vintage Books.

Chapter 3

"OK, So Zion's Not a Sissy Anymore He's Gay, So Let's Call Him That"

From Elementary School to College: Schooling Experiences of Black Gay Males Leading to Understanding and Self-Possession of Their Intersecting Racial and Sexual Identities

Michael D. Bartone

Presented here are narratives of navigation and understanding of and appreciation of the participants' intersecting identities, a self-possession rarely given attention in the literature (Bartone 2015). This attention becomes important because currently the field of public education has a workforce dominated by White female educators: 81 percent of K–12 public school teachers are White and 77 percent are female (National Center for Educational Statistics, n.d.). From participants' narratives emerged several themes, most notably: self-determination (taking the initiative to seek information and relationships to learn about sexual identity), experiential evolution (understanding that experience translates into growth and self-affirmation), thick skin (increasing ability to face and conquer challenges based on negotiation of past challenges), racial shelving (bracketing race in majority-Black environments to contend with sexual identity issues); and defying/transcending stereotypes (refusing to conform to dominant narratives about Black gay males); all of these themes developed due to the effect of the school environments they navigated, as well as the effect of other institutions they encountered, but the focus here is their schooling experiences.

Within this chapter, attention is given to how the participants' experiences in schools led them to learn (overtly and covertly) about and begin to accept and appreciate their racial and sexual identities. Further, implications for educators working with Black gay youth addresses ways educators can understand the importance of knowing how to support Black gay youth, which includes bringing in the Black sexual minority community in their instruction through myriad of units of study. From these units, and learning from the participants' experiences, the hope is schools can become educative places of race and sexuality and where racism and heteronormativity are known, dismantled, and schools and society made safe for Black queer youth, and in turn all youth for the future of humanity.

BLACK AND GAY YOUTH AND IDENTITY

For Black sexual minority youth, forming and understanding one's racial identity consists of relying on family members and peers (Cardabo 2005; Jamil et al. 2009). Peers and family members help the navigation through a racist society, but what about helping youth know their sexual identity which differs from many peers and family members? Living in a heterosexist society, youth are taught early that being of the sexual majority is "normal" and all else is "othered," not "normal"; sexual majority peoples rarely have to question their sexuality since their feelings of mental and physical attraction to the opposite sex is what is expected in society and reinforced daily. Thus, studies show Black sexual minority youth turn to the internet and/or community-based organizations to get a better understanding of their sexuality (Harper, Serrano, and Jamil 2009; Jamil et al. 2009); in some instances, unless specific to racially subaltern peoples, these spaces may not include or address an understanding of one's intersecting racial and sexual identities, thus causing tension for some youth.

A question White sexual minority people rarely, if at all, have to answer is, "what you identify with first: race or sexuality?" Since whiteness is normalized and the community of sexual minorities is seen by society largely as White, race becomes a non-factor (Dubé and Savin-Williams 1999). However, for Black sexual minority peoples this question gets asked (M. A. Hunter 2010; Meyer and Ouelette 2009), adding another layer to their identification and process for knowing their identities. The question is problematic because it demonstrates the idea one must choose and be either their racial community *or* into the community of sexual minorities because they must choose one or the other, which can cause stress (Meyer and Ouelette 2009). Yet, this is an important piece to examine because it affects Black sexual minority youth, whose identities should not, and cannot, be divorced from one another; these multiple intersecting identities must be front and center when discussing the lives and experiences of Black sexual minority youth so as not to ignore the influences of each identity on the person.

This identity process, and choosing how one presents oneself, demonstrates how racism (or whiteness) and heteronormativity function as social structures influencing how sexual minority people must live; they must choose to privilege a racial or sexual identity over the other and they must choose some category in which to place themselves based off of sexual majority social norms (e.g., in a relationship there must be gendered roles, one must be the "man" or husband, while the other must be the "woman" or wife and one must be in a biologically opposite-sex relationship to be "normal"). Complicating how one understands identity is the reality that for Black gay males, society has presented two dominant binaries: flamboyant and/or effeminate *or* a homo-thug, reinforcing tropes of Black men as sexual deviants (Hill Collins 2005).[1]

Sexual Minority Youth in School

Navigating through school for sexual minority youth is not easy, as many encounter hostile attitudes and microaggressions by peers, educators, and administrators; policies protecting sexual majority youth; and curricula often leaving the sexual minority community out in many subjects from history to language arts to sexual education (Kosciw et al. 2016; Mayo 2013). Also, schools are places where heteronormativity is reproduced and policies are often not supportive of sexual minority youth (Mayo 2013).

To underscore schooling experiences of sexual minority youth, of the over 10,000 youth ages 13–21 participating in The Gay Lesbian Straight Education Network's (GLSEN) 2015 Climate Survey (Kosciw et al. 2016; xvi–ii) data from responses show such hostility sexual minority youth face:

- 57.6 percent of LGBTQ students felt unsafe at school because of their sexual orientation, and 43.3 percent because of their gender expression.
- 63.5 percent of the students who did report an incident said school staff did nothing in response or told the student to ignore the harassment
- 56.2 percent of students reported hearing homophobic remarks from their teachers or other school staff, and 63.5 percent of students reported hearing negative remarks about gender expression from teachers or other school staff.
- Eight in ten LGBTQ students (81.6%) reported that their school engaged in LGBT-related discriminatory policies or practices.

Additionally, sexual minority youth express often missing days of school because of the hostility. Lastly, while other factors need to be included, the data from the survey shows sexual minority youth who "experienced higher levels of victimization" on average have lower grade point averages than those who report a lower level of harassment.

While the GLSEN Climate Survey is very important and illuminates the hostility sexual minority youth face, and the work that needs to be done to support sexual minority youth, it should be noted that 68 percent of the respondents are White, while 3.2 percent of the respondents are Black. Though the authors dedicate a brief section to exploring the responses by race and ethnicity, including "Black/African American students were less likely to feel unsafe due to sexual orientation" (Kosciw et al. 2016, 81), much more needs to be attended to and studies focusing solely on each groups response which would show a more complex and complete picture of how one's intersecting identities and their school setting informs their lives as sexual minority youth in school.[2] For instance, Mitchum and Moodie-Mills examined disciplinary data of LGBT youth and found that Black and Brown students face a system of criminalization, where "LGBT youth make up between 5% and 7% of the overall youth population, [but] they represent 15% of those in the juvenile justice system, and the vast majority of these youth are black and Latino" (Mitchum and Moodie-Mills 2014, 5). Like their racial and ethnic sexual majority peers, sexual minority youth from subaltern communities are no more violent or aggressive than their sexual majority and/or White peers: they are in a system where they are challenging the heteronormative school and where many of their teachers may have negative perceptions of them based on their racial identity (Ferguson 2000). Conjointly, for Black and Brown youth, schools are places of historic and continued disinvestment (Ladson-Billings 2006), where teachers come from and implement Eurocentric units and lessons (Asante 1991), have a deficit ideology of Black students (Howard 2013), and many White pre-service teachers have dysconcious racism (King 1991).

Knowing these tensions for Black sexual minority youth, this study aims to break the deficit ideology throughout much of the literature (Bartone 2015) to know how Black gay youth, in their words, successfully navigate through schools and other institutions to have a self-possession of their intersecting identities.

THEORETICAL FRAMEWORK AND POSITIONALITY

In order to analyze, code, interpret, and retell the participants' life histories centered around their intersecting identities, critical race theory (CRT) and quare theory are utilized. Briefly, CRT has several tenants, two of which are important for this study: racism is endemic to and woven throughout society, becoming a part of the national fabric, and race is the central focus of any analysis (Taylor 2009). For this study, in order to best know participants' experiences, knowing their navigation through a racist system and how this affected their knowing of their racial identity, means a researcher needs to attend to the institutionalized racial system in which these experiences occur and are in reaction to and from, to know what it means to be Black; Black is central to their identity as they learned from their family and peers about being Black and less explicitly about being gay from these peoples. Thus, their racial identity cannot be divorced from their experiences within the racist system.

Johnson explains that quare studies (or theory) "is a theory for gays and lesbians of color" (Johnson 2005, 127) in which researchers should be "refocusing our attention on the racialized bodies, experiences, and knowledges of transgendered people, lesbians, gays, and bisexuals of color, quare studies grounds the discursive process of mediated identification and subjectivity in a political praxis that speaks to the material existence of 'colored' bodies" (Johnson 2005, 136). In other words, quare studies acknowledges the embodied existence of Black sexual minority people, unlike queer theory, and quare studies allows a space for Black sexual minorities within discussions of blackness because "heterosexuality is no blacker than homosexuality" (Johnson 2005, 144). For this study, it is important to understand the embodied existence of Black gay youth and how they negotiate through school and society, putting their sexuality at the center with their racial identity.

Of importance too is understanding my positionality as a White cis-gender gay male. From the design and implementation of the study, and through the analysis and interpretation of and retelling of the data, I never lose sight that I am an outsider, that my racial privilege is never forgotten and is constantly checked to ensure I am not "whitewashing" or employing a "colorblind" lens to knowing and retelling their experiences; I do not believe in a colorblindness ideology. Additionally, when explaining their experiences to knowing their racial and sexual identity, I bracket my own knowing of my sexual and racial identity; knowing my racial identity, in fact my identity, has always been tied less to whiteness and more to being Italian American, which growing up I did not consider the same or offshoots of one another, and my racial identity was often covertly understood in juxtaposition to Black peoples: they are racial and we are not. Lastly, it became important to understand that my participants and I grew up in two different worlds of being sexual minorities: for me, in an era of less visibility and few rights but constant fights for rights by people, yet for the participants, they grew up in a time when sexual minority rights were front and center with much more visibility on television, in presidential elections, legal fights, and the participants, had the internet in which to turn and learn, while the internet did not exist in the same fashion for me.

METHODOLOGY

Using narrative inquiry, with a focus on life histories (Hatch and Wisniewski 1995) during the summer of 2014, five Black gay males (nineteen to twenty-four years of age) who spent most of their lives in metro-Atlanta were interviewed using semi-structured questions (Kvale and Brinkmann 2009) at least three times: first interview focused on birth-middle school; second, on high school-present; and, third explored their use of and presentation of self on social media; the focus on social media was to see how they presented themselves and their intersecting identities to the world knowing they love and embrace and these identities, but is not addressed here since this was not tied to their schooling experiences of learning about their intersecting identities.

Narrative inquiry provides a framework for understanding where these young males have come from and how they are progressing in their lives. Following from Polkinghorne, the participants' narratives are understood as a means for people to create an understanding of their experience and the significance of the experience (Polkinghorne 1988). Concurrently, according to Hatch and Wisniewski, the terms "life history" and "narrative" are often used interchangeable (Hatch and Wisniewski 1995). However, they note that for some researchers, there is a slight difference and it is this difference that guides this study, with Zellner noting the distinction being "all life histories are narratives, not all narratives are life histories" (Hatch and Wisniewski 1995, 114). In other words, someone can write a story or they can answer questions in an interview telling a story but not necessarily *their* story, *their* history. Lastly, Clandinin notes that as researchers we enter the participants' lives at a certain moment and must be conscious of that fact; in essence their life history is not done, so one's writing of participants' narrative should never be a finished product (Cladinin 2006).

According to Tierney there are three questions a researcher should ask themselves while they are conducting life histories: (a) What is the reason for this narrative? (b) What constitutes the truth in these narratives? and (c) Who is writing this narrative? (Tierney 2000). First, in this study I intend for life histories to inform educators in ways to best support Black gay youth in their personal, social, and educational growth. While the participants' narratives are not meant to be generalizable to *all* Black gay males, their narratives can provide a glimpse into ways educators, policymakers, and leaders of other institutions can better understand and/or begin to engage with their Black gay students to meet these students'/youths' needs. Second, taking from critical race and quare theories, truth is in the voices and histories and self-presentations of the participants, from their standpoints (Johnson 2008; Solorzano and Yosso 2009). As Harding notes, due to the marginalized position of many based on gender, race, class, sexuality, and other identifiers of marginalization, particular experiences and ways of knowing have been devalued (Harding 1993). Thus, by placing value on their experiences and ways of knowing and doing, may assist in challenging majoritarian beliefs regarding a universal truth experienced by all.

Worth noting is why Atlanta was chosen as the site of study. As previously noted, Atlanta is often viewed as the Black gay mecca (Jarvie 2006) due to the visibility and engagement of many organizations and peoples in the Black sexual minority community. Thus, in what way does the location of growing up in a city, or metro area, considered a Black gay mecca, affect how one comes to understand their intersecting racial and sexual identities? Knowing this about Atlanta, as another "player" in this study, is front in center in this study, whether or not the participants understood this about Atlanta as they were growing up.

The five participants' experiences are explained next with the themes found highlighted in their experiences. At the time of the study, Charlie[3] was twenty-one and on hiatus from college and living in a suburb of Atlanta with his mom, who knows he is gay but he has never officially "come out" to her, and Charlie had a steady boyfriend; they have since broken up. Slick Rick was twenty-four and also on hiatus from college and was working full-time and living about forty-five minutes outside of Atlanta proper with his parents who did not know at the time nor do they currently know of his sexual orientation; after the sturdy was in a long-term relationship and is living in downtown Atlanta with his boyfriend but they are no longer together. Tae was twenty-three and enrolled in college in Atlanta, and he has since graduated. Theodore was nineteen at the time and had left college to pursue a career in modeling. Zion was twenty in 2014 and enrolled in college in Atlanta and living with his parents just outside of the city of Atlanta, but during the last interview he noted he had moved to Atlanta with his boyfriend.[4] Before continuing, it should be noted that none of the participants knew what gay meant, even if the term, or other sexual epithets, were hurled their way, but many knew they had an unexplained physical, mental, and emotional attraction to boys and that gay was a negative thing, something one did not want to be. Also, when discussing their physical sexual explorations, it is not to sexualize the participants in a demeaning manor or reinforce negative dominate narratives that Black males are merely sexual beings (Hill Collins 2005) but should be understood in the same way that sexual majority boys flirt with, find attraction to, explore female physicality from afar, and/or are told to like girls.[5]

Charlie

> Putting both together and having to fight to prove that I am gay and Black but
> I don't have to fit into your stereotype, because if I'm gay and Black I have to

carry a purse, be flamboyant, get a whole bunch of weave all that stuff. I have to be a thug and be on the down low. I can't be in the middle because I'm gay and I'm Black?

For Charlie, society told him to be one or the other: a flamboyant Black gay male or a thug and on the down low, a term not used for White gay males (Hill Collins 2005). Yet, Charlie was neither: he did not want to be and fit into society's ideas of what society believed was to be Black and gay, a rigid binary he actively pushed against. Whether in school, hearing from family members, seeing media representations, or what was learned in church, Charlie learned what these categories meant, but knew he was more than these two categories.

As a child Charlie was expressive, always making jokes and dancing at school and around his family; he was "theatrical" and fed off the attention. Many in his elementary classes perceived him to be gay for such mannerisms yet he had no idea the meaning of gay or that his theatrical manners held a certain, if any, connotation—he was having fun. Additionally, during his time in elementary school, Charlie explains he did not understand "race" as a concept but saw the variations in skin color with his Black peers. However, he notes in one of his elementary classes race was quite present, even if he was unaware of the meaning of race and racism, because there were "five Black people in my class. We were a team, a few of us in there like "power." Thus, his racial identity began to be formed as he unofficially "organized" with other Black kids to stick together because they knew they were the "outsiders" in a class of White kids and a White teacher. Also, during this time, Charlie was attending church and was "saved," and thus ensued a few years where he was heavily involved in the church, influencing what he understood about sexuality and grappling with the tensions of his love for Christ and his burgeoning questions of his sexuality.

When Charlie entered middle school, he became much more conscious of and began grappling with his racial and sexual identities. In seventh grade Charlie was attending a majority-Black school and admitting he was "bisexual," told two close friends, and then all of a sudden, almost all of the seventh and eighth graders knew his sexual identity. Charlie explains the tensions of his intersecting identities, and how racial shelving came to be:

Next thing I know the whole grade knows and I was like "I don't even talk to you all. How you all [know]? Well yeah I'm bi." Every Black person was so disgusted with me and every time I would walk by "So are you really bisexual? Are you really bisexual?" I cried all the time, I was scared of being bullied, well I was bullied, but nobody stepped to me because I may have been in seventh grade, I may have been a little shorter but I was this big boy. People were intimated by my size, but then me being gay [brought stares], but nobody tried me, nobody got bucked, so I was just like "you gonna talk all that [negatively about his sexuality]?"

Though nobody "stepped to him" to fight him due to his size, he was constantly barraged with questions and looks, which played with his mind and emotional state; Black classmates criticized him for his sexual identity rather than being barraged with questions about his racial identity, although many may have believed he was not "a Black man" because Black men are not supposed to be gay. At one point, Charlie did have enough, and due to his size, knew he could fight almost anyone, particularly when one peer yelled "'You a faggot.' Then we just going [verbal attacks] and he got up and I said 'What? Yeah, what's good?' I pushed him and he pushed me back, I pushed him and they said 'Charlie hit his ass. Charlie hit him.'" The teacher ended up coming back in the room, but, in this moment, Charlie was getting mixed messages from his peers: many calling him faggot and looking down upon him for his sexual identity yet in the same breath some are encouraging him to "be masculine," to fight and beat someone up who was harassing him for being a "faggot." Was Charlie aggressive in the sense of how Black men have been historically portrayed? No, Charlie was standing up for himself in part because the school was ignoring the sexual minority students, and Charlie was unaware of any policies that existed protecting sexual minority students.

Outside of school, Charlie was taking control of better understanding his sexuality by going online and watching gay porn and entering sites dedicated to gay men; since Charlie's school was not teaching sexual education which included queer peoples, he had to employ self-determination and find out on his own.

Entering high school, Charlie was in an emotionally difficult place: he was being harassed even more in ninth grade for his sexuality and began cutting himself and getting into more fights freshman year. Having had enough, Charlie's mom agreed to let him transfer to the demographically diverse arts high school, a school where Charlie was surrounded by people like him, with similar interests and where many did not mock him for his sexuality. In high school, Charlie found a few teachers who embraced their sexual identity as lesbians and mentored Charlie, showing Charlie what it means to be proud of one's sexual identity in-spite of being told otherwise. Throughout his life experiences, Charlie interacted with adults who did not acknowledge his sexual identity or told him being bisexual or gay is wrong (e.g., pastors and therapists he saw for his cutting). In his experiences with his two lesbian teachers, Charlie felt at peace, and was able to have one-on-one conversations with them, something that allowed him to ask questions and seek guidance on ways to navigate the queer community and relationships; Charlie was engaging in experiential evolution, learning that adults do not have to be the enemy and can be supportive.

When at home Charlie was watching shows like *RuPaul's Drag Race* ("Who is this Black man runnin things?" Excuse me "Black queen runnin thangs cause she doin it.") and *Noah's Arc* helping him to see the varied identities within the queer and Black gay community. Again, taking control of understanding these identities, through self-determination, junior year of high school Charlie went with friends to Black Gay Pride in Atlanta and saw a beautiful varied Black queer community:

> [Pride] was so much fun. Seeing the drag queens and different kinds of men that were there. There were feminine men, the thug guys, you had the in-betweens, you had people with their shirts off, no pants on . . . all drawls, thongs, you saw angels and wings, you saw dance teams. I was like "There is so much culture in this little vicinity." It was so much fun to see we as a people can come together and be one, we're separate but we're one. We're all our own individual person but we all live the same situations.

All of these experiences helped Charlie come to love himself and helped him build a thick skin where he is now able to deflect any criticism and be the Black gay male he wants to be, not what society tells him where he should be categorized. In a testament to his strength and love of self, in college he began doing drag on the side and has invited his family members to see one of his shows, something he never believed would happen when he was a child.

Slick Rick

> Just anytime a gay scene or something [was on] my mom would react violently like "Ughhhhh, that's so nasty" or "Why?" or I mean she wouldn't go on a rant about it but she would definitely react.

Seeing his mother react negatively to gays was common for Slick Rick, as this was his normal. Having parents who immigrated to the United States from a West African nation, Slick Rick grew up very conscious of his heritage and how his identity differed from many of his peers. Though rarely teased in school and, by his own admission, a happy child in school, from an early age, Slick Rick encountered teachers and peers who showed their ignorance of his heritage, putting this difference front and center in school, helping him understand how he differed from his Black peers who did not have first generation African immigrant parents:

> Elementary school was when I was most self-conscious about my last name. I knew how to spell it, I knew how to pronounce it, but I changed the

pronunciation to make it easier on everybody else, because I was tired of giving *Hooked on Phonics* lessons every single time somebody asked my last name. I'm gonna pronounce it for the easiest way I know, leave me alone . . . I did that and then of course I got the whole "Oh you don't look African" or the "Speak African."

Besides the teasing about his name and knowing he was "not like" his Black American peers, even though Slick Rick was born in the United States, elementary school was easy. In middle school Slick Rick did not make waves, but made friends with many, did his work, and kept a positive attitude. However, during this time he began a friendship with Jeron, who was teased by others on the perception he was gay. Being Black, Jeron was teased by Black and White peers for his sexuality, to which Slick Rick was learning about racial shelving: one can be Black but the focus of teasing was less overtly about race and more about one's perceived sexuality. Not knowing the definition of gay, Slick Rick ignored others and became fast friends with his peer; in fact, Slick Rick was more concerned with his studies and friends and did not have physical or emotional attractions to anyone during his middle school years, so gay was something not on his radar. Also, since Slick Rick attended middle school in a conservative county, sexual education was limited and focused much more on abstinence only education, therefore making any queer sexualities null.

When he entered high school, things began to change for Slick Rick with regards to understanding his sexuality. Still ignored by educators, Slick Rick was learning more about what it could mean to be Black and gay. First, a Black gay male transferred into Slick Rick's school and taught Slick Rick Black males can have myriad of identities:

He was a cross dresser, he wore heels. Black homosexual out queen. Some days he would just wear his red pumps and be pumpin around these high school hallways. Of course, being from [town name], these White people, they didn't know how to deal with that. That created an uproar. Maybe in that instance, maybe I heard some not so friendly words or whatever like "He's doing too much." But then again that didn't really faze me too much. That wasn't my style, like I have no desire to be in female clothing or shoes or accessories, well maybe like a bracelet.

Still friends with Jeron and coming to terms with his burgeoning sexual desires, Slick Rick began exploring his sexuality online with Jeron. Since their school ignored the queer community in curricula and in providing policies to protect sexual minority students and Slick Rick having parents who were telling him to marry a woman, going online was the only option during this time for Slick Rick, thus employing self-determination: to understand what it meant to be Black and gay. The sites he visited had many different purposes, from dating to essays and articles about the community. Slick Rick used these sites, such as Black Gay Chat Live (BGC Live), as a way to talk with others but to read the essays, to understand experiences of Black and Latinx gays navigating through society. On these sites, Slick Rick began to learn that Atlanta had a visible and sizable Black gay community, but, unlike other participants, he did not go out into the community until well into college.

Even though Slick Rick did not face teasing in school from people who may perceive him to have been gay, seeing how others were treated based on their actual or perceived sexual identity, and the lack of having the sexual minority community represented in curricula or being visible and active in school, did play a factor in what Slick Rick did and did not know about the community: he had to learn on his own, or with a trusted friend, the feelings he was having because he had little context for these physical and emotional feelings. From his experiences seeing how Jeron was treated for being himself, how the Black classmate challenged ideas of blackness, sexuality, and gender, and from the men he met or read about online, Slick Rick saw many forms of Black gay identities, and he chose to defy stereotypes and, like all other participants, not fit into one of the rigid binaristic categories, and live his authentic self.

Tae

> So, regardless what my skin is, if you know I'm gay, "Oh, fuck you being Black, n**** you gay." And then you disowned right there. I don't got time for that. You not gonna hurt my feelings or destroy who I worked so hard to become because I'm not straight.

Herein lies the tensions for Tae as he was navigating through school: being a Black male but not being Black enough because of his gayness. For Tae, racial shelving was often at the core of his schooling experience. When Tae was in elementary school his mother left him with her parents, solidly middle class and loving, in a mostly White county abutting Atlanta; though the county was majority White, when Tae was a child, he lived in the racially mixed but more Black area of the county. In elementary school Tae was emotionally missing his mother and though his grandparent's support was strong, he struggled academically and emotionally in school. Also, during this time Tae would hear his grandfather talk about the privilege of White people while trying to teach Tae about the rich culture and history of Black Americans; his grandparents never discussed sexuality. This came to a head for Tae in elementary school, because he was not learning overtly about race and the contributions of Black Americans and there was no attempt to show a safe and educative environment about and for the sexual minority community. However, in fifth grade Tae began to grapple with the real emotions of being attracted to someone of the same sex:

> I had a crush on a guy; he was Latino. He had slick backed hair, very nice complexion, and was in fifth grade; I was in third grade when I started noticing him. He left [the school] and I started cryin because he was gone. . . . Did I understand it? No. What I felt, I had a funny feeling as "Oh gosh he's so cute." But I didn't realize what was going on. Looking back at it, I know what I was thinking, but when I was in the emotion at the time at that young age it was just like I would stare at him and then look down. Then I looked back at him, he looked at me I looked away again like "oh no, he saw me. . . . It was kinda like a flirting thing but we really weren't, it was just kids, harmlessness."

Lacking words for what was happening, Tae knew there was a connection, which he would begin to explore in the coming years in middle school. In fact, when he was in sixth grade, Tae and his neighbor, a White boy, explored their bodies with one another. When Tae's grandmother came down in the basement and saw them exploring, she screamed hysterically—either for the same-sex exploration or the age of the two or a combination of both, banished Tae from ever seeing his friend again, and taught Tae in that moment what he was doing was wrong. While his grandmother may have been horrified, Tae did not have any words for what was happening and his school did not acknowledge through formal curricula or schoolwide polices of support, the sexual minority community, which may have helped as a place for Tae to learn what was happening; through teasing he heard, and then lobbed at him, and the term "gay" used in a negative way, Tae was learning about same-sex sexuality but with little context and depth of understanding, which could have come through formal curricula.

Attending a majority-Black middle school, Tae was still shy and was not one who enjoyed sports. For many of his male peers, they conflated the shyness and the lack of athletic ability, meaning Tae was gay, for which he was constantly teased, often leading to fights or encounters off of the school grounds. Tae did not tell anyone about the bullying because he did not believe the administrators would do anything and this would also show a sign of weakness. Concurrently, in middle school, Tae's mother came back to Georgia and he went to live with her and began exploring the internet to help him understand the physical feelings he was having for males; he freely admits he was intrigued by the male physique and would go online and watch pornography to see the male physique in action. Keeping these feelings hidden from peers and his mother, his mother eventually found out and scolded Tae for

searching online and looking at gay porn. Confused because his mother had
gay friends and not realizing her concern might have been more of that the
content of sex for a middle schooler was too much, Tae felt feelings of guilt
and shame and vowed to never look again, though he did eventually. Also,
being teased was not easy on Tae, and he began to build a thick skin, which
would be tested in high school, and Tae also employed self-determination:
standing up for himself from attacks and going outside of school to learn
about his burgeoning sexual identity.

Once in high school, Tae began causally dating females but knew deep
down he wanted to date a male. Going online to dating websites, he began
talking with and meeting up with gay men. However, there were several gay
males at his school, and he took a chance and contacted one of them, even if
the fear of being "outed" was real. As they began their clandestine meetings,
Tae's friends began to suspect something was happening since he was either
skipping step team practice or his stories of where he had been or what he was
doing had holes. Tae had finally found a solid group of Black male friends
and feared they would leave him if they found out the truth, but Tae found
the opposite to be true, challenging his ideas of Black ideology and sexuality;
since he had been teased by Black peers, he believed the Black community to
be very homonegative, another example of Tae encountering racial shelving.
In relating his "outing" to his friends, Tae's story shows the beginning of his
experiential evolution, that not all Black people are homonegative:

> "Tae, where were you?" I kept sayin "Restaurant." They said "Ok, so whatchu
> have for lunch there? What did you have to eat?" I said "The lunch special."
> They all looked and everybody started laughing and was like "Tae, tell us the
> truth." I said "Ok, first of all before I tell you what's going on, I have to tell you
> that, I'm gay, I like dudes." And they were like "Ok." Some started laughing,
> some was like "I knew it. I told you." But not in a disrespectful [way], just like
> "I knew something was going on, I'm not stupid." Then they said "So, who'd
> you do it with?" and I told them that the guy who it was and they said "Ewe,
> Tae really? Him? At least do it better with someone else," and we just all started
> laughing. I was like "Yo, I didn't think you all would be like this open or cool
> with it." They were like "You know we don't care cause you still our dude at
> the end of the day. Like you know we just don't appreciate you tryin' to lie and
> tryin' to pull [anything] over our head like we stupid." I was like "I didn't know
> what to tell y'all, I didn't know how to feel, because I thought y'all's gonna stop
> being my friends and something like that." They said like "Nah, Tae, like you
> our friend for life, you're really our best friend for life, so there's nothing [that]
> can really push us away." And they started laughing and clowning for the rest
> of the time. After I came out to them I felt so much better.

Even though he was feeling safe with friends, Tae did begin to emotionally
spiral out of control since his family found out his sexuality in less than

pleasant terms (he was about to be exposed by a man he dated who was ten years his senior and living in Florida and his best female friend told him to tell his mother which he did in a very quick and rash manner causing her to cry, hurting Tae's feelings) and a peer in school had died unexpectedly; Tae retreated. His friends told him to either stay in the "hole" and leave their group or move forward with their support; support was exactly what Tae needed and is forever grateful.

Even though Tae's school had an LGBT club, and he was not hiding his sexual identity, nor was he fitting into either of the binaristic categories society has for Black gay males, Tae chose to attend one or two meetings, but as McCready (2010) argues about gay-straight alliances, Tae too found the club to be mostly female and White; he never went back. Also, in another example of Tae's experiential evolution, while on the step team he had a male coach and the females had a female coach. The male couch was very supportive, particularly when the female coach pulled Tae aside and told him "'Hey, I heard that you were gay' and she told me to tone it down or not broadcast it so much because people could judge or it may not look good on you [me] especially at this age. She pretty much said don't be outwardly gay." Not only was Tae perplexed because he was not "outwardly gay" and did not understand her comment, his male coach supported him and told him to be himself, reinforcing the idea that not all sexual majority-Black men are homonegative.

Theodore

> I'm [coach] so thankful to have you [Theodore] in my life. You have opened up my eyes to a lot of different things. I would have never thought in a million years that I would have had a gay athlete that's openly gay and isn't different than my straight athlete.

By the time Theodore entered a new high school senior year, he was already "out" to his family, four brothers and a sister and a mother. The journey to accepting himself and sharing his identity with his family and peers was not easy. While living in a northern city until the fifth grade, Theodore often heard his father's family invoke the Bible and demonize homosexuality. During this time at school, he began having crushes on his male classmates but never had words for these feelings. As the family was poised to move to Atlanta, his biracial mother, her White husband, and her sister, often spoke about Atlanta being full of Black gay men, and that women need to be careful. Again, not fully understanding, but by this time knowing gay means two men and is something bad, Theodore had another image of Atlanta, far from the Civil Rights capital his mother had showed him in prior visits, but this time as a place full of Black gay men. To his dismay, Theodore grew up in a suburb about thirty minutes outside of Atlanta and saw Black lesbians more than gay men. Also, Theodore was living with brothers who were not gay, mocked gays, and picked on Theodore to the point where Theodore had to build a thick skin, a protective armor, to prove he was not gay. However, starting in fifth grade and lasting until early high school, Theodore would sneak downstairs and search online for images of men to which he was found out by his bothers; Theodore never confirmed the searches were his but his brothers continued to tease him. Like Tae, Theodore was entranced by the male physique and engaged in self-determination to learn more about his feelings.

As with all the participants, Theodore attended schools that ignored the sexual minority community and reproduced a Eurocentric curriculum. In school, Theodore ran track and had a girlfriend to keep up appearances, but knew she was merely a cover. Also, people in school did not tease Theodore because he was muscular and had older brothers; even if they teased him at home, he was still their brother and would stick up for him at school. Due to the lack of learning about the sexual minority community, not mention ignoring of the Black sexual minority community, Theodore had to find his own way to learn and know. Therefore, Theodore not only went online to learn about the community, but also saw media representations of what it meant to be Black and gay, images he disliked and made him distance himself from his Black identity. For instance, when watching *A-List New York*, Theodore resonated with the White characters on the show and the show taught him:

> Independence, that I could be successful and not be judged. I feel like they made it, I can make it too, I can be independent in this world and make a living. They were out. They had boyfriends, they went to events. So, it was like ok I can be that way. I can go to dinners, I can go out in public and hold hands with somebody that I'm with and stuff like that. That's why I enjoyed that show.

However, in his assessment of a Black gay series, "But *Noah's Arc* was the cliché of gay men," showed him what not to be, even if all of the main characters had a shared racial identity as Theodore.

For the first few years of high school, Theodore was "outed" by someone who saw his profile on MySpace which stated he liked "men and women." This is not how Theodore wanted to tell his family and friends, but he was comforted when his mother said she supported him, just as she did his openly lesbian friends. In school, people knew and did not tease Theodore nor did they treat him as the voice for all gays. Even though Theodore was distancing himself from his *Black* gay identity, defying and transcending stereotypes like all participants, Theodore made friends with other Black gay and lesbians at school; he began dating a White gay male from another county because he was only attracted to White gay males at the time.

When Theodore entered his new high school senior year, he knew immediately the school was safer and more accepting than his previous school:

> The openness like people accepting one another, whatever you wanted to be they supported it no matter what. So, it wasn't a judgmental school like how [former high school] was, like if you wore shorts above your knees you were considered gay. So, it was different, like people dressed any kinda way they liked. . . . It's like everybody always wanted a gay best friend. So, it was [with one girl] it was like, "ok well I can be your best friend but you not my best friend." I actually felt good about it [being the gay friend] because I could express [my feelings] and I talk about guys with them, that's something I always wanted to do is meet somebody I could talk about guys with and stuff like that. So, it was just like, she told me about her boyfriend and I would tell her about mine.

In fact, an encounter with one teacher eased his mind that he could be himself even if she made a judgment without confirmation from Theodore of his sexuality, "I really came out, and one of the teachers [lovingly] said 'Boy I been knew.' We talked and they [peers] would ask me about the experiences and stuff like that. And it seemed like with me, it's like, every time I met somebody and I talked to somebody it was like 'oh my God, I gotta new gay best friend.'"

Like with the track coach at this new high school who accepted and appreciated Theodore's openness of being gay, Theodore was engaging in experiential evolution: not all coaches or teachers or peers were homonegative or ignored one's sexual identity and some would embrace and support students and peers who were gay.

Charlie and Tae both attended Black Gay Pride during high school and embraced the myriad of identities within the Black queer community, but Theodore had a different assessment of Pride when he went with his lesbian friends:

> I was kinda uncomfortable. I used to say that I didn't wanna go back because I didn't like the way gay people presented themselves. I would think "y'all don't act like this every day, so why on this day of our celebration, why are y'all dressin' half-naked and doin all this extra stuff? Dressin like females and drag queens." I was like, I don't have to do all that, and I'm still comfortable in my skin.

The tensions of having a Black and gay sexual identity for Theodore demonstrates the grappling of identity White gay males rarely, if ever, have to contend. But, like all of the participants, Theodore has since embraced both identities, remembering the racial pride his mother instilled in him, and knowing he need not fit into stereotypic roles of being Black and gay.

Zion

> You've come from generations of strong Black men just to spit on their graves
> and not even populate . . . I want a family. You're my first born. . . . As a Black
> man in today's society you already have a disadvantage. . . . You being gay and
> Black is already making it even more disadvantaged.

The aforementioned words of Zion's father are seared in his memory,
words that get to the core of intersecting identities. His father taught that
being gay is not what Black men are to be, they must procreate with a woman
and keep the race alive; here is the example where Zion was encountering and
participating, unwillingly, in racial shelving. However, while not disagreeing
about the double disadvantage, Zion has been determined to prove his father
wrong, to show him and the world that being Black and gay is not a bad thing
and that he will be successful, whatever the cost. Though loving his intersecting identities today, this was not always the case for Zion growing up. Like
Theodore, at times he wanted to distance himself from being Black because
of the representations of Black gays and, like Tae, he was mostly teased by
his Black peers for his perceived, and then actual, sexual identity.

As with everyone else, when Zion heard the word "gay" he was confused,
especially in school because of who his father was forcing him to become at
home. When Zion was seven, his father retired from his job that took him
away from home for weeks on end and Zion's ability to be himself, when
it was just he and his mother and older sister, dissipated when his father
returned. From the beginning, his father disliked the way Zion walked and
talked:

> I would talk like this*ah*, say things like that*ah*, like with the extra "*ah*." And he
> [father] was like "*Stop talking like that!*" . . . I remember one day I was outside
> walking and he got super-duper mad at me. I was like, "why did he get so mad at
> me?" He yelled "*Come back here and walk differently!*" I was like "what?" He
> made me go up and down my driveway and practice walking for like an hour, in
> the hot sun . . . I was like "why the fuck am I doing this?" But of course in that
> household you didn't have a say so, it was his way or the highway, so my happy
> ass shut the fuck up and walked up and down those gravel and rocks. . . . It [the
> butchening up of his walk] was [a] subconscious [act] because after that I was
> like "well if he has a problem with it, I wonder what other people think?" I'd
> never thought about the way I was walking but in the back of my mind I would
> think "well if my dad is making me walk back and forth, how do I look when
> I'm walking? . . . How am I walking, what's wrong with it?" He would never
> answer me. He would just say "Just fix the way you walk."

At his racially diverse elementary school, Zion was shy and tried to make
friends with the other kids, but many teased him calling him gay and sissy,

which confused Zion because he was doing "masculine, non-sissy" things at home, laborious things outside for his father. During this time, Zion began exploring his sexuality, and he would have a friend over to play video games and the boys would also touch one another's penises. Then, the summer between fifth and sixth grades, Zion's friend slept over, and they began fondling one another and the young boy motioned for intercourse but Zion resisted. All night Zion thought about that moment and how much he wanted to be intimate with his friend and told his friend the next morning he was willing to try intercourse, to which the friend ignored him, crushing Zion. These feelings were so alive for Zion but he had no place to learn, nobody at school was bringing forth the sexual minority community through lessons or through visibility of support. At home, Zion was learning what it meant to be Black, to be strong and love one's blackness and culture, but what about his sexual identity?

Middle and high school were trying times for Zion. At first, he was in a majority-Black school where the teasing by his Black peers was nonstop and he ended up befriending a group of Black peers who were into art like himself. This juxtaposition was something he grappled with since, partially based on his father's reactions and his peers' teasing, Black people were homonegative, so why would one embrace their blackness? He surely was not considered "truly Black" if he liked boys or was less masculine than others, yet now he found Black peers who accepted him and who he was able to slowly open up to regarding his sexuality. High school was where Zion learned how to use his thick skin to his advantage and where he stood up for himself. After a very dramatic manner in which his father and mother found out he had a boyfriend early in high school, Zion was a stranger in his own home. He had no outlet but music and his art. Taking solace in artists who challenged society's norms, like Grace Jones and Erykah Badu, Zion realized he was not alone and he was not wrong for his sexuality, his "otherness" within society. However, high school was a different story, and at school one day, he tired of the teasing and publicly confronted someone who was bullying him:

He called me gay and tried to make a scene in the lunchroom. He did it really dramatically: "Hey look at this fag blah blah blah." I was like "Oh, I'm a faggot? Ok, but [pointing to others standing around watching] I'm sleeping with your brother and I'm definitely sucking you up and I would suck you up too. So, like are there any takers?" I did it in front of a very large crowd, no one could say anything because it's like, "he knows what? . . . The only thing that you have on me is gay, what next?" In that moment all those past times, the bullying and the annoying boys, it all clicked and was ok. Then eleventh and twelfth grade years were the best years of my high school life because literally no one fucked with me.

As Zion notes, after this moment nobody challenged him. While not perfect, Zion felt more at ease at school, especially because at one point he held power over many of the "straight boys." Since he was known for his artistry, he began getting inquiries through text from male peers to design tattoos. When he agreed, the males would then begin texting him asking how sex was with a guy and if Zion was up for it, that they would like to try being sexual with him. Often, he would meet the males in the bathroom and they would engage in oral sex. The power came when Zion told them to treat him well, or else, he had text messages between the two of them and he would share with the whole school. While thrilling at first, Zion tired of being the gay these sexual majority males chose to live out their curiousness; he was open and accepting of his sexuality and had fought this hard, why should he be "used" for those who chose not be as open?

Like all other participants, his schools and teachers, through curricula or in every day actions, very rarely acknowledged the sexual minority community. From his past encounters with teachers ignoring the teasing and parents who punished him for being gay, Zion had all but given up on adults. That all changed when he was in Mr. Karl's art class. Zion's birthday occurred when he was grounded and his privileges taken away and he relayed to Mr. Karl he had no plans. On his birthday he was depressed and walked in the class to see all of his classmates sitting around one table. Approaching the table, Zion saw a cookie cake with a rainbow and candles, wishing him a happy birthday. As Zion began to cry, he realized not all adults were horrible homonegative people and neither were all of his peers. However, what struck Zion the most was the fact that a stranger took the time to show care and kindness when his own parents had all but banished him to his bedroom with little to no celebrating. This experiential evolution was very important for Zion, for he felt safer and more understood at school by an adult, something he would have needed much earlier in his schooling.

IMPLICATIONS FOR EDUCATORS

The narratives of the participants is important for educators for several reasons: (a) to know what some Black gay males face when understanding identity in school and to support Black gay males as they navigate through schools; (b) to provide educative lessons about intersecting identities, in particular making visible the Black gay community, and creating educative lessons to confront, deconstruct, and dismantle racial and sexual systems of oppression; and (c) to help blunt ideas that Black gay males may be at a deficit due to their socially constructed liminal identities.

Supporting Black Gay Males
as They Navigate Through Schools

There are many ways educators can support Black gay males in school, but from the participants' experiences, it becomes clear one way is acknowledging the thick skin some may grow due to bullying or negative encounters due to their sexual identity and being judged for their sexual identity, possibly over their racial identity, resulting in racial shelving; growing thick skin from the bullying should not be a given just because this is what kids do, because bullying should be stopped and administrators should intervene. For instance, if teachers understand how thick skin is grown, that experiences Black gay males face in myriad aspects of life, but particularly in school which is influenced by racist and homonegative ideologies, ideologies often reproduced in school (Asante 1991; Mayo 2013), which produces such thick skin, then teachers should know the nuances of why and how this harassment occurs, moving from a surface level to deconstructing racism and heterosexism. Further, knowing how participants knew their racial identity, while a factor in why they were being taunted by others because of their sexuality (not being a *real* Black male), could help teachers address this issue and acknowledge to youth how and why this racial shelving occurs, the complexities with intersecting identities; this is detailed in the next section. Also, as was expressed by many participants, having that one teacher who acknowledged their intersecting identities, in particular their sexual identity, and knowing they had an adult to confide in, helped many successfully navigate through school; this is akin to Irvine's "Other Mothers," when Black teachers become "other mothers" to their Black students (Irvine 2003). By teachers being that one, or one of many, may be socially, emotionally, and academically invaluable to Black gay males as they navigate through school.

Educative Lessons about Intersecting Identities

Every participant noted their schools ignored bringing in any lessons regarding same-sex sexuality; many lessons and actions of teachers reinforced and informally taught heterosexual relationships are what is expected and normal. Also, many participants expressed they were not taught Black history from a perspective where Black contributions to society and the world were known; either Black history was relegated to February, focused only on enslavement and Dr. King and Rosa Parks, or they did not remember any teachings of blackness and Black and African-related history in school.

Teachers can begin the process of creating educative units and lessons that are not tertiary to other topics but where race and sexuality are the core of what is being studied. For instance, in elementary school, the National Council of the Social Studies C3 Framework asks students to explore the concept of community and identity (focused more on state, regional, and national). This becomes an opportunity for educators to bring in the queer and Black communities as such, a community, not merely a group of people whose identity is only sexual. Students can then deconstruct why and how these communities contribute to the larger idea of community and the nuances within communities; students can dig deeper and explore the nuances within the Black and queer communities. Further, for educators who have the freedom and are not tied to restrictive non-relevant standards, they can engage with students to know what they want to study and explore when it comes to identity, particularly with race and sexuality. It is incumbent for the teacher to then create pragmatic and educative units and lessons where students study the nuances of identity and community, and in the process begin to understand racism and heterosexism. As with using experience and creating educative lessons (Dewey 1938), the lessons then lead to more lessons regarding race and sexuality, being pragmatic in nature, to the studying of these topics, so students are able to delve deep and more lessons of race and sexuality emerge from the previous lessons, lessons laying the foundation with purpose for the study of these topics.

As is often noted, the queer community is left out of sexual education courses, especially in abstinence only courses (Bartoné 2015; Hoshall 2013). All of the participants engaged in self-determination, to learn and know about not only their community and burgeoning sexual identity, but also about sex, often hearing and reading many different things from others online or viewing gay pornography. When brought into sex education courses, students will know there are myriad sexualities and can better understand how sex occurs, the act, in myriad of communities, especially when learning about safe sex. Further, teachers can also bring in lessons about PreP (pre-exposure prophylaxis) and PeP (post-exposure prophylaxis), showing a commitment to not just all students but especially to the gay students' sexual health and well-being; this requires teachers branching out and knowing medical advances affecting many in the gay community. Lastly, teachers can build educative lessons where the queer community is included in relationships, how the queer community faces many of the same issues sexual majority peoples face: abuse, euphoria, general navigation of a relationship, etc. The sexual minority community must not continue to be ignored and must be included in all lessons for all students to know, thus helping to combat heterosexism for all.

Blunting Ideas That Black Gay Males May Be at a Deficit
Due to Their Socially Constructed Liminal Identities

While the participants had to endure much as they navigated through racist and heteronormative schools and society, many came out on the other side with self-love, but they often had to do this alone or find others to help them through schooling and the process of knowing their intersecting identities; this finding is tricky as one never knows who to trust. From these narratives, educators can see that Black gay males are Black *and* gay, that, while grappling with the tensions, they do not view their identities as a deficit or separate and privileging one over the other; they love and embrace their identities. Also, knowing that the participants employ self-determination to learn about their identities, and finding the strength within themselves to know themselves, to not fit into the two dominant categories of being Black and gay, shows that the participants refused to be categorized. Since they refused to be categorized, this shows they are not and did not view their identity as a deficit, as a shunning of their identity but rather as an acceptance of their identity and making their identity fit for them, not shying away from being Black and gay. For these participants, Black is also gay, not limited to White males, and they show the Black community they are just as Black as sexual majority-Black males.

CONCLUSION

The participants' experiences in school, of how they have come to know, love, and accept their intersecting identities, shows the complexities of being Black and gay, a complexity White gay youth do not face; their racial identity just is, because gay equals White (Berubé 2003). A lot of this, the self-determination and thick skin, while admirable, is telling: why must the burden be on the youth? Where are the educators tackling these issues and knowing and infusing curricula with these communities rather than making the kids responsible? Where is the reasonability of the adult, the "educated" adult who supposedly knows what is best for youth? Why must students endure bullying as a "rite of passage" and develop a thick skin? Thus, what becomes crucial here, especially in a profession that is overwhelming White and female, is that teachers must know and understand the system of racism and heteronormativity. If they do not know and come in with their limited views, or from a White savior or colorblind and/or sexualblind ideology, then all can be lost with these educative experiences and providing support. It is important teachers know and understand how these systems unfold in society but more importantly in school, teachers' possible complicitness in how they teach, interact with students and what they include/exclude in their instruction in relation to race and sexuality.

The hope is that once the Black queer community is made visible in a positive manner, all students will not only know the value and contributions of the community but also see what the Black queer community faces due to racist and heterosexist ideologies and policies, policies they hopefully will one day dismantle rather than reproduce and reify.

NOTES

1. The term "down low" (DL) is also used to portray "straight" Black men as deviants for clandestinely seeking out sexual relations with other men, reinforcing narratives of Black males as sexual deviants, lacking honesty. Further, the term "DL" is not used for White straight males clandestinely seeking out sexual relations with other men, to which Whiteness provides a cloak of innocence or an excuse for these males (Hill Collins 2005).

2. Huang et al. conducted a "content analysis of the past decade (1998–2007) of psychological scholarship about lesbian, gay, and bisexual (LGB) people of color" (Huang et al. 2009, 363). What they found is a scarcity of research focused specifically on individual racial or ethnic groups and if studies did focus on an individual racial or ethnic group that group was compared to another racially and/or ethnically marginalized group.

3. All participants have been anonymized through the use of pseudonyms.

4. Due to unforeseen circumstances, I am unaware of the current state of life of Tae, Theodore, and Zion.

5. In no way I am arguing males must stare at and sexually and physically objectify females. The point here is that growing up and navigating through puberty, males attracted to females go through hormonal processes of attraction, in the same way gay males do with an attraction to other males.

REFERENCES

Asante, Molefi K. 1991. "The Afrocentric Idea in Education." *The Journal of Negro Education* 60 (2): 170–80. doi: 10.2307/2295608.

Bartone, Michael D. "Navigating and Negotiating Identity in the Black Gay Mecca: Educational and Institutional Influences That Positively Impact the Life Histories of Black Gay Male Youth in Atlanta." PhD diss., Georgia State University, 2015.

Carbado, Devon. 2005. "Privilege." In *Black Queer Studies: A Critical Anthology*, edited by E. Patrick Johnson and Mae G. Henderson, 190–212. Durham, NC: Duke University Press.

Clandinin, D. Jean. 2006. "Narrative Inquiry: A Methodology for Studying Lived Experiences." *Research Studies in Music Education* 27 (1): 44–54. https://doi.org/10.1177/1321103X060270010301.

Collins, Patricia Hill. 2005. *Black Sexual Politics*. Abingdon-on-Thames: Routledge.

Dubé, Eric M. and Ritch C. Savin-Williams. 1999. "Sexual Identity Development Among Ethnic Sexual-Minority Youths." *Developmental Psychology* 35 (6): 1389–398. http://dx.doi.oCollinsrg/10.1037/0012-1649.35.6.1389.

Ferguson, Anne A. 2001. *Bad Boys: Public Schools in the Making of Black Masculinity*. Ann Arbor: The University of Michigan Press.

Fisher, Christopher M. 2009. "Queer Youth Experiences with Abstinence-Only-Until-Marriage Sexuality Education: 'I Can't Even Get Married So Where Does That Leave Me?'" *Journal of LGBT Youth* 6 (1): 61–79. https://doi.org/10.1080/19361650802396775.

Harper, Gary W., Douglas Bruce, Pedro Serrano, and Omar B. Jamil. 2009. "The Role of the Internet in the Sexual Identity Development of Gay and Bisexual Male Adolescents." In *The Story of Sexual Identity: Narrative Perspectives on the Gay and Lesbian Life Course*, edited by Phillip L. Hammock and Bertram J. Cohler, 297–326. Oxford: Oxford University Press.

Hatch, J. Amos and Richard Wisniewski. 1995. "Life History and Narrative: Questions, Issues, and Exemplary Works." In *Life History and Narrative*, edited by J. Amos Hatch and Richard Wisniewski, 113–31. London: The Falmer Press.

Hill, Patricia. 2005. *Black Sexual Politics: African Americans, Gender, and the New Racism*. New York: Routledge.

Hoshall, Leora. 2013. "Afraid of Who You Are: No Promo Homo Laws in Public School Sex Education." *Texas Journal of Women and the Law* 22 (2): 219–39.

Howard, Tyrone. 2013. "How Does It Feel to Be a Problem? Black Male Students, Schools, and Learning in Enhancing the Knowledge Base to Disrupt Deficit Frameworks." *Review of Research in Education* 37 (1): 54–86. https://www.jstor.org/stable/24641957.

Huang, Yu-ping, Melanie E. Brewster, Bonnie Moradi, Melinda B. Goodman, Marcie C. Wiseman, and Annelise Martin. 2010. "Content Analysis of Literature About LGB People of Color: 1998–2007." *The Counseling Psychologist* 38 (3): 363–96. doi: 10.1177/0011000009335255.

Hunter, Marcus. A. 2010. "The Nightly Round: Space, Social Capital, and Urban Black Nightlife." *City & Community* 9 (2): 165–86. https://doi.org/10.1111/j.1540-6040.2010.01320.x.

Irvine, Jacqueline. 2003. *Educating Teachers for Diversity Seeing with a Cultural Eye*. New York: Teacher's College Press.

Jamil, Omar B., Gary W. Harper, M. I. Fernandez, and Adolescent Trials Network for HIV/AIDS Prevention. 2009. "Sexual and Ethnic Identity Development Among Gay-Bisexual-Questioning (GBQ) Male Ethnic Minority Adolescents." *Cultural, Diversity, and Ethnic Minority Psychology* 153 (3): 203–14. doi: 10.1037/a0014795.

Jarvie, Jenny. "Voice of Atlanta's Black Gays is Emerging." *The Los Angeles Times*, May 9, 2006. http://articles.latimes.com/2006/may/08/nation/na-blackgay8.

Johnson, E. P. 2005. "'Quare' Studies, or (Almost) Everything I Know About Queer Studies I Learned from My Grandmother." In *Black Queer Studies: A Critical Anthology*, edited by E. Patrick Johnson and Mae G. Henderson, 124–57. Durham, NC: Duke University Press.

Johnson, E. P. 2008. *Sweet Tea: Black Gay Men of the South an Oral History*. Chapel Hill, NC: The University of North Carolina Press.

King, Joyce E. 1991. "Dysconcious Racism: Ideology, Identity, and the Miseducation of Teachers." *Journal of Negro Education* 60 (2): 133–46. http://www.jstor.org/stable/2295605.

Kosciw, Joseph G., Emily A. Greytak, Noreen M. Giga, Christian Villenas, and David J. Danischewski. 2016. *The 2015 National School Climate Survey: The Experiences of Lesbian, Gay, Bisexual and Transgender Youth in Our Nation's Schools*. New York: GLSEN. https://www.glsen.org/sites/default/files/2015%20National%20GLSEN%202015%20National%20School%20Climate%20Survey%20%28NSCS%29%20-%20Full%20Report_0.pdf.

Kvale, Steinar and Svend Brinkman. 2009. *Interviews: Learning the Craft of Qualitative Research Interviewing*, 2nd ed. Los Angeles, CA: Sage Publications.

Ladson-Billings, Gloria. 2006. "From the Achievement Gap to the Education Debt: Understanding Achievement in U.S. Schools." *Educational Researcher* 35 (7): 3–12. jstor.org/stable/3876731.

Mayo, Cris. 2005. "Unsettled Relations: Schools, Gay Marriage, and Educating for Sexuality." *Educational Theory* 63 (5): 543–58.

McCready, Lance. 2010. *Making Space for Diverse Masculinities: Difference, Intersectionality, and Engagement in an Urban High School*. New York: Peter Lang.

Meyer, Ilan H. and Suzanne C. Ouelette. 2009. "Unity and Purpose at the Intersections of Racial/Ethnic and Sexual Identities." In *The Story of Sexual Identity: Narrative Perspectives on the Gay and Lesbian Life Course,* edited by Phillip L. Hammock and Bertram J. Cohler, 79–106. New York: Oxford.

Mitchum, Preston and Moodie-Mills, Aisha. C. 2014. "Beyond Bullying: How Hostile School Climate Perpetuates the School-to-Prison Pipeline for LGBTYouth." *Center for American Progress*. Accessed June 30, 2018. https://cdn.americanprogress.org/wp-content/uploads/2014/02/BeyondBullying.pdf.

National Center for Educational Statistics. "Table 209.10: Number and Percentage Distribution of Teachers in Public and Private Elementary and Secondary Schools, By Selected Teacher Characteristics: Selected Years, 1987–88 through 2011–12." Accessed June 28, 2018. http://nces.ed.gov/programs/digest/d13/tables/dt13_209.10.asp.

National Council of the Social Studies C3 Framework. "College, Career, & Civic Life: C3 Framework for Social Studies State Standards." Accessed August 2, 2018. https://www.socialstudies.org/sites/default/files/c3/C3-Framework-for-Social-Studies.pdf.

Polkinghorne, Donald E. 1988. *Narrative Knowing and the Human Sciences*. Albany, NY: State University of New York Press.

Solórzano, Daniel and Tara Yosso. 2009. "Critical Race Methodology: Counter-Storytelling as an Analytic Framework for Educational Research." In *Foundations of Critical Race Theory in Education*, edited by Edward Taylor, David Gillborn, and Gloria Ladson-Billings, 131–47. New York: Routledge.

Taylor, David. 2009. "The Foundations of Critical Race Theory in Education." In *Foundations of Critical Race Theory in Education*, edited by Edward Taylor, David Gillborn, and Gloria Ladson-Billings, 1–13. New York: Routledge.

Tierney, William G. 2000. "Undaunted Courage: Life History and the Postmodern Challenge." In *Handbook of Qualitative Research* (2): 537–35. Thousand Oaks, CA: SAGE Publications.

Chapter 4

Gay Latino Greeks

Finding a "Familia" in a Latino Fraternity

Manuel Del Real

LATINO/A FRATERNITIES AND SORORITIES

Currently, there are over thirty-five established Latino/a Greek-letter organizations in the United States (Muñoz and Guardia 2009). The origins of Latino/a-oriented fraternities and sororities can be traced back to Sigma Iota, founded in 1904 at Louisiana State University and Phi Lambda Alpha in 1919 at Rensselaer Polytechnic Institute in New York. These two organizations decided to merge in 1931 to form Phi Iota Alpha Fraternity, Inc. (Kimbrough 2003; Miranda and de Figueroa 2000). Fraternities and sororities were founded to cultivate service and social responsibility that members pledge to uphold and promote in their community. Members are provided with opportunities for volunteering as well as leadership development (Astin 1993). Latino/a fraternities and sororities grew out of these directives because Latino/a students wanted to both "be a part of mainstream culture yet preserve one's own heritage" (Miranda and de Figueroa 2000, 7). To meet the needs and interests of Latino/a students, founders of these organizations added a cultural paradigm focusing on uplifting Latino/a communities compared to the traditionally exclusionary white institutions (Torbenson and Parks 2009). The primary purposes of Latino/a fraternities and sororities were to (1) advance Latino/a cultural awareness, (2) advocate for Latino/a goals, (3) provide a family atmosphere at a college or university campus, and (4) solidify the Latino/a population (Miranda and de Figueroa 2000). Latino fraternities provide a *hermandad* (brotherhood) among members that becomes a support group away from home and enhances their ethnic and gender identity (Guardia and Evans 2008). Guardia and Evan's study found that hermandad and the pride of earning Greek-letters contributed to being a Latino man but did not include sexual orientation (Guardia and Evans 2008). This case study will focus specifically on one, Sigma Lambda Beta International Fraternity, Inc., and the importance and construction of a queer "home" created by five gay identifying brothers that serves as an empowered support system for the organization.

Sigma Lambda Beta International Fraternity (SLB) was founded on April 4, 1986, at the University of Iowa. The founding chapter consisted of eighteen men of various backgrounds, including Latinos, East Asians, and South Africans. SLB is an organization that "adheres to our principles of Brotherhood, Scholarship, Community Service, and Cultural Awareness on an everyday basis to become productive members in society" (SigmaLambdaBeta 2018). Today, SLB is the largest, fastest growing Latino-based fraternity with multicultural membership consisting of 110 chapters that "stretch across 29 states from California to New York, Florida to Washington, and even have reached the shores of Puerto Rico" (SigmaLambdaBeta 2018). SLB was founded with the following motto and mission statement:

> Opportunity for Wisdom; Wisdom for Culture
> Our mission is to nurture and further a dynamic, values-based environment, which utilizes our historically Latino-based fraternity as a catalyst to better serve the needs and wants of all people. (SigmaLambdaBeta 2018)

This espoused motto and mission statement for SLB promotes cultural awareness, advocates for the community through leadership, service, and scholarship, while fostering a *hermandad* (brotherhood) among members (Atkinson, Dean, and Espino 2010; Muñoz and Guardia 2009).

Staying true to the mission of serving as a catalyst, gay identifying brothers of SLB created a private group or rather a familia within a familia for gay/bi/queer brothers designed to help connect them across the nation, provide networking opportunities, and build community. The group originated using a Yahoo group listserv and shifted to social media such as Myspace and currently through Facebook. Recruitment of brothers who self-identify occurred through social media and at national fraternal events starting in 2005. Today, there are more than 300 members who participate in this virtual network that is local, regional, and national. In this chapter, the author examines the importance of finding a queer "familia" within SLB and concludes with suggestions for the group and the fraternity overall.

THEORETICAL FRAMEWORK

The theoretical framework that guided this study was queer theory, which addresses the notions that sexual power runs through social life and is enforced through boundaries and binary divides and a willingness to interrogate areas which normally would not be seen as the terrain of sexuality (Gamson and Moon 2004; Stein and Plummer 1994). Research on how sexuality shapes and is shaped within Latino Greek fraternities is minimal. Using queer theory is essential to making sense of how ethnicity, gender, and sexuality contribute to the construction of the meaning of "familia" for members who identify as gay/queer.

METHODOLOGY AND PARTICIPANTS

The purpose of this exploratory case study of five members of Sigma Lambda Beta International Fraternity, Inc., across the United States was to provide an in-depth understanding of the importance and construction of a queer "familia" created by gay/queer identifying brothers that serves as an empowered support system within the organization. Using a structured interview protocol (Yin 1994), interviews took place starting in August 2018 and lasted between sixty and ninety minutes. To develop a measure of triangulation, field notes and memorandums were taken. The participants interviewed consisted of four alumni and one undergraduate member of SLB. Pseudonyms were used for all participants; a few sentences provide a brief description of their lives at the moment of the interview.

Daniel identifies as a homosexual Mexican man that was born in California. He majored in electrical engineering and joined the fraternity the spring semester of 2001. Currently, he serves as a litigation paralegal for a law firm in southern California. He volunteers for the Education Foundation of the fraternity and is a current board member for an LGBT community center.

Aiden is a Mexican American from Gary, Indiana, and identifies as queer. He is a first-generation college student, majored in political science and received a master's degree in education/student affairs. He joined the fraternity in his first year of college in the spring semester of 2009. Currently, he lives in Oregon, working with LGBT student services.

Martín was born in Nicaragua, and identifies as a gay male. He majored in recreation, parks, and tourism. He became a brother of the fraternity in the spring semester of 2007. He previously held leadership positions within the executive office of the fraternity. At present day, he lives in south Florida as a technical expert.

Eddie was born in Mission, Texas, and identifies as a homosexual male. He majored in interdisciplinary studies with a specialty in bilingual education. Eddie became a brother of the fraternity in the summer of 2013. At present day, he is a paralegal for a law firm assisting in claims and legal assistance in south Texas.

Jose is a Peruvian American that grew up in Denver, Colorado, and identifies as a gay male. Currently, he is a third-year first-generation student, majoring in theater and psychology with minors in ethnic studies and dance. He joined the fraternity in the spring semester of 2017 and currently serves as the marketing chair for a chapter in Colorado.

ANALYSIS

To answer the research question, traditional forms of qualitative data analysis were used starting with coding and then looking for patterns across the codes to create the themes, which were the focus of the findings. Creswell's (2009) six-step interactive practice assisted with coding and analyzing the data. Data was uploaded into Dedoose (platform app for analyzing data) to provide a description of the participants, how they found a familia within the fraternity, as well as a queer familia. The following section provides examples of how we can use queer theory as a lens to think about and understand how ethnicity, gender, and sexuality intersect within a Latino fraternity.

FINDINGS

Using queer theory provided a lens to examine how ethnicity, gender, and sexuality contribute to the construction of the meaning of familia for members who identify as gay/queer within a cisgender and heteronormative Latino fraternity. Building a familia within a familia illustrates how sexual power is enforced through binary divides and boundaries within the organization. The analysis exposed themes around boundaries and divides related to finding a familia within the fraternity, finding a queer familia, as well as challenges (Gamson and Moon 2004; Stein and Plummer 1994). In addition, implications are provided for taking action on sexuality as a national organization.

Finding a Familia

Similar to previous research (Atkinson, Dean, and Espino 2010; Miranda and de Figueroa 2000; Muñoz and Guardia 2009), the majority of participants joined the fraternity because they viewed it as a familia and a brotherhood for Latino and men of color. There were specific brothers in leadership roles that influenced participants to join the organization. For example, Eddie mentioned that the brother who took him to events and introduced him to other members in the chapter and the region also served as a mentor and teacher for the Upward Bound program and as a Resident Assistant. When coming out to their specific chapters, three of the participants were open about their sexual orientation during the recruitment and education process to join the fraternity, while the other two came out a year or two after joining the organization. Daniel explained, "When I came out, I was making a really big step being an open gay brother from California in general, my chapter, and region. I came out to my line brothers, my membership educator and had a very positive experience that I came out to the whole chapter at a chapter meeting."[1] Coming out in this space is powerful because there is a great amount of trust developed among the chapter that they will not be casted out or be afraid of rejection. All participants received support from their chapters when they came out which Daniel summarized, "The brotherhood teaches us about loving us for who we are. We all go through the same educational process and we all bond." Experiencing oppression as men of color and participating in the education process taught members to respect the views and values of others regardless of their identity.

Being a part of a chapter that embraced the participant's intersecting identities allowed them to thrive in important leadership positions within the fraternity. Three participants were the president of their chapters and two served as vice president. There were two who served as secretary and two who worked with the executive office of SLB. One participant helped create the Multicultural Greek Council on campus and became the first president. Three participants either worked or volunteered with LGBT student services, community, or student organizations. One participant currently volunteers as an alumnus with the SLB Education Foundation. These leadership opportunities helped participants develop skills, get involved, and contribute to the success of their chapter and fraternity.

Finding a Queer Familia

All participants found a familia within the fraternity and also found a sub-familia that allowed their sexual orientation to flourish. This familia, Daniel states, "was created just for us to have a space to be ourselves. We want to be who we are with other people like us in the fraternity." Martín and Daniel helped create the Facebook group and recruit brothers. The group tries to maintain discretion and privacy, which allows for brothers to join that are not out to brothers or family.

This virtual network provides a media platform for members to share advice, LGBT job opportunities, social gatherings, supporting local fundraisers, pictures of brothers together, and posts or memes related to gay culture. Eddie mentioned, "If you are going through a breakup, you can post on the group chat and brothers will reply." Others have sought advice related to higher education regarding studying abroad or engaging in a national exchange program. One undergraduate member, who serves as the brotherhood chair for his chapter, asked for advice related to planning a homecoming event. There is also a large amount of posts from members who are traveling to various parts of the United States and inviting brothers in the area to meet up or provide recommendations. Brothers also host other brothers that are traveling in the area and usually post pictures when they get together. All of these examples illustrate a strong brotherhood among familia.

This media platform allows brothers to share and comment on topics within gay culture, such as the upcoming new season of RuPaul's Drag Race All Stars, memes, and gatherings for national Pride events. One member shared a link to a podcast on a former president of Kappa Sigma fraternity at the University of Alabama talking about how an underground network of gay brothers helped him come out. This post is evidence that support groups like this exist and help other men who identity as gay/bi/queer within Greek-letter organizations.

This network helped Aiden find a Latino/queer community that he didn't find within the different cultural centers on campus. Aiden explains, "When I was in specific Latino communities, I didn't find queerness or when I was in specific queer communities, I wouldn't find people of color. I was trying to find that unison, that community and to be honest, I ended up finding it within SLB, specifically where I was trying to find both." Aiden was able to connect with brothers who also identified as queer and Latinx either in person or virtually on the Facebook group. The term "Latinx" is an attempt to decolonize the Spanish language and neutralize gender that has emerged through social media and adopted by individuals like Aiden (Salinas and Lozano 2017).

This familia also allows brothers to interact in person at national events such as the convention and the leadership institute. Aiden shared his experience presenting this year at the national convention, "I shared with brothers who I am, how I identify, letting them know who is in front of you and what my frame of reference is coming from. After the presentation, I had brothers who identify come up saying 'hey can you tell me more about that,' wanting inquiry but also trying to find community." These are the type of connections being made at the fraternity's national events because brothers have the opportunity to engage with one another.

Challenges

When we think about sexual boundaries and divides, participants being among brothers in the familia group allowed each other the freedom to express gender and femininity which is not accepted being around cisgender heterosexual members (Gamson and Moon 2004; Stein and Plummer 1994). Aiden states, "When other familia brothers are around, I feel more comfortable expressing gender and femininity than when I am around straight brothers." Jose shared, "I love the unity that we have and freedom of expression that we can share or talk about issues." The familia gives brothers an opportunity to express all of their intersecting identities.

Even though participants have found a supportive network among familia and their chapters, some have faced isolated challenges related to homophobic alumni and brothers. Jose mentioned overhearing an alumnus talking with other alumni stating, "When did we accept a bunch of nerds and faggots." When he tried to address the statement with the alumnus, he did not seem interested in having the conversation. Martín shared his experience, "When I was going through the process, there were some brothers in the chapter that were vehemently opposed to giving me a bid to join the fraternity. Members that would actively find ways to discourage me from continuing so that I did not join their fraternity." Aiden described his experience visiting the central region of the fraternity and sharing his sexual orientation, "When I shared my sexual orientation, it was not a negative or positive response, but it was like a chilled response. Clear distinction of brothers from different areas and how they viewed it." These examples illustrate both when it has been accepted to be gay/queer in the fraternity with the familia and instances when it has not been the case in the larger brotherhood. These challenges highlight and speak to the homophobia and hypermasculinity that continue to exist within SLB, fraternities, and the larger United States.

CONCLUSION

Using a queer lens helps us think about ethnicity, gender, and sexuality within Latino fraternities. This exploratory case study provides an in-depth analysis (Yin 1994) of how members of SLB have found a familia within a familia where they can feel accepted as gay/queer. This case also underlines the need for taking action at the national level of education and intentionality around sexuality and addressing homophobia and hypermasculinity. There is also a call to action for members in the familia group to engage and lead advocacy efforts for the fraternity. The following are recommendations for the fraternity at a national and individual chapter level, and the familia group to be more supportive of members who identify as gay/queer.

Relating back to the primary purposes of Latino/a fraternities and sororities (Miranda and de Figueroa 2000), the national fraternity could advocate
or support a cause related to the LGBTQ Latinx community. Daniel suggests
the fraternity "support an LGBTQ cause because it would make a huge statement for an ethnic minority group to support a cause that is uncommon from
that area of the community." This suggestion also relates back to the motto
and mission of the organization of serving the needs and wants of all people.
Daniel also recommends looking internally at the fraternity documents. He
asks, "Has anyone ever reviewed our documents and made sure there was no
hyper-masculine sentiment in the vocabulary? Why aren't we talking about
our fraternity in a way that we do not have brothers in chapters that feel
they cannot come out? Why aren't we addressing that as a group?" This is
a call for the national fraternity to be intentional when engaging in partner-
ships and critical of discourse underlining homophobic or hypermasculine
sentiment.

At the individual chapter level, Aiden mentioned that he would like to see
the fraternity be more intentional about conversations and education about
sexuality especially at the national events. He states, "Advocacy in relation to
the brotherhood. What would it be like at convention or at leadership institute
specifically talking about sexuality? Not putting it in a lump when we talk
about intersectionality or multiple identities but actually talking about it and
what that means for brothers." Daniel suggests chapters can put on workshops
or cosponsor with an LGBTQ group and do something that addresses some of
those issues as a community service opportunity. These type of workshops
or collaborations can help chapters be more mindful of microaggressions and
create an inclusive space for brothers who identify as gay/queer. These types
of collaborations do exist because chapters of SLB in the Midwest region of
the United States have collaborated with an Asian Sorority and LGBTQ Center to educate members of the community about sexual assault and domestic
violence (Del Real 2017).

In the familia group, Aiden stated they could be more resourceful. He
thinks the group should provide a "sense of advocacy, what are the ways
to advocate in the community that we are respectively living in, especially
moving to a conservative or liberal area. I think of that as community sharing
or community advocacy in that way." Although Daniel recognizes that the
familia group was created just for members to have a space and not necessarily seeking to be change agents, he feels that the group could do more. He
states, "We do not do enough with the mobilization abilities that we have
been able to create." Overall, participants agreed that the familia group could
do more work around advocacy and providing resources to members.

In conclusion, these recommendations can help SLB as well as other Greek-letter organizations be more cognizant and supportive of their LGBTQ members. Having a familia within a familia speaks to the importance of having a space where members can embrace all of their identities within a cisgender and heteronormative culture.

NOTE

1. Pseudonyms were used for all participants.

REFERENCES

Astin, Alexander W. 1993. *What Matters in College: Four Critical Years Revisited.* San Francisco: Jossey-Bass.

Atkinson, Eric, Laura A. Dean, and Michelle M. Espino. 2010. "Leadership Outcomes Based on Membership in Multicultural Greek Council (MGC) Organizations." *Oracle: The Research Journal of the Association of Fraternity/Sorority Advisors* 5 (2): 34–48.

Creswell, John W. 2009. *Research Design: Qualitative Quantitative, and Mixed Methods Approaches*, 3rd ed. Thousand Oaks, CA: Sage.

Del Real, Manuel. 2017. "Living the Creed: How Chapters of Sigma Lambda Beta International Fraternity, Inc., Contribute to Civic Engagement." PhD diss., Iowa State University.

Gamson, Joshua and Dawne Moon. 2004. "The Sociology of Sexualities: Queer and Beyond." *Annual Review of Sociology* 30 (1): 47–64.

Guardia, Juan R. and Nancy J. Evans. 2008. "Factors Influencing the Ethnic Identity Development of Latino Fraternity Members at a Hispanic Serving Institution." *Journal of College Student Development* 49 (3): 163–81.

Kimbrough, Walter M. 2003. *Black Greek 101: The Culture, Customs, and Challenges of Black Fraternities and Sororities*. Madison: Fairleigh Dickinson University Press.

Miranda, Monica L. and Martin de Figueroa. 2000. "Adelante Hacia el Futuro! (Forward to the Future) Latino/Latina Students: Past, Present, and Future." *Perspectives* 8: 6–8.

Muñoz, Susana M. and Juan R. Guardia. 2009. "Nuestra Historia y Futuro (Our History and Future): Latino/a Fraternities and Sororities." *Brothers and Sisters: Diversity within College Fraternities and Sororities*. Madison: Fairleigh Dickinson University Press.

Salinas, Cristobal and Adele Lozano. 2017. "Mapping and Recontextualizing the Evolution of the Term Latinx: An Environmental Scanning in Higher

Education." *Journal of Latinos and Education*: 1–14. https://doi:10.1080/15348 431.2017.1390464

Sigma Lambda Beta. "Sigma Lambda Beta International Fraternity." Accessed August 3, 2018. http://sigmalambdabeta.com/.

Stein, Arlene and Ken Plummer. 1994. "'I Can't Even Think Straight': 'Queer' Theory and the Missing Sexual Revolution in Sociology." *Sociological Theory* 12 (2): 178–87.

Torbenson, Craig L. and Gregory S. Parks. 2009. *Brothers and Sisters: Diversity within College Fraternities and Sororities*. Madison: Fairleigh Dickinson University Press.

Yin, Robert K. 1994. *Case Study Research: Design and Methods*, 2nd ed. Thousand Oaks, CA: Sage.

Chapter 5

Gayborhood Change

The Intertwined Sexual and Racial Character of Assimilation in Chicago's Boystown

Jason Orne

Oh shit, now we're equal to people. Now we're normal. Is that what we fought for?

—Sam, mid-thirties biracial Black gay man

In this chapter, I aim to demonstrate that the assimilation of a minority group contains intertwined sexual and racial assumptions due to what I've called the *intersectional knot* (Orne 2017). The *intersectional knot* refers to a puzzle that I observed within my fieldwork in Boystown, Chicago's gay neighborhood, or gayborhood as they are colloquially called. First, instances of heterosexism between queer men and straight women fed into sexism demonstrated by these men. Second, situations in which a particular community space managed to ameliorate one aspect of inequality (such as the sexy communities I studied having less racism) often relied on other forms of inequality to maintain rigid boundaries to create instances of cross-racial interaction (such as the sexism and "no women allowed" policies of these spaces, to continue the example).

Intersectionality (McCall 2005; Collins 2005) argues that systems of inequality and power are mutually reinforcing. A classic dictum is, "Where is the sexism in this racism? Where is the racism in this sexism?" Intersectionality *does not* merely refer to looking at the experiences of those experiencing multiple marginalized statuses, or "accounting" for the effects of multiple marginalized peoples within one's model, but rather that the experience of those at intersecting statuses reveals important aspects of how these systems of inequality interact. The *intersectional knot* (Orne 2017) further argues that these systems are tangled, and that attempts to loosen one strand that do not consider the totality of the systems of power will tighten other strands within the knot, magnifying those forms of inequality as a result.

In this chapter, I examine the intersectional knot by examining the intertwined sexual and racial consequences of assimilation of a minority group into the mainstream. I argue assimilating a cultural group involves acculturating that group into mainstream sexual norms, restructuring sexual fields to discourage marginalized sexual behavior, and whitening that group's cultural heritage to fuse it with the mainstream. I use data from my ethnography of Chicago's Boystown neighborhood (Orne 2017). First, I demonstrate some gay men in Boystown are acculturating, adopting mainstream sexual norms. Next, I show that restructuring Boystown's sexual fields reinforces sexual assimilation through changes to the neighborhood's gay bars as straight White women consume them. Finally, I discuss the racial consequences. As gay men become "ethnically straight" (Hicklin 2012) and integrated into straight society, racial boundaries in the neighborhood harden, whitening the area, and casting gay men of color as violent outsiders. These results demonstrate sexual assimilation involves a racializing component. By extension, I argue that to understand assimilation, we must proceed intersectionally to understand not only how it acculturates ethnic groups to mainstream White values, but that those values include heteronormative sexual mores.

ASSIMILATION

Assimilation is a core concept of twentieth-century sociology. From Park's 1926 race relations cycle to contemporary articulations (Alba and Nee 1997; Portes and Zhou 1993), scholars examine how racial and ethnic groups integrate into the White American mainstream. Assimilation researchers focus on the spatial assimilation and place stratification of ethnic groups (Pais, South, and Crowder 2012), the structural assimilation of minority groups (Gordon 1964), and acculturation to majority norms (Zolberg and Woon 1999).

Assimilation theories often privilege ethnic groups' sexuality and family formation demographics. To illustrate, Portes and Zhou discuss the expectations of immigrant Sikh families that female children marry quickly, require parental consent to date, and avoid dancing. They saw successful passing of such norms to second-generation children as evidence these families selectively assimilated, resisting Americanization (Portes and Zhou 1993). Alternatively, problematic depictions of Black sexuality and family structure in the 1965 Moynihan Report marked African Americans as unassimilatable. Park originally placed emphasis on intimate relationships as the method that would break down barriers between racial groups (Park 1914). Therefore, unsurprisingly, scholars use interracial relationships as markers of assimilation, (Bonilla-Silva 200; Zhou 2008; Song 2009). Relationship demographics and family structure are forms of sexuality, more tactfully named.

Surprisingly though, sexuality researchers ignore racial assimilation scholarship when discussing sexual minorities. In the gay context, assimilation refers to integrating gay individuals into heterosexual society and adapting queer sexual cultures to mainstream straight cultures. Homonormativity (Duggan 2012) is the "new normal" focusing gay political activism on integrating into neoliberal institutions like the military and marriage. With the repeal of "Don't Ask; Don't Tell" and marriage equality across the United States, the political assimilation of gay sexual minorities into the American mainstream is well on its way.

Gayle Rubin's charmed circle is a helpful lens on assimilation diagraming how sexual practices interrelate. The circle's inside wedges are mainstream and hegemonic (e.g., heterosexuality, sex in the home, same-generation, vanilla, procreative, married, monogamous), while those outside are subversive, stigmatized, and, I would say, queer (e.g., homosexuality, sex in public, intergenerational, BDSM, for pleasure, out of wedlock, with multiple partners). As the stigma of homosexuality fades, society expects queer people to follow the other parts of hegemonic sexuality like marriage, monogamy, and procreation (Rubin 1992).

Therefore, society accepts same-sex partners, but only if they look like straight relationships. Political victories like marriage focus on acculturating, not equalizing, a separate queer culture. As such, these social movement victories are markers and drivers of assimilation of queer people. How are these macro changes influencing the micro- and meso-level sexual lives and sexual cultures in gayborhoods?

In December 2012, after winning *Out Magazine*'s Person of the Year, Nate Silver told the magazine, "I'm kind of sexually gay, but ethnically straight" (Hicklin 2012). The White *New York Times* journalist and former Boystown resident does not "want to be Nate Silver, gay statistician." His desire to be "ethnically straight," embracing straight norms while maintaining a nominal gay identity and engaging in same-sex relationships, is evident in his favorite club in Boystown, Chicago's gay neighborhood. He likes Berlin because it is mixed. While it has gay clientele, straight people regularly attend late into the night to enjoy the throbbing house music and two-dollar PBR Tuesdays.

Berlin's mixed atmosphere is increasingly common in more traditional male gay bars. Straight people are integrated, both residentially and commercially, across gay neighborhoods (Ghaziani 2014). Queer people's destigmatization strategies (Lamont 2009; Saguy and Ward 2011)—for instance, coming out—mostly worked. Some scholars argue queer people are now "beyond the closet" (Seidman 2002) and "post-gay" (Ghaziani 2014). However, LGBTQ people's lived experience remains mixed (Williams, Giuffre and Dellinger 2009). They still must employ a strategic outness (Orne 2011) and they continue to use traditional sexual identity labels (Orne 2013). Post-gay theorists contend gay identity is disappearing. Instead, gay people are assimilating, becoming "ethnically straight," gay but not queer (Orne 2017).

"Ethnically straight" or ethnically gay, only people who perceive themselves as raceless (e.g., White people) could think of themselves as such. Queer of color critique emphasizes this distance, one that has been perpetuated by the academy, especially sociological understandings of queer communities (Ferguson 2004). Positioning homosexuality as an ethnic-like cultural group whitens gay identity, rendering queer people of color invisible. Queer people's race is often unmarked, thus raced White. For instance, the mass media in the aftermath of Proposition 8's passage—the California antigay marriage amendment—reported the story as the Black community versus the gay community, as though queer people of color (QPOC) did not exist. As Moore articulates in her book on Black lesbian families, QPOC are often "invisible" (Moore 2011).

Because of this invisibility within communities of color presumed to be homophobic (Connell 2014), queer communities presumed to be White, and the academic community itself invested in this monolithic distinction (Ferguson 2004), work on the assimilation of gay people into American society pays inadequate attention to the legacy of work on assimilation in the sociology of race and ethnicity. Assimilation literature provides a wealth of concepts: acculturation, structural assimilation, spatial assimilation, gentrification, and so on. When these encounter the previous ethnographic work on gay neighborhoods that focus on gay identity and social movements (Ghaziani 2014) and the structure of their sexual fields (Green 2011), the fusion reveals the intersectional character of assimilation. The assimilation of sexual groups has racial consequences and, I argue, vice versa.

I would like to stress that, as I discussed in *Boystown* (Orne 2017), the goal here is not to reproduce the argument of queer of color critique (Ferguson 2004). Instead, I seek to demonstrate how our understanding of a central concept within sociology—assimilation—can be deepened through understanding its intersectional knot. To understand the connection, we turn to a classic site in which its effects are often studied.

Enclaves and Gayborhoods

Enclaves are the metropolis's visible marker of assimilation. The presence of an enclave signals the degree of the group's assimilation or separation. The activity occurring within enclaves indicates the resistance or accommodation to assimilation. Gayborhoods are cultural enclaves serving a primarily gay male clientele. Like other cultural enclaves—such as religious enclaves like Chicago's Skokie for Jewish people or racial enclaves like Chicago's historic Brownsville for African Americans—they insulate stigmatized communities from outsiders and employ members who might be able unemployable outside the enclave (Portes and Jensen 1989). Enclaves might be dissolved through assimilation into mainstream society, moved around the city through gentrification, or remain as a historic neighborhood although the "old-timers" represent only a minority share of residents (Brown-Saracino 2009). The enclave allows a separate lifestyle from the mainstream, often allowing entrepreneurs to setup businesses that would be otherwise impossible and workers to use cultural social networks to secure jobs (Nee, Sanders and Sernau 1994). Cultural enclaves are not uniformly helpful to their minority residents, with some evidence that wages, for instance, would be higher if they sought work outside of the enclave (Nee, Sanders, and Sernau 1994).

Scholars have not examined classic assimilation theories in gay neighborhoods. Instead, they examine sexual identity politics or gay men's sexual networks. The first tact tracks the meaning of gayborhood change to sexual identity social movements and sexual identity politics (Ghaziani 2014). In this vein, scholars trace changes in the need for gayborhoods as queer people move into a "post-gay" era. The rise and fall of gayborhoods is related to other historical forces shaping sexuality and the creation of a homosexual minority group post-World War II (D'Emilio 1983). For instance, some work looks at the vicarious citizenship gay men feel with gayborhoods when not residents (Greene 2012). These studies reveal the context for assimilation, but do not themselves situate the structural integration or segregation within their studies within classic assimilation frameworks.

The second tact maps the sexual networks of gay men. Laumann et al.'s Chicago Health and Social Life survey took special care to include the same-sex sexual networks of gay men and lesbians. Work in this vein looks at gayborhoods as a nexus of sexual activity and relationships for men who have sex with men (MSMs), primarily through a sexual markets lens (Ellingson and Schroeder 2004; Laumann et al. 1993). More recently, scholars like Green draw upon Bourdieuian field theory as an alternative to sexual markets (Martin and George 2006) to trace sexual fields' creation and transformation. Sexual fields are collective social worlds with their "own particular social organization, status hierarchy and regulative principles" regarding sexual activity (Green 2008a, 2008b, 2011, 2012). One sexual field would be the hookup scene at a college's Greek fraternity life, with all the sexual scripts, stratification, and interactional strategies that scene entails. This tact similarly reveals activity within the sexual fields of gayborhoods that is useful for tracing the resistance or accommodation to assimilation, but does not itself comment on assimilation.

This chapter examines assimilation on the ground, a meso-level approach synthesizing these two tacts by looking at gayborhood change through the lens of scholarship in the sociology of race and ethnicity. I trace the transformation of the sexual field of Boystown and connect it to the structural assimilation and acculturation of the neighborhood due to the transformation of the meaning of gay people in society. This approach reveals that assimilation has an intertwined sexual and racial character, an intersectional knot (Orne 2017). Examined intersectionally, Rubin's "charmed circle" is hegemonically White and a group's assimilation into the center racializes that group as White. This chapter also connects how sexual organization creates and maintains shifts in collective identity. Work in both sexuality and racial scholarship needs to consider the intersectional character of assimilation. Before we examine what this intersectional assimilation looks like in Boystown, I turn to my methods.

METHODS

Starting mid-2011, I conducted an ethnography of the Chicago neighborhood Boystown (Orne 2017), in the style of classic Chicago-style ethnographies like *Black Metropolis* (Drake and Cayton 1993) and *Street Corner Society* (Whyte 1993). Multiple data collection methods triangulated information, giving me a comprehensive picture of the neighborhood. Over three years, I conducted participant-observation at community events, neighborhood bars and clubs, and private social gatherings. I collected 26 hours of formal interviews with twenty participants. I also conducted countless informal interviews with bartenders, club patrons, shop clerks, and passersby. On a number of occasions, I conducted nonrandom establishment surveys and tallies to assess neighborhood consumers using the phenotypic gender, race, and sexual identity as they appeared to me, a longtime resident of the Midwest. I also examined my auto-ethnographic experience of these spaces through a daily journal that I completed in addition to traditional fieldnotes.

Given the digital nature of modern life, I included online components of Boystown. There are a number of print and online publications that follow Chicago's queer life. I comprehensively followed these throughout my fieldwork, with an eye to discussions of race, sexuality, and Boystown. I also examined social media like Facebook and Twitter discussions by participants and others. I collected over 600 of these print and social media accounts. Following the lead of Nakamura, I also analyzed the structural organization of race and sexuality on online dating and hookup websites participants identified (Nakamura 2002), such as Grindr or Adam4Adam, both of which use location data, thereby identifying Boystown.

I selected Boystown for theoretical reasons. The project began with an interest in the interracial dynamics of gay male relationships and communities. Boystown combines Chicago's tumultuous racial history, Fryer's finding that the Midwest has the least interracial relationships (Fryer 2007), and previous studies of gay sexual networks in the city (Ellingson and Schroeder 2004). These findings led me to explore the neighborhood as a possibility during early 2011. The Take Back Boystown event, which I describe later, crystalized the racial issues in the neighborhood. Thus, mid-2011, I began ethnographic fieldwork in the area, ultimately moving to Boystown in January 2012, living there for over a year before following White gay participants' residential patterns north. I did not restrict my fieldwork to Boystown. When participants invited me to other parts of the city, I followed. These other neighborhoods—like "lesbian" Andersonville, Latinos in Pilsen, White queers in Edgewater, or gay Black communities on the south side—often were reference points when groups discussed the neighborhood.

I primarily spent my time in Boystown split between six different social groups that crossed racial and class scenes: JJ's Latinx group, Frank's "anti-racist" White queer friends, Darrin and Jon (a pair of QPOC friends), Marcus's racially diverse leather family, a largely White group of "poz" (HIV positive) friends, and the "Boat People," an upper-class White group known for parties afloat Lake Michigan. My interview sample evolved through theoretical sampling (Charmaz 2006), selecting participants through ongoing analysis, and did not generally overlap with the ethnographic groups. Participants and I co-constructed interviews (Corbin and Morse 2003), conversing about Boystown, queer life, race, and sex. Key informants were in community organizations, bartenders, club promoters, club personnel, journalists, and people that both frequented Boystown and hadn't gone back in years. Analysis using the tools of constructivist grounded theory (Charmaz 2006) led me to several insights about the structure and evolution of queer life and racism. One such follows.

BOYSTOWN AND GENTRIFICATION

Located in Chicago's Lakeview East neighborhood, Boystown is the center of gay male community life. Although tendrils of queerness extend throughout the city, Boystown is the only area Chicago designates as a gay village, the first in the country to have such a designation. During the early 1980s, gay men moved up Halsted Street from the Lincoln Park area to what was then called NewTown. The largely Puerto Rican residents began to be displaced as gay men, from a variety of races but mostly White, began to settle in the area. In 1998, Mayor Daley arranged beautification projects—often involving large public art to mark the area—to four neighborhoods in the city: three neighborhoods identified with Chicago's major ethnic groups and Boystown, solidifying the neighborhood's official status as the gay enclave. In the last decade, the neighborhood continues to change. This time, straight White women and heterosexual families are displacing Boystown's gay residents.

Boystown's history is an almost textbook case of gentrification. Brown-Saracino (2009) divides gentrification into two different stages. In early-stage gentrification, White people with high cultural capital, but low economic capital, push people of color out of a neighborhood through a series of "cleanup" projects and rising rent prices. These gentrifiers are often White gay men, due to marginalization from their homosexuality that prevents them from fully accessing their White and male privilege in the housing market. As the neighborhood changes, becomes more fashionable, and more hip, "yuppies"—White young professionals with high economic capital—begin to move into the area. This late-stage gentrification is much less analyzed. It involves straight White people, often families, exchanging their greater economic capital to move into the trendy new area. The early-adopters are pushed out and into a new area, starting the cycle again. Boystown is experiencing late-stage gentrification.

As one would expect from a neighborhood that completed early-stage gentrification, a previous study identified the area as almost completely White (Ellingson and Schroeder 2004). However, my fieldwork indicates this claim overly relies on residential status, ignoring the lengthy history of queer people of color traveling to the area for entertainment from other parts of the city.

Thus, this chapter concerns itself less with the demographic change in residential status and more with the demographic change in neighborhood consumption my participants believe to be tied to changes in society. Although the residents that have lived in Boystown may have been predominantly White, the consumption of the neighborhood was not. Although they did not live in the neighborhood, queer people of color came from across the city to hang out on Boystown's streets and in its gay bars. Similarly, regardless of true residential changes, participants believe the area now is settled and consumed increasingly by straight White women.

Ethnographic observations lent credence to my participants' views that the area is experiencing an influx of straight White women living in the area and consuming its nightlife. As an illustration, table 5.1 describes a tally that I took of people on the streets of Boystown on December 6, 2012. At 7:30 p.m., a few of these people were coming into or out of bars and restaurants, but many of them were walking home, carrying exercise clothing, walking dogs, or pushing strollers. This tally is conceptually representative of the new face of Boystown. For an area purportedly for gay men, the presence of

Table 5.1   Count of Boystown Pedestrians

Thursday, December 6, 2012, 7:30 p.m.	
Count	*Demographic*
41 (53%)	White Women
8 (10%)	Men of Color
26 (34%)	White Men
2 (3%)	Women of Color

an overwhelming majority of White women, I argue, has an influence on the community life of the area.

The area has become a destination for many people, straight and gay, to consume a "gay lifestyle" that includes a kind of nightlife and shopping popularized by media depictions of gay men. As Adam, a gay Black man in his forties, put it, "It's a mall. You go to the mall to hang out or to shop, but you don't live at the mall." Many people expressed similar sentiments. Frequently, they referred to the area as a "gay Disneyland." Asked what this meant, Jackson, a late twenties Black gay man, described it as "everything that you would want if you were going to visit a gay neighborhood some-where. Fifteen clubs, everyone is adorable, and people are roaming around in groups. It's like, you know, a TV gay neighborhood." The area is now a destination. A place where one does not necessarily live (Ghaziani 2014), but a place they still return to consume. This chapter looks at the change in who and how people come to consume the neighborhood, and what that change indicates about assimilation.

The neighborhood has not followed the typical gentrification cycle, which would involve another area of the city rising up as the new major gay area, just as Boystown moved north transforming NewTown. Although many White gay men have moved north to Buena Park, Edgewater, or Rogers Park, none of these places have displaced Boystown as the gay capital of Chicago. There are three reasons that the neighborhood hasn't moved.

First, the official recognition by the city gave the neighborhood a historical character. The city erected pylons along Halsted St. from Belmont to Grace. These large golden pillars topped with rainbow colors—my participants sometimes referred to them as Boystown's "golden phalluses"—were later supplemented in 2012 by plaques that listed famous LGBT people and their historical significance. Many people referenced these pylons as marking the neighborhood as *the* gay neighborhood. They are literal stakes in the ground.

Second, legal differences exist between the neighborhood when it moved into the area and today. Today, many of the buildings on the block are owned by the backers of the clubs. Those that do not own the building their clubs reside in are more transient, opening and closing regularly. Some of these—like a Black and Latino club Circuit that briefly closed after arguments over rent with building owners—reopen in another part of the city, only to return later. Others, like Cocktail, frequently open and close, change ownership and even names, but remain in the neighborhood. Both major landmark bars, Sidetrack's and Roscoe's, own the building they are located in. Owning their locations means they are rooted in a way that discourages moving further north to follow White gay male residential movement.

Third, in 2008, a major LGBT community center opened in the neighborhood called The Center on Halsted. The Center, a major target of the Take Back Boystown campaign described later, is a multimillion dollar facility and nonprofit organization. They provide space for community groups to meet, host social events, and provide many social services. For instance, the Center supplies mental health services, HIV testing, a youth program, and job training. Their senior program will expand in the coming years to include a new senior living building close by. The Center is another stake in the ground, identifying this area as *the* gay area of Chicago. That The Center is in Boystown, rather than several smaller community centers across the many areas of Chicago where queer people live (as was originally a proposal), gives Boystown a special emphasis as the gay center of Chicago, a destination to come to consume either the thriving nightlife or the Center's social services.

I asked one new resident, George, a mid-thirties White gay man who returned to the neighborhood after having moved away for nearly ten years, what had changed since he last lived there. He responded, "When I moved back here, I wanted to live in Lakeview [the official city name for the area that includes Boystown] because it's a fun place to fuck and like hang out. And my husband and I were looking and we're like 'Oh my god. It's fucking Lincoln Park.' It's the demographic that I do not want. You know? It's not the neighborhood that it was ten years ago. It's less gay, it's less diverse, it's more of a tourist spot." This transformation of Boystown from a stigmatized gay enclave to a thriving gay Disneyland represents the assimilation of the neighborhood into the fabric of traditional mainstream society.

Assimilation's Intertwined Character

The late-stage gentrification of Boystown and its transformation into a "gay Disneyland" reflects the assimilation of gay men. It has an intertwined sexual and racial character. I first present evidence that some gay men are taking up mainstream straight sexual values. Next, I show how sexual assimilation is reinforced through restructuring sexual fields, changing the ways people find sexual partners. Finally, I document the racial consequences of sexual assimilation: racial boundaries in the neighborhood harden, whitening the area, and, thereby, casting queer people of color as outsiders.

Sexual Assimilation

Sexual assimilation is the spatial assimilation, structural integration, and acculturation of a sexual minority to mainstream straight sexual values. Acculturation is the taking up of a belief, attitude, or cultural practice by a minority group. Acculturation is not one way. It can also occur through the blurring of boundaries between the two groups, transforming a stigmatized practice associated with the group into a commonplace occurrence no longer associated with the group. It need not be totalizing to have occurred.

To understand the queer cultural ethos that some gay men are acculturating from, return to Rubin's charmed circle. Some queer communities have an alternative queer sexual lifestyle and culture (Orne 2017), separate sexual fields from straight culture with their own social organization and interactional rules (Green 2012). Perhaps because gay men are marginalized along one part of the pie (i.e., homosexuality), their sexual field does not stigmatize some of the other parts of the pie (e.g., nonmonogamy and public sex), resulting in acceptance of multiple partners, casual sex, public sexuality, adult toys, and other sexual activities marginalized by mainstream straight culture. Although it was threatened by the AIDS/HIV epidemic, this queer sexual ethos survives today in the plethora of gay hookup websites, some bathhouses, and in niche gay male communities like bears, leather, and the HIV positive "poz" community.

This section discusses how some gay men are acculturating to mainstream straight sexual culture that devalues the outer circle and emphasizes inner circle activities like marriage. Now that the possibility of marriage exists for gay men, a traditional marriage like their parents has become the goal. For example, Frank, a gay mid-twenties White Catholic, wants to get married. He expectantly waits to find the right guy. When asked who the "right guy" looks like, he specifies this means a monogamous relationship, marriage, and a family. He "wants the same things as everyone else," meaning straight people. When he discusses the straight White women in Boystown's gay bars, he only disapproves of bachelorette parties because they "rub my face in it. It's just rude when they have rights I don't have."

In the meantime, he's not going to let that stop him from going on sexual hookup websites, but he feels shameful doing so because "that's not the type of relationship that [he's] looking for." Again, acculturation need not be totalizing to have occurred. In this case, hookups are accepted in some straight cultures, although not to the extent in queer culture, as long as that the eventual goal is marriage and monogamy (Currier 2000). His shame also reflects a change in attitudes toward what is often seen as "normal" gay sexuality, a shift toward the beliefs of the straight sexual majority. The boundary between the alternative sexual culture of queers and the straight people has blurred one kind of acculturation (Zolberg and Woon 1999).

However, many gay men do not wish to participate in the hookup culture associated with queerness. Alexander doesn't want to be involved in the hookup culture and "slut shames" those who do. During several of our conversations, Alexander, a mid-twenties White gay man who immigrated to America as a teenager, talked to me about two different men that he's had sex. His sense of shame was palpable. He stressed that if they only want him for sex, well, "I'm not a slut" and would not continue to see them. Through ethnographic triangulation, I observed Alexander out with one of these two men during fieldwork. The potential boyfriend appeared to genuinely desire a relationship with him. Alexander, however, rejected him, primarily because of the man's history of hooking up and large number of previous sex partners. Men like Alexander have acculturated to straight sexual norms, more closely reflecting their parents' traditional sexual systems.

The neighborhood also reflects acculturation through a change toward valuing the "stroller set," as Sam puts it, over other neighborhood groups. These refer both to queer families and nonqueer families. More straight families are hanging around and moving into the neighborhood, but also queer families now desire the gayborhood to be "more quiet" and less "a party scene." One of the most noticeable consequences has been several complaints about the sex-toy shops with open windows on the street. At a doctor's appointment at a neighborhood clinic, my phlebotomist, who looked to be in his early thirties, told me that he sees Boystown's streets as much different than when he first came out: "During the day, it's a family area now, not really a gay one." The shift toward families represents favoring the procreative segment of Rubin's charmed circle over the non-procreative.

These forms of acculturation are not totalizing. Acculturation is not a one-way street, it involves the blurring and, to an extent, the queering of these boundaries. While some men are slut shaming and/or desiring of marriage, they still participate in casual sex, but in ways consistent with straight culture. Each of these attitude changes represents a shift from the outside of the charmed circle toward a hegemonic inner circle value. Changes to the sexual field of Boystown reinforce these attitudes, making queer sexual culture increasingly hard to actualize regardless of one's sexual ethos.

Sexual Field Restructuring

"NO BACHELORETTE PARTIES," read the sign outside of Cocktail, a gay bar on one of Boystown's most bustling corners. Yet, inside I couldn't tell. For a gay bar, the place probably had as many women as gay men. Surely, a few of these women were lesbian, bisexual, or otherwise queer, but a good many were straight. Near the stage, a male stripper in his underwear—who often tells me he only strips to support his wife and children—caressed a woman in leopard print pants and open-toed strapped high heels, a style of shoe thought to be so alluring to men that the late neosoul diva Amy Winehouse called them "Fuck Me Pumps." He gyrated into her, moving her hands along his body as her two other female friends laughed beside her. Over the next half hour, this routine continued only occasionally punctuated with a quick dollar down his waistband from one of the few gay men standing around.

I've dragged my partner along for the night and he tells me that he's had enough of what has become a strip club for straight women. After quickly taking a few more jottings of the situation on my iPhone, we decided to head across the street to Roscoe's, perhaps the most popular gay bar in the area. After seeing three separate groups of women head out the door, he threw up his hands, "Can we go somewhere gay?"

I relented. We walked toward the Lucky Horseshoe, a gay strip club raunchy and literally dirty enough to resist the changes overtaking Boystown's other bars. Along Halsted St., Boystown's main thoroughfare, I continued taking notes on my phone, categorizing the groups we passed along the street. It was a busy night, a definite girl's night out.

These nights are common in Boystown. It is not just gay men who come to consume "gay Disneyland." The late-stage gentrification of the area has brought more women into the area, most of which my participants believe to be straight. There are consequences of the real and perceived structural assimilation of straight women into the bars and clubs, the community "third spaces" of Boystown. As gay men sexually assimilate to straight norms, the structural assimilation of straight women into gay male bars restructures the sexual field gay men navigate, reinforcing mainstream sexual norms.

The sexual field of Boystown is restructured by the presence of large quantities of straight White women primarily because it breaks down the interactional rules that once governed the space. Sam, a biracial Black gay man, says the result is that gay men in these bars feel objectified, like they exist for straight White women's entertainment:

> It's become this petting zoo where they come and look and gawk at the gays. It's not as much just the gay neighborhood as it is where people go to see the gay people. A lot of people don't like that. I can't stand it when women will come up to me at a bar like, "You're gay, you're my best friend." Just because you've seen a gay on TV doesn't mean I'm going to be your best friend.

This feeling of objectification means that they no longer feel comfortable engaging in the hookup rituals, public sexuality, and other actions the queer sexual field entails. In Sam's words:

> Those days [before straight women were present], you go to the gay bar to be
> gay. There are a lot of guys who want to go to a gay bar to be free. To like take
> off your shirt, be raunchy, and just have at it without this whole table full of
> straight girls, "Oh, gay men are so safe and pretty and I love you." Bitch, get
> off of me I'm trying to suck this guy's dick. I'm sorry just being completely
> open here.

These changes reinforce assimilated straight, inner charmed circle, values.
When gay men no longer feel comfortable engaging in the behavior, it reinforces mainstream straight sexual beliefs. In this case, as Rubin's charmed
circle shows, sex belongs in the home. The segments of the circle are mutually reinforcing.

I even saw this reinforcement out at some leather events, a raunchier queer
subculture. At a Tom of Finland, a gay leather artist known for his hypermasculine drawings, themed event at Hydrate, Jon and I were astounded to see
five young White women come inside off the street. I struck up a conversation
with them as they gawked at their surroundings. They didn't know it was a
leather themed event, but were walking along the street and thought the venue
looked like fun. When Jon and I turned to go to the back "No Shirts Allowed"
dance floor—a rule meant to foster a sexually charged atmosphere—they followed us. The bouncer stopped them. "No shirts," he reminded them. While
two of the women were reluctant at first, the other two convinced them, negotiating the bouncer down to bras only. As they entered the dance floor clad
only in their bras, they gleefully yelled, telling me what a wild time they were
having. The men around me on the floor moved away slightly, shooting me
dirty looks. While I did see sexually charged dancing, I didn't see any of the
making-out or groping I had witnessed at previous themed events. At least,
not near us, and, not until the women left the bar a few hours later.

This reinforcement is not just discouraging gay men that might wish to
engage in alternative sexual behavior. It also discourages gay men from identifying as a separate culture from the mainstream straight world. Frank, the
gay Catholic whose marriage views I describe earlier, for instance, doesn't
mind that more women are in the gay clubs he frequents. When I asked him
about how he feels about more women in gay clubs, he responded:

> What's the difference? We're always bringing our girlfriends with us. At least
> I do. My two girlfriends are the ones I come to Boystown with. I never come
> to boystown with gay guys. It's not a big deal. I don't belong to this culture of
> I can only be around other gay men.

This culture he explains is one that wants to maintain itself as "separate" from the straight world. To Frank, women in the clubs represent the

acceptance by the straight world that he mimics in his beliefs about marriage and monogamy. The structural changes to the sexual field blur group boundaries that maintain queerness as a separate cultural group and enclave.

Thus, the sexual assimilation of gay men in Boystown is reinforced on two levels by the structural integration of straight White women into Boystown's night life. First, they restructure the sexual field of the neighborhood, discouraging behavior that is not aligned with mainstream straight values—the hegemonic inside of the charmed circle. Second, the integration demonstrates to people like Frank that gay men are accepted by straight culture, they are not a separate group, and Boystown is a district for a certain consumer.

Racial Consequences

As the neighborhood assimilates, queer people of color, because of their racial difference, become the most visible affront to the hegemonic "gay Disneyland" model of the neighborhood. The assimilation of the neighborhood, including its integration into straight society, racializes the neighborhood as a White neighborhood. Queer people of color in the area are "outsiders" and racial boundaries harden.

"Make sure that when you are writing this book, you write about both the good and the bad changes to the neighborhood," an older affluent White gay man admonished me after I told him about my project. We were drinking whiskey in Buck's, a gay bar on Halsted St. known for its older clientele. The good changes, he explained are "how nice everything is nowadays," evoking the same language others used when referencing Boystown's late-stage gentrification and "gay Disneyland" atmosphere.

The bad changes? "The ghetto trannies and gay kids on the street" who are "loud" and don't realize that they can be "respectable" now. I hear these references frequently toward the young Black men, drag queens, and transwomen who come to Boystown, like gay men of other racial groups, for entertainment and social services.

He is not the only one to feel that the presence of queer people of color is a change in the neighborhood. In the summer of 2011, a stabbing in the neighborhood was caught on video by the White gay owners of a condo overlooking Halsted St. The video shows two groups of young Black men coming together, a short argument, and then a burst of violence as one man stabs another. The owners leaked the video to the mainstream Chicago media, prompting articles and a wave of hysteria to grip the neighborhood about the sudden "crime wave" in Boystown. The accused culprits of this crime wave were clear: young Black and Latino men hanging out on the street.

The Take Back Boystown event and accompanying Facebook page formed shortly after. Take Back Boystown was meant to be a "community loitering" event, where "residents" of Boystown would band together and hang out on the street to show "those that don't belong here" that the neighborhood would not be intimidated. The event was protested by a queer community group, GenderJUST, calling the event racist and an attempt to prevent queer people of color from coming to the neighborhood.

Much of the blame was placed on The Center on Halsted, the multimillion dollar LGBT center that opened in 2008, for attracting "outsiders" to the neighborhood with its social services. In an interview with the *Windy City Times*, the major gay newspaper of Chicago, The Center's CEO Modesto Tico Valle similarly expressed his beliefs that the Take Back Boystown event was driven by racism:

WCT: The Center has been controversial for a lot of Lakeview residents worried about safety, especially last summer with the "Take Back Boystown" Facebook page campaign. Why do you think that is?
MV: We are a significant presence on Halsted Street. This is the go-to place…I think the issue is a lot more complicated and it involves a lot of the "isms" of our society. Some of it has to do with fear and facing your own prejudices. When you really have the opportunity to speak to some individuals in the community and challenge tone and language, people can pause for a minute and realize "hmm, maybe there is a bit of racism."
WCT: What were you hearing from youth [*author: the codeword* for *young black men* in *the area*] in the Center last summer when this was going on?
MV: I heard from a lot of young people a roller-coaster of emotions: anger that they were being blamed for something that they had no role in, sadness because they came into a community that they thought was going to embrace them and be safe after being beaten, raped, abused in their neighborhoods, in their families. They kind of saw this as their safe haven and their family. The community—not everyone, but some—slammed the door in their face in a very ugly way. (Sosin 2012)

It should surprise no one in the sociology of race and ethnicity that a belief in rising crime rates was connected to the visibility of queer people of color on the streets of Boystown. The perception of crime in a neighborhood is not related to the level of reported crimes in a neighborhood, but to the percentage of African Americans seen on the street in the area (Quillian and Pager 2001). In fact, Boystown was experiencing some of the lowest crime rates in years (Demarest 2012).

Most importantly, queer people of color in the neighborhood are not a new phenomenon. Instead, because of the changing assimilated status of the neighborhood as a "gay Disneyland" to be consumed, queer people of color in the neighborhood *began* to be seen as outsiders to the neighborhood.

Pauline, a Black bisexual woman in her early 40s, remembers when she was a young Black woman engaging in precisely the same kind of street activity in the early 1990s that Take Back Boystown suddenly identified as new and the cause of crime. She used to visit the neighborhood from her home on the south side of Chicago—where most of Chicago's Black population lives—to hang out with her friends on the Belmont Rocks, a popular destination for people under twenty-one when Boystown first formed. Queer people of color coming to Boystown is not new.

However, it is now seen as new, or at least noteworthy. The comments on the Take Back Boystown Facebook page vividly show that the neighborhood is now seen as a White space:

> It's the blacks tearing the neighborhood apart. They're a bunch of monsters.
>
> Most of the drama is caused by black a**holes who live in other neighborhoods who come here and I [*sic*] respect the area.
>
> I've lived in Chicago for 46 years. These comments arten [*sic*] racist. They are true.
>
> Go back to your hoods!!!

Such posts—and the often sixty plus comment threads that followed them debating whether the post was racist—demonstrate the area is now seen as a White area.

While the area did not have an exclusively White reputation earlier, that does not mean that it did not have racism. There is a difference between racism in a space where both White gay men and gay men of color are assumed to be present and the racialization of Boystown as a White area. Boystown, like all of society, has had plenty of interpersonal and structural racism. For example, they did not have a Black bartender in the area until 1998.

I argue not that Boystown was a place of racial harmony, but rather that the new vividness of race in the area and the hardening of its racial boundaries is bound up in its new status as an assimilated space, a "gay Disneyland." Queer people of color, rather than being members of the gay community that have always been present in the space, are newly salient as out of place. The area has been recategorized as being aggressively White.

DISCUSSION AND CONCLUSION

Assimilation has an intertwined sexual and racial character. Through ethnographic fieldwork, interviews, and content analysis, I demonstrated a cultural group assimilates along multiple lines. Assimilation involves acculturation to mainstream sexual norms. Demographic change and structural integration conspire to restructure sexual fields discouraging unassimilated sexual behavior. Concurrently, these changes whiten the area, fusing it with the mainstream.

Specifically, this chapter demonstrates gay men are a cultural group that is assimilating in American society and the consequences are mixed. Some gay men have profoundly conservative sexual attitudes. These gay men engage in "slut shaming," express concern over how to find "good" relationships within gay culture, and look to forward to marriage and children. Neighborhood institutions reflect this as well with increased family programming, concern for children in the neighborhood, and efforts to "clean up" the party atmosphere of the entertainment district. Of course, these are not negative, unless they come at the expense of alternative queer cultures that celebrate non-hegemonic sexual values.

Structural integration and spatial assimilation reinforce this acculturation. The neighborhood has experienced demographic change, with White straight women moving in and increasing their consumption of Boystown's institutions and nightlife. Structural assimilation of this kind changes the way that gay people use the bars and clubs. Previously "raunchy" sexually charged places are de-queered, straightened up, and desexualized. However, these places are still read as gay. It is a more commodified and commercialized form of gayness.

This data also shows that as sexual fields in the neighborhood reshape, the area is not only mainstreamed heterosexually, but also whitened. The Take Back Boystown event is the most vivid example of the policing of the neighborhood's racial boundaries. The neighborhood is cast as a White area. Queer people of color are outsiders to a neighborhood they had long been a part of. This is of course not a bastion of racial harmony previously, but the area is recast as exclusively White—gay as a White ethnicity—rather than an area in which queer people of color were expected albeit under conditions of discrimination. The distinction is important.

This finding goes against the cultural predictions of post-gay theorists, who argue, however unevenly the process occurs that the cultural distinctiveness of gay identity is disappearing (Ghaziani 2014). Rather, I demonstrate that due to assimilation tensions within the gay community that have always been there have begun to rise to salience. The cracks in the foundation binding the assimilationist gay community and separatist queer community have begun to become visible. Separate community spaces supporting gays and queers will continue to diverge: one mainstream, commercialized and supported, and the other separatist and continually marginalized. Equality has not brought liberation. It has merely separated the few to be lifted up, as long as they act like their former oppressors.

Theoretically, I argue there is an intersectional character to assimilation. As one would expect, scholars of a particular axis of privilege—gender, ability, sexuality, race, class, and so on—typically focus on assimilation in their area. Throughout this paper, I have demonstrated assimilation of gay men in Boystown has both a sexual aspect—acculturation to straight sexual norms—but also a racial aspect—whitening of the gayborhood and ethnicizing gay identity.

The most important extension of these findings is that racial assimilation likely also has a sexual character. For instance, immigrants to America often are struck by the radically more liberal sexual norms in mainstream American culture (for a Canadian example, see Uskul 2007). Assimilation of cultural and racial groups erases their family structures and unique sexual cultures as they become acculturated to the mainstream American norm. Research that looks at single motherhood in Black-American communities (e.g., Edin and Kefalas 2007) might be illuminated by the possibilities of "queerness" in their participants. These alternative family structures only appear alternative to a heterosexual middle-class White norm. By illuminating the racial character inherent to sexual assimilation, we should be more attentive to the sexual character inherent to racial assimilation.

Furthermore, as I demonstrated in the case of Boystown, the hegemonic forms of sexuality in Rubin's charmed circle also carry with them the whiteness that is inherent to mainstream sexuality in American society. I urge scholars to continue to examine the ways that the charmed circle is both hegemonicly straight, as well as raced and classed.

ACKNOWLEDGMENTS

Thanks to Loka Ashwood, Michael Bell, and Amanda Ward for their comments on earlier drafts of this chapter. Some material presented also appears in my book, *Boystown: Sex and Community in Chicago*.

REFERENCES

Alba, Richard and Victor Nee. 1997. "Rethinking Assimilation Theory for a New Era of Immigration." *International Migration Review* 31 (4):826–74.
Brown-Saracino, Japonica. 2009. *A Neighborhood that Never Changes*. Chicago: University of Chicago Press.
Charmaz, Kathy. 2006. *Constructing Grounded Theory: A Practical Guide through Qualitative Analysis*. Thousand Oaks, CA: Sage Publications.
Collins, Patricia Hill. 2005. *Black Sexual Politics*. Abingdon-on-Thames: Routledge.

Connell, Catherine. 2014. *School's Out: Gay and Lesbian Teachers in the Classroom.* Oakland: University of California Press.

Corbin, Juliet and Janice M. Morse. 2003. "The Unstructured Interactive Interview: Issues of Reciprocity and Risks when Dealing with Sensitive Topics." *Qualitative Inquiry* 9 (3): 335–54.

Demarest, Erica. "Citywide Crime Down in 2011, Slight Decline in Lakeview." *Windy City Times*, April 4, 2012. http://www.windycitymediagroup.com/lgbt/Citywide-crime-down-in-2011-slight-decline-in-Lakeview/37107.html.

D'Emilio, John. 1983. *Sexual Politics, Sexual Communities: The Making of a Homosexual Minority 1940–1970.* Chicago: University of Chicago Press.

Drake, St. Clair and Horace R. Cayton. 1945. *Black Metropolis.* Chicago: University of Chicago Press.

Duggan, Lisa. 2012. *The Twilight of Equality?* Boston, MA: Beacon Press.

Edin, Kathryn and Maria Kefalas. 2007. *Promises I Can Keep.* Oakland: University of California Press.

Ellingson, Stephen and Kirby Schroeder. 2004. "Race and the Construction of Same-Sex Sex Markets in Four Chicago Neighborhoods." *The Sexual Organization of the City*, edited by Edward O. Laumann, 94–123. Chicago: University of Chicago Press.

Fryer, Roland G. 2007. "Guess Who's Been Coming to Dinner? Trends in Interracial Marriage Over the 20th Century." *The Journal of Economic Perspectives* 21 (2): 71–90.

Ghaziani, Amin. 2010. "There Goes the Gayborhood?" *Contexts* 9 (4): 64–66.

Ghaziani, Amin. 2014. *There Goes the Gayborhood?* Princeton, NJ: Princeton University Press.

Gordon, Milton M. 1964. *Assimilation in American life: The Role of Race, Religion and National Origins.* Oxford, UK: Oxford University Press.

Green, Adam Isaiah. 2008a. "Erotic Habitus: Toward a Sociology of Desire." *Theory and Society* 37: 597–626.

Green, Adam Isaiah. 2008b. "The Social Organization of Desire: The Sexual Fields Approach." *Sociological Theory* 26 (1): 25–50.

Green, Adam Isaiah. 2011. "Playing the (Sexual) Field: The Interactional Basis of Systems of Sexual Stratification." *Social Psychology Quarterly* 74 (3): 244–66.

Green, Adam Isaiah. 2012. *Sexual Fields: Toward a Sociology of Collective Sexual Life.* Chicago: University of Chicago Press.

Greene, Theodore. 2012. *Sexual Orientation, Sexual Identity and the Politics of Place.* Evanston, IL: Northwestern University Press.

Hicklin, Aaron. "Nate Silver: Person of the Year." *Out Magazine*, December 18, 2012: 1–6. http://www.out.com/news-opinion/2012/12/18/nate-silver-person-year.

Lamont, Michèle. 2009. "Responses to Racism, Health, and Social Inclusion as a Dimension of Successful Societies." *Successful Societies: How Institutions and Culture Affect Health.* Cambridge, UK and New York: Cambridge University Press.

Martin, John Levi and Matt George. 2006. "Theories of Sexual Stratification: Toward an Analytics of the Sexual Field and a Theory of Sexual Capital." *Sociological Theory* 24 (2): 107–32.

Moore, Mignon. 2011. *Invisible Families.* Oakland: University of California Press.

Nakamura, Lisa. 2002. *Cybertypes.* London: Psychology Press.

Nee, Victor, Jimy M. Sanders, and Scott Sernau. 1994. "Job Transitions in an Immigrant Metropolis: Ethnic Boundaries and the Mixed Economy." *American Sociological Review* 59 (6): 849–72.

Orne, Jason. 2011. "'You Will Always Have to "Out" Yourself'." *Sexualities* 14 (6): 681–703.

Orne, Jason. 2013. "Queers in the Line of Fire: Goffman's Stigma Revisited." *The Sociological Quarterly.* Abingdon-on-Thames, UK: Routledge.

Orne, Jason. 2017. *Boystown: Sex and Community in Chicago.* Chicago: University of Chicago Press.

Pais, Jeremy, Scott J. South, and Kyle Crowder. 2012. "Metropolitan Heterogeneity and Minority Neighborhood Attainment." *Social Problems* 59 (2): 258–81.

Park, Robert. 1914. "The Concept of Social Distance." *Journal of Applied Sociology* 8: 339–44.

Portes, Alejandro and Leif Jensen. 1989. "The Enclave and the Entrants: Patterns of Ethnic Enterprise in Miami Before and After Mariel." *American Sociological Review* 54 (6): 929–49.

Portes, Alejandro and Min Zhou. 1993. "The New Second Generation: Segmented Assimilation and Its Variants." *The Annals of the American Academy of Political and Social Science* 530 (1): 74–96.

Quillian, Lincoln and Devah Pager. 2001. "Black Neighbors, Higher Crime? The Role of Racial Stereotypes in Evaluations of Neighborhood Crime." *American Journal of Sociology* 107 (3): 717–67.

Rubin, Gayle. 1992. "Thinking Sex: Notes for a Radical Theory of the Politics of Sexuality." In *Pleasure and Danger: Exploring Female Sexuality*, edited by Carole S. Vance. London: Pandora.

Saguy, Abigail C. and Anna Ward. 2011. "Coming Out as Fat: Rethinking Stigma." *Social Psychology Quarterly* 74 (1): 53–75.

Seidman, Steven. 2002. *Beyond the Closet.* London: Taylor & Francis Group.

Song, Miri. 2009. "Is Intermarriage a Good Indicator of Integration?" *Journal of Ethnic and Migration Studies* 35 (2): 331–48.

Sosin, Kate. "Center on Halsted CEO on Controversies, Five-Year Anniversary." *Windy City Times*, April 18, 2012. http://www.windycitymediagroup.com/lgbt/Center-on-Halsted-CEO-on-controversiesfive-year-anniversary/37316.html.

Whyte, William Foote. 1943. *Street Corner Society.* Chicago: University of Chicago Press.

Williams, Christine, Patti A. Giuffre and Kirsten Dellinger. 2009. "The Gay-Friendly Closet." *Sexuality Research and Social Policy* 6 (1): 29–45.

Zolberg, Aristide R. and Long Litt Woon. 1999. "Why Islam is like Spanish: Cultural Incorporation in Europe and the United States." *Politics & Society* 27 (1): 5–38.

Chapter 6

Queer Loneliness, Queer Hopefulness

Toward Restaging the Intersectionality of Gay + Asian/American from the Southwest

Shinsuke Eguchi

During one of the weekends in July 2016, I went to Albuquerque's gay night-club *Effex* with my friends and their acquaintances. As soon as we walked into the dance floor located in the first floor, I noticed two Asian buffed-out Adonis dancing together. One is very tall. Another one is little taller than me. To me, they look like American born and raised Asians. Since I rarely see Asian/American men in my Albuquerque's social scene, I told my friend "Oh my god! There are Asians. I got to talk to them!" Little later as we passed by the bathroom, they came out of there. So, I approached them by asking, "Do you live in Albuquerque?" They replied to me that they were visiting. Then, without embarrassment I asked them "What kinds of Asian backgrounds are you part of?" With the standard American English intonation, the tall guy responded to me, "I am Filipino and my partner is Chinese." I followed up this by saying that "I am Japanese . . . I just wanted to say hello to you guys because I rarely see Asians in this place."

Next morning I felt quite embarrassed as I rethought of my *exciting* encounter with these two Asian/American men in *Effex*. I said to myself, "Oh geeze. I am major awkward. I just asked them about their ethnicities. Then, I moved on. I bet they thought I was rude not carrying on the conversation." At the same time, I also questioned why I was quite excited to see the couple in that space through which I assume I rarely see other Asian/American men. Technically speaking, I have nothing in common with these men. I am a foreign-born Asian/Japanese effeminate male who speaks accented English. I probably have a different history of becoming and being *gay* and *Asian/American* from them. The U.S. racial paradigms of "Asians" and "Asian Americans" are socially constructed fictions (Nishime 2012). So, perhaps I should not have excited to see the couple. Yet, I still felt something inside of me as I saw them dancing together in *Effex*.

*****

With this personal account, I remake an intellectual and political move to complicate the intersectionality of *gay* and *Asian/American* as a multiple, unstable, and dynamic construct in this chapter. By intersectionality, I mean an analytical framework that attempts to explicate, elucidate, and elaborate how interlocking systems and distributions of power (such as race, ethnicity, gender, sexuality, class, language, and empire) simultaneously affect sexual minoritarians of color and their everyday interactions, relationships, and contexts (Muñoz 1999; Yep 2013). In recent years the transdisciplinary collections of academic literatures have increasingly advanced understandings about Asian/American male identities in and across North American gay sexual cultures (Han 2015; Hoang 2014; Lim 2014). Asian/American men are historically represented as *unattractive* and *undesirable*. They are often seen as falling short of the normative White gay masculine appearances and performances. Consequently, they are often marginalized as *soft, feminine,* and *submissive Others* from the center through which buffed-out White gay Adonis are already privileged. C. Winter Han reminds that "the illusion that Asian men are somewhat naturally more feminine than White men may be more of a treatment to the White imagination than the result of actual physical traits of Asian men" (Han 2015, 23). Still, Asian/American men are likely to internalize such White supremacy. As a result, they develop negative feelings of their bodies, identities, and performances. Thus, Asian/American men are often known to struggle with low self-esteem and low self-worth as they participate in U.S. American gay sexual cultures (Poon and Ho 2008).

Simultaneously, the discourse of victimization, essentializing gay Asian/American male identities, has been repeatedly problematized as the limitation (Eguchi 2011; Poon 2006). In fact, gay Asian/American male identities are much more complex and contradictory than simple and consistent. For example, the discourses of victimization privilege a master narrative, that is, White men sexually and romantically rejecting Asian/American men. At the same time, some Asian/American men also actively chase after buffed-out White gay Adonis. They admire, aspire, and buy into the logics of normative White gay masculine norm. As a consequence, they are almost always not known to be interested in sexual and romantic relations with other men of color, including Black/African Americans and Asian/Pacific Islander Americans (Eguchi 2015; Phua 2007). The way in which Asian/American men aspire to be with White men ironically recenters the power and privilege of whiteness as a normative gay beauty, style, and value. Thus, Asian/American men must also own up to the material reality through which they are active participants and consumers of gay sexual cultures rooted in whiteness. Therefore, the social and performative aspects of gay Asian/American male identities still require ongoing interrogations.

More precisely, the ways in which Asian/American men develop, negotiate, and modify their affective meanings with and relational proximities to "Gaysian [meaning Gay + Asian] America" throughout their lifetimes are quite overlooked. Indeed, the conception of Gaysian America remains extremely vague and intangible in and across the lines of differences. In reality, there is no such single, stable, and essentialized category as "Asians" and "Asian Americans" operating in and across gay sexual cultures. Accordingly, the foundational assumption of Gaysian America requires the collective shared mechanism. The White/Western/U.S. American politics of racialized gender always make and remake the intersectionality of gay and Asian/American as a political identity. As such C. Winter Han argues, "'Gay Asian American male' identity is an entirely new creation, predicted on both the racial oppression experienced by people of color in the United States and the sexual oppression experienced by gay men" (Han 2015, 187). Thus, I call to interrogate cultural and communication processes of becoming and being gay and Asian/American as "a collective political becoming" (Muñoz 2009, 187).

As a referencing point of this critical qualitative engagement, I exemplify how my relocation to the Southwest for my academic job offers me an additional opportunity to question, struggle with, and renegotiate the performative rhetoric of *gay* and *Asian/American*. I pay close attention to my feelings of relational and communal isolation from Gaysian America as I live in the Southwest. That is, where I find Gaysian American communities are not as big and strong as other cities such as New York, San Francisco, Los Angeles, and Washington, DC. At the same time, I am not interested in presenting such feelings through a lens of victimization. Instead, I problematize and critique how I feel lonely. I reframe my loneliness as a queer pedagogical product of the present that "this world is not enough, that indeed something is missing" (Muñoz 2009, 1). I translate my loneliness as hopefulness for the future, that is, "a spatial and temporal destination" (Muñoz 2009, 185). By writing about the paradoxes of my loneliness (and hopefulness), I call into question undisrupted ideas and social relations surrounding the material realities of gay Asian/American male identities.

In what follows, I first orient this chapter in the genealogy of queerness and queer autoethnography. Then, I demonstrate my queer autoethnographic critique of becoming and being *gay* and *Asian/American* in the Southwest. The following themes, *feeling suffocated by the present*, *missing the past*, and *bringing the past into the future*, organize my critique. I end this chapter by rethinking of the broader implications of Gaysian America that require queer (of color) restaging for the future.

METHODOLOGY

I draw the genealogy of queer of color critique to politicize, historicize, and contextualize the intersectionality of gay and Asian/American as a performative method of change in this chapter. By change, I mean an indefinite possibility for the future. For example, Gust A. Yep, Karen E. Lovaas, and John Elia have previously argued that the conception of queerness is to approach sexualities as multiple, fluid, and unstable assemblies intersecting with other identity markers such as race, ethnicity, gender, class, and the body (2003, 4). The normative paradigm of a straight-gay binary can never stabilize, fix, and essentialize sexualities in and across the lines of differences. Indeed, the embodied performance of coming out of the closet is a social and cultural fiction of self-discovery and self-journey rooted in whiteness. The closet symbolically misrepresents the White normative imagination of a gay-straight binary through which homosexuality remains as an essentialist concept (McCune 2014). The conception of queerness becomes not only about sexual identities but also political identities in order to disrupt the normal and ordinary. Queerness is about destabilizing and denaturalizing the (hetero) normative sets of categories, ideas, social relations, and power organizing the structural systems of institutional lives (Yep 2013). Queerness not only offers a path to resist the institutional norms but also seeks alternative modes of knowing, being, and acting through which ideological and material lines of differences are no longer problems. Yet, such conception of queerness philosophically remains idealistic (Muñoz 2009, 1).

Discursive and material effects of liberalism, rooted in the logics of individualism, merit, responsibility, and choice, reproduce and reconstitute the idealistic problems of queer theorizing. David L. Eng reminds, "Queer liberalism relies upon the logic of color-blindness in its assertion that racial difference has given way to an abstract U.S. community of individualism and merit" (Eng 2010, 3). The conception of queerness, focusing on micro-acts/ processes of sexual multiplicity, fluidity, and instability, can easily ignore the historical and structural constraints of racism, sexism, heterosexism, and classism that ironically produce and constitute the culture-specific and text-specific knowledges of sexualities (Johnson 2001; Lee 2003). According to the White Western U.S. American normative imagination, lesbian-gay-bisexual-transgender-queer (LGBTQ) people of color have been always already constructed as embodied markers of the homophobia and/or transphobia reflecting their racial/ethnic/cultural/migrant communities (Puar 2007). Here, people of color are collectively framed to represent the logics of sexual and gender conservatism. In opposition, White people are assumed to enjoy their sexual freedoms and liberations. This misrepresentation redefines the advancement and progressivity of White Western U.S. American liberalism through which the discourse of LGBTQ equality is globally becoming visible. In so doing, whiteness becomes a sexually exceptional symbol. This discursive practice implicates the way in which certain kinds of gays and lesbians, who are particularly White, cisgender, able-bodied, and affluent, are increasingly incorporated into the U.S. nation-state today (Ferguson 2005). So, the normal and ordinary can be invisibly sustainable through the capitalistic expansion.

Accordingly, I am methodologically committed to the conception of queerness troubling the reproductions and reconstitutions of whiteness as invisible and universal power. In order to avoid the misuse of queerness as an alibi of whiteness, I adapt José Esteban Muñoz's conception of queerness as a futuristic ideality. He asserts, "Queerness is a structuring and educated mode of desiring that allows us to see and feel beyond the quagmire of the present. The here and now is a prison house" (Muñoz 2009, 1). Queerness is like a utopian formation of the future through which the question of differences is no longer relevant (Abdi and Calafell 2017). Simultaneously, the historical and structural constraints of power relations such as heteronormativity, patriarchy, whiteness, healthism, and capitalism always already occupy the present. Consequently, the present reproduces and reconstitutes the negative feelings such as loneliness, hopelessness, and depression (McRuer 2006). Sexual minoritarians of color may suffer complex layers of depression produced by intersections of multiple identity positionings that go against the forms of majoritarian belongings (Calafell 2017). They may be quite lonely because of feeling simultaneously isolated from multiple relationships and communities. Thus, the present is always imperfect and not ideal for sexual minoritarians of color. Queerness becomes and is "primarily about futurity and hope" (Muñoz 2009, 1). Therefore, queerness requires constant revisions of the present. It is like a dream that allows us to vision possibilities of the future.

As I draw such genealogy of queerness described above, I engage in the critical cultural method of autoethnography in this chapter. I argue that autoethnography focuses on personal experiences in order to critically and performatively investigate social, cultural, political, and historical concerns in an in-depth manner (Eguchi 2011, 2015). Autoethnography is about the way in which the self implicates the complexities and contradictions of ideological and material environments. Bryant Keith Alexander reinforces, "Autoethnography asks and allows others to begin to look critically at the ways in which articulated lived experiences might provide a template for social investigation of everyday lived experiences; a template as a critical methodology" (Alexander 2012, 141). At the same time, autoethnography has been also a controversial site of ongoing critiques from the intellectuals. For instance, even after writing her collaborative autoethnography with me, communication scholar

Mary Jane Collier still feels autoethnography as self-indulgent (Eguchi and Collier 2018). However, I reject the perspective that reconstitutes the rigor of social science ignoring the embodied involvements of scholar(s) in research. Autoethnography, being transparent of where scholar(s) write from, disrupts the comfort zone of readers who consume what has been traditionally defined as academic research (Boylorn 2008). The anti-normative tastes and irrational expectations of autoethnography as the research method bring to the fore voices of minoritarians that are hidden by the majoritarian ways of knowing. Autoethnography is a critical cultural strategy that complicates easy binarism of power relations such privilege and oppression and/or majoritarian and minoritarian producing the contemporary discourse of identity politics. Thus, autoethnography has the potential to provide thick descriptions of differences that are intersectional and paradoxical at the same time.

Accordingly, I reiterate that autoethnography is, indeed, queer. The methodological intersections among queerness and autoethnography explicitly trouble the normative sets of ideas, social locations, and power organizing the productions of knowledge in the academy (Adams and Holman-Jones 2011). Queer autoethnography is an intellectual and political commitment that destabilizes and denaturalizes the normal and ordinary sustaining the heteronormative logics of present-ness. So, we can step toward a future though which queerness is no longer an ideality. With this methodological lens, I move to write about the ways in which I redevelop the performative rhetoric of *gay + Asian/American* as I relocate to the Southwest next.

*****

June 27, 2018, Thursday

It is little after 4:00 p.m. I have just received the email about my tenure and promotion from the university. So, I texted my friend/colleague at another university, "I guess I am now tenured!" She immediately replied back to me, "Congratulations! How do you feel now?" As soon as I saw her text, I told myself "ha. I probably should reply to her as I say something like 'I am happy!' or 'I am so relieved!' But, I am not feeling so. I do not want to lie either." So, I wrote back to her, "I do not feel any changes yet." Later in that evening, I started to want to make sense of this *strange* feeling as I sit on a sofa in the living room. On the one hand, I felt like, "This is it! I will never be able to move to other place(s)." Over the few years I have seen many tenured colleagues who wanted to relocate remain stuck in where they are. The academic job market is extremely competitive due to the limited number of tenure-stream lines. On the other hand, I recognize my privilege to get tenured and promoted to be an associate professor. Since I have heard the horror stories about the faculty of color not getting tenured and promoted, I know I must appreciate my case. I definitely would not want to experience a *career failure* in the system of academy through which faculty members (of color) are always already subjected to competitions. However, I cannot just say I am simply happy. Something personal, which makes and my intersectional significance of gay and Asian/American, has been missing from my life for last six years.

*****

FEELING STUCK IN THE PRESENT

Quite frankly, since I moved to the Southwest in 2012. I have not felt that Albuquerque is one of my homes. Victoria Chen reminds, "Home can be conceptualized as a place of belonging that offers a sense of comfort and relational connections. It is a geographical construction and a spatial metaphor" (2010, 484). The historical complexities of explorations and colonialisms make the unique particularities of New Mexico as the state. The legacies of Native American inhabitation, Spanish conquest, Mexican governance, and U.S. American occupation create a New Mexican culture of borderland. That is, "a vague and undetermined place created by the emotional residue of an unnatural boundary" (Anzaldúa 2012, 25). Under such continuity of border makings, I feel I am always already a visitor in this space and place. Yet, I chose to come to this land because of my academic commitment. The academic industry almost always reproduces the cultural norm, that is, "you got to go to where a job is." So, I took this job regardless of my personal ties to this city, this state. However, the academy has not been also hospitable to people of color, in general, and queer people of color, in particular (Calafell 2017; Yep 2003). The system sustains historical and existing power relations of race, gender, sexuality, and the class. The academy is not going to fulfill my desire to feel a sense of home either. So, I everyday daydream of the possibility of moving back to Washington DC, New York City, San Francisco, or Greater Los Angeles Area where I have felt my senses of home. These cities offered me the spaces and places where I developed the intersectional meanings of performing *gay* and *Asian/American* since I had moved from Japan to the United States in 2001. So, I long for belonging to home(s) since I have been sacrificing my personal life for my academic life. Still, I recognize that the everyday presence of my body in this land implicates the discursive and material effects of globalization.

The elites from both Western and non-Western nations are freely moving in and across the national borders requiring "proper" travel documentations. As Sachi Sekimoto has suggested, I also own global mobility, economic privilege, and cultural capital attached to the Global North branding of my Japanese nationality (Sekimoto 2014). It allows me to get to where I am in the U.S. academic system. My Japanese nationality signifies a safe and nonthreatening category according to the contemporary realities of U.S.

international relations with Japan as their ally. I never had any trouble obtaining nonimmigrant U.S. visa status such as F-1 student visa (2001/2011), J-1 visitor's visa (2012), and H1-B foreign worker visa (2012/2013). In addition, my transitioning process from H1-B visa to permanent residency (also known as green card) was relatively fast and easy. It took only a year. Moreover, my accessibility to resources helped me to easily go through such long processes of documentation. At the same time, everyone is not socially, politically, and economically situated to be able to become international students and scholars in the U.S. academic system. Thus, I have been lucky and fortunate. This is a particular social space of privilege through which I come to develop my standpoint as *gay* and *Asian/American*. Consequently, I must work through such complex and paradoxical layers of my intersectionality to make sense of my present. In fact, my Gaysian narrative is never simply disadvantaged. It is the rhetorical and performative form of position and status representing tensions between privileges and disadvantages. *I am a part of the settler colonialism taking place in the indigenous land of New Mexico.* So, I must critique and suspend how I feel lonely being in Albuquerque through a lens of victimization. Yet, I remain feeling that something personal is missing from my body. I no longer feel the same way about the intersectionality of *gay* and *Asian/American* as I used to.

My everyday social interactions reinforce and reconstitute how others see me through (gay) Japanese first. Indeed, many colleagues and friends I have come across in Albuquerque have almost always asked me a lot about Japan. This micro-act and process of communication implicates how popular cultural discourses about Japan as an attractive tourist destination are well circulated in the United States in recent years. At the same time, I have been in the United States almost two decades. While I travel back to Japan at least once a year, I no longer feel I am just (gay) Japanese. Even though I of course understand that I am Japanese, it is very strange for me to be regularly constructed as a representative of Japan. Simultaneously, I become more confused with what I mean by *gay* and *Asian/American* than ever. I feel I am losing my identification with Gaysian America because I feel I am no longer in that space. Consequently, I am trying again and again to remember my racialized, gendered, and sexualized memory of embodying the rhetoric of gay and Asian/American. I do not want to forget my intellectual and political consciousness as gay and Asian/American that has allowed me to feel the United States is my home at one point. This is why I internally felt something *hot* and *strong* when I ran into the Asian/American couple in *Effex* described in the introduction. I was reminded of my past that is missing from my present. However, I was not able to explicitly articulate it at that time. It took almost two years for me to understand what I was missing.

*****

July 1, 2018, Sunday

It is around 8:00 p.m. I have a one-day layover at Los Angeles International Airport (LAX) while on my way to Tokyo. So, my Japanese cisfemale friend picked me up at the hotel and took me to a Sushi restaurant near Marina del Ray. As soon as we entered into the restaurant, I immediately noticed multiple Asian/American hosts and servers who speak standard American English or English with foreign accents. Then, as I sit down at our table, I also realized that many Asian/American customers are in the restaurant. They do not seem to come from one particular ethnic and cultural background. They are very eclectic representations of Asian/Americans. Then, a waiter approached us to take our order. Her name is Japanese. So, I code-switched to speak to her in Japanese. Later when I was comfortable with her, I asked, "Are your servers and customers normally Japanese?" She replied to me, "No, they aren't normally Japanese. Our servers and customers are very diverse." As soon as she says so, I experienced an "Aha!" moment.

*****

MISSING THE PAST

While this particular restaurant is not a Gaysian space, I realize what I have been lonely of. I am longing to belong to Gaysian America where possibilities and impossibilities of border-crossings are negotiated in and across the power lines of differences such as ethnicity, nationality, class, and the body. Such an ambiguous, ambivalent, and subtle interstate is my intellectual and political home. It best characterizes my in-between positionality, that is, I am neither perfectly gay nor Japanese. For example, I can only perform being gay questionably. My non-White body is always already a discursive marker of *the Other*. The appropriate and proper cultural conception of gay men is socially, politically, and economically rooted in whiteness as a normative beauty, style, and value. C. Winter Han asserts that "coming out as gay and entering gay spaces may cause some [Asian/American men] to feel further isolated and alienated to their racial difference" (Han 2015, 187). At the same time, I do not also perform my Japaneseness correctly because of my transnational and transcultural life experiences. Japanese citizens who live abroad for so long are oftentimes questioned as *strange* or *different* because they do not subscribe the mononational and monocultural imagination of Japaneseness. The historically particularized conception of Japaneseness as a cultural purity is rooted in ethnocentrism, patriarchy, and cis-heteronormativity (Toyosaki and Eguchi 2017). Thus, a messy interstate of Gaysian America becomes a necessary fiction for me to find a home. That is where I long to belong with others who may be like me. Simultaneously, I do not fantasize that Gaysian America is free from the material realities of power relations. Becoming and being a part of Gaysian America is, indeed, to actively recognize and work with how power relations create and recreates differences. So, this is a discursive and material space of power where I have been almost always frustrated with *gay* and *Asian/American*.

As I think of my past, I admit the notion of *sexual competitions* has guided how I related to other Asian/American men participating in gay sexual cultures. C. Winter Han has also argued that "the perceived limited number of White men willing to date Asian men led many gay Asian American men to see other Asian men as potential competitors for the affections of White men" (Han 2015, 107). When I first started to go to gay clubs in West Hollywood, I felt "disgusted" by younger feminine Asian men dating older masculine White men. In my eyes, such colonial couplings signified my dissatisfaction to be *Asian/American* in gay sexual cultures. That is, being subjugated to the power and privilege of White cisgendered masculinity. Under the ideology at play, I did not want to become such Gaysian queen. I despised the gay sexual cultural norm of Asian/American men exclusively seeking after (older) White men as "the desirable sexual partners" (Han 2015, 107). So, I made my political choice to romantically surround myself around Black/African American men. At the same time, my choice has been also paradoxical (see the detail critique for Eguchi 2015). I have been "sucked" into what Claire Jean Kim suggested is "Asian Americans in a triangulated position vis-à-vis Whites and Blacks" (Kim 1999, 107). My relational proximity to Black/African Americans, whom I find symbolize U.S. insider status, have become a site in which I validated my belonging to U.S. gay sexual cultures. I have remained operating my same-sex desire according to the racial paradigm of a White-Black binary. That is, making and remaking Asian/Americans as forever foreign.

Here, I critique how I was almost avoiding other Asian/American men in and across gay sexual cultures. By having chosen to be around Black/African American men, I, as a foreign-born subject, literarily wanted to be *different* from the rest of Gaysians who subscribe the homoerotic logics of a White-Asian colonial coupling. Whenever I met some men through gay social networking sites, they almost always initiated their conversations with me by asking "Do you like an older White man?" This illuminates the way in which the gay colonial-transnational frame of foreign Asian men "is a subcultural category referencing the racialized fetishes of an older White male" (Lim 2014, 27). Because I was structurally framed as if I needed a sugar daddy, I was frustrated. Coming from Japan as a global economic tiger, I carried my ethnocentric pride to feel that "I am not that kind of Asian who needs a sugar daddy." I critique that such thought of mine was a historical product of Japanese colonialism benefited from political and economic hierarchies in Asia. Simultaneously, I was frustrated with how the lines of differences among Asian/Americans were easily ignored. I was also frustrated with how I could not get away from the racialized sexual stereotypes associated with the intersectionality of gay and Asian/American. Moreover, I was frustrated with my subcultural location from which I perform my same-sex desires. Thus, I imposed my racialized sexual insecurities onto other Asian/American men. I intentionally disassociated myself from other Gaysians who remind me of my frustrations.

Then again, I critique my contradiction of how I remember such frustrations described above. In the present time, I actually miss how I was dissatisfied with the intersectionality of gay and Asian/American. My dissatisfactions have been a major part of how I found a sense of home(s) while participating in U.S. American gay sexual cultures. Despite of my intension to disassociate myself from Asian/American men, I could never get away from Gaysian America in cities like Los Angeles, New York, San Francisco, and Washington DC. Whenever I went for dining, drinking, and clubbing in the gay sexual cultural spaces, I saw Asian/Americans including some Japanese/American men. I ended up interacting with some of them as well. In addition, the discursive implications of Gaysian America have been a contextual background in which I performed my racialized sexuality in relationships with non-Asian/American men. I was never their first Gaysian friend or lover. Since they previously had some encounters and ongoing contacts with Gaysians, they were a bit culturally sensitive to differences among Gaysians. I was comfortable in that space. Accordingly, I acknowledge how I was always already a part of Gaysian America whether or not I recognized so at that time. Thus, I now reflect that my dissatisfactions with the intersectionality of gay and Asian/American have been social and performative sites in which I develop a political identity as a sexual minoritarian of color. This identity negotiation process offered my relational spaces of home "as a fluid context that holds one's changing identity" (Chen 2010, 488).

*****

August 2, 2018, Saturday

It is around 4:00 p.m. in the middle of my pool party. I am celebrating my tenure and promotion with my group of friends. So, I can reframe my loneliness I have felt back in June when I officially got tenured and promoted. As I look around the pool, I notice that most of them are cisgender gay men in their thirties who are not affiliated with the University. Going into my seventh year being in Albuquerque, I am thankful of having made personal friends outside of my academic work. Perhaps, this is something I have been dreamed of. I always wanted to have a bunch of gay male friends since I had moved to the United States in 2001. I envisioned the (White/Western/U.S. American) gay social capital as the measurement of my assimilation. However, I feel something is still missing from who I am, what I do, and how I make sense of what

I do. The more I am around (White or Whitened) gay men, the more I feel
suffocated. Somehow, I feel I am no longer gay these days because I do not
fit into gay cultural norms rooted in the heterosexual standard. I do not feel
confident in identifying with gay as it is like an almost heterosexual symbol.
The more I am around White or Whitened gay men, the more I realize I am
queerer than ever. I feel my intersectionality of gay and Asian American is
shifting to be *queer*.

*****

BRINING THE PAST INTO THE FUTURE

Sometimes I hate how naïve I can be. Over the last few years, I have been
repeatedly critiquing the global and transcultural circulations of White gay
normativity through my scholarship. As the professoriate, I spend most of
my times in writing my scholarly essays like this one everyday. So, I should
have better known how the political is becoming the personal; the personal is
becoming the political. I develop and redevelop my intellectual and political
commitment to (racialized) queerness more and more as I question how the
academy reinforces the technology of heteronormativity intersecting with cis-
genderism, patriarchy, whiteness, U.S. American imperialism, and ableism.
So, I should have known better. I can never get away from my political com-
mitments. The truth is that I find extremely boring that gay men are becoming
like *almost heterosexuals*. Gay men are the U.S. American nationalist and
patriotic agents who help police, discipline, and sustain the logics of heteronormativity. That is, "the presumption and assumption that all human experience is unquestionably and automatically heterosexual" (Yep 2002, 168).

As becoming in mid-late thirties, I have increasingly noticed that my gay
male friends from diverse backgrounds almost always talk about topics such
as marriage, wedding, home buying, family, child adaption, and retirement.
Of course, my friends often remind me that I better get married as soon as
I can. This idea of life path implicates how the logics of heteronormativity
organize and reorganize the naturalized temporality of straight time for gay
men. Because of such ideological reinforcement, I have one time contacted
the professional gay matchmaker to see if there may be some options for
me to meet men. So, I won't be lonely forever. However, as I learned about
extremely expensive service pricing for the first time, I truly thought, "why
do I need to go through this? What is wrong to be single?" Indeed, I do not
need to buy into the U.S. American hetero-patriarchal capitalistic ideality
of searching a life partner/lover as a way to become happy. So, I need to
try again and again to resist how the logics of heteronormativity guide my
present. If I could completely step out of such straight time's present-ness, I

would not know why I would be lonely right now. I am only lonely because I make sense of my life according to the logics of heteronormativity. José Esteban Muñoz reminds that the present "is impoverished and toxic for queers and other people who do not feel the privilege of majoritarian belonging, normative tastes, and 'rational' expectations" (Muñoz 2009, 27). So, I need to accept that I do not want to live up to the heterosexual standard. I need to stop caring if I am a strange and peculiar minoritarian of color.

With this realization, I reclaim that my loneliness I have been experiencing in the Southwest pedagogically allows me to feel something is missing from my present. I have been nostalgic of Gaysian America where I was visibly and invisibly being a part of in the past. Simultaneously, the more I am getting older, the more I am getting sick of hetero-patriarchal and masculinist norms of cisgender gay male life. Lately there has been an instance through which I was reminded of how gay men reproduce and reconstitute the historical continuities of anti-femininity and homophobia. For example, my gay Asian/American friend tells me that he does not understand why some gay men wear makeups because makeups are women's things. This perception implicates the rhetoric of stigma around symbolized and material forms of male-femininity. E. Patrick Johnson reminds, "Because femininity is always already devalued in patriarchal societies, those associated with feminine are also viewed as inferior" (Johnson 2003, 227). The majoritarian logics of belonging, tastes, and expectations can be almost always reproduced and reconstituted. Accordingly, I critique that gay Asian/American men are in need of checking their unearned cis-male advantages provided by the patriarchy. They are also a part of the structural system sustaining historical and existing power relations. Gay Asian/American male identities are social and performative sites in which often invisible power relations (implicated by whiteness, patriarchy, heteronormativity, and capitalism) produce multifarious paradoxes between privileges and disadvantages. Thus, possibilities and impossibilities of Gaysian America as racialized queerness are to teach us what we are collectively failing in the present time. Recognizing collective shared dissatisfactions to be *imperfect* and *impossible* only allows us to take a step toward the hopefulness of the future.

CONCLUSION

In conclusion, I have begun this chapter by sharing my contact moments with two Asian buffed-out Adonis in the Southwest where I find is that Asian/Americans are not historically as visible. My momentarily perceived spatial connection to the gay Asian/American couple taught me to realize why I feel lonely. I am longing to belong to Gaysian America. Han reminds, "It is here that gay Asian American men finally come to find a 'home,' a place of belonging with others 'like them'" (2017, 187). At the same time, I recognize that Gaysian America is a politically shared space in which multiple subjects identifying with gay and Asian/American are essentially lumped together. Simultaneously, there is something about Gaysian America through which Asian/American male sexual minoritarians identify with. The historical and ideological forces of marginalization from gay cultures as *White* and Asian/American cultures as *heteronormative* create and recreate a collectively shared space of dissatisfaction as Gaysian America. Yet, such seemingly liberatory space is problematic at the same time. Thus, the intersectionality of gay and Asian/American requires ongoing queer restaging for the future as a hopeful destination. Therefore, I end this chapter by reiterating that transdisciplinary queer (of color) interventions of Gaysian American are still necessary.

REFERENCES

Abdi, Shadee and Bernadette Marie Calafell. 2017. "Queer Utopias and a (Feminist) Iranian Vampire: A Critical Analysis of Resistive Monstrosity in A Girl Walks Home Alone at Night." *Critical Studies in Media Communication* 34 (4): 358–70.

Adams, Tony E. and Stacy Holman Jones. 2011. "Telling Stories: Reflexivity, Queer Theory, and Autoethnography." *Cultural Studies↔Critical Methodologies* 11 (2): 108–16.

Alexander, Bryant Keith. 2012. *The Performative Sustainability of Race: Reflections on Black Culture and the Politics of Identity.* New York: Peter Lang.

Anzaldúa, Gloria. 2012. *Borderlands/la Frontera: The New Mestizo,* San Francisco: Aunt Lute Books.

Boylorn, Robin M. 2008. "As Seen on TV: An Autoethnographic Reflection on Race and Reality Television," *Critical Studies in Media Communication* 25 (4): 413–33.

Calafell, Bernadette Marie. 2017. "When Depression is in the Job Description #realacademicbios." *Departures in Critical Qualitative Research* 6 (1): 5–10.

Chen, Victoria. 2010. "Authenticity and Identity in the Portable Homeland." In *The Handbook of Critical Intercultural Communication,* 483–94. London: Wiley-Blackwell.

Eguchi, Shinsuke. 2011. "Negotiating Sissyphobia: A Critical/ Interpretive Analysis of One 'Femme' Gay Asian Body in the Heteronormative World." *Journal of Men's Studies* 19 (1): 37–56.

———. 2015. "Queer Intercultural Relationality: An Autoethnography of Asian-Black (Dis)connections in White Gay America." *Journal of International and Intercultural Communication* 8 (1): 27–43.

Eguchi, Shinsuke and Mary Jane Collier. 2018. "Critical Intercultural Mentoring and Allying: A Continuing Struggle for Change in the Academy." *Departures in Critical Qualitative Research* 7 (2): 49–71.

Eng, David L. 2010. *The Feeling of Kinship: Queer Liberalism and the Racialization of Intimacy.* Durham, NC: Duke University Press.

Ferguson, Richard A. 2005. "Raceing Homonormativity: Citizenship, Sociology, and Gay Identity." In *Black Queer Studies: A Critical Anthology*, 52–67. Durham, NC: Duke University Press.

Han, C. Winter. 2015. *Geisha of a Different Kind: Race and Sexuality in Gaysian America*. New York: New York University Press.

Hoang, Tan Nguyen. 2014. *A View from the Bottom: Asian American Masculinity and Sexual Representation*. Durham, NC: Duke University.

Johnson, E. Patrick. 2001. "'Quare' Studies or (Almost) Everything I know about Queer Studies Learned from My Grandmother." *Text and Performance Quarterly* 21 (1): 1–25.

———. 2003. "The Specter of the Black Fag: Parody, Blackness, and Hetero/Homosexual B(r)others." *Journal of Homosexuality* 45 (2–4): 217–34.

Kim, Claire Jean. 1999. "The Racial Triangulations of Asian Americans." *Politics & Society* 27 (1): 105–38.

Lim, Eng-Beng. 2014. *Brown Boys and Rice Queens: Spellbinding Performances in the Asias*. New York: New York University Press.

Lee, Wenshu. 2003. "Kauering Queer Theory: My Autocritography and a Race-Conscious, Womanist, and Transnational Turn." *Journal of Homosexuality* 45 (2–4): 147–70.

McCune Jr., Jeffery Q. 2014. *Sexual Discretion: Black Masculinity and the Politics of Passing*. Chicago: University of Chicago Press.

McRuer, Robert. 2006. *Crip Theory: Cultural Signs of Queerness and Disability*. New York: New York University Press.

Muñoz, José Esteban. 1999. *Disidentifications: Queers of Color and the Performance of Politics*. Minneapolis: University of Minnesota Press.

Nishime, Leilani. 2012. "The Case for Cablinasian: Multiracial Naming from Plessy to Tiger Woods." *Communication Theory* 22 (1): 92–111.

Phua, Voon Chin. 2007. "Contesting and Maintaining Hegemonic Masculinities: Gay Asian American Men in Mate Selection." *Sex Role* 57: 909–18.

Poon, Maurice Kwong-Lai. 2006. "The Discourse of Oppression in Contemporary Gay Asian Diasporal Literature: Liberation or Limitation?." *Sexuality & Culture* 10 (3): 29–58.

Poon, Maurice Kwong-Lai and Peter Trung-Thu Ho. 2008. "Negotiating Social Stigma among Gay Asian Men." *Sexualities* 11 (2): 245–68.

Puar, Jasbir K. 2007. *Terrorist Assemblages: Homonationalsim in Queer Times*. Durham, NC: Duke University Press.

Sekimoto, Sachi. 2014. "Transnational Asia: Dis/orienting Identity in the Globalized World." *Communication Quarterly* 62 (4): 1–18.

Toyosaki, Satoshi and Shinsuke Eguchi. 2017. "Powerful Uncertainty for the Future of Japan's Cultural Diversity: Theorizing Japanese Homogenizing Discourses." In *Intercultural Communication in Japan: Theorizing Homogenized Discourse*, 1–23. New York: Routledge.

Yep, Gust A. 2002. "From Homophobia and Heterosexism to Heteronormativity." *Journal of Lesbian Studies* 6 (3, 4): 163–76.

———. 2003. "The Violence of Heteronormativity in Communication Studies: Notes on Injury, Healing, and Queer World-Making." *Journal of Homosexuality* 45 (2–4): 11–59.

———. 2013. "Queering/Quaring/Kauering/Crippin'/Transing "Other Bodies" in Intercultural Communication." *Journal of International and Intercultural Communication* 6 (2): 118–26.

Yep, Gust A., Karen E. Lovaas, and John P. Elia. 2003. "Introduction: Queering Communication: Starting the Conversation." *Journal of Homosexuality* 45 (2–4): 1–10.

Chapter 7

Navigating the Spaces between Racial/Ethnic and Sexual Orientation

*Black Gay Immigrants' Experiences
of Racism and Homophobia
in Montréal, Canada*

Sulaimon Giwa, Kofi Norsah, and Ferzana Chaze

Despite advances in their civil rights, lesbian, gay, and bisexual (LGB) people continue to face discrimination in the form of homophobia and biphobia. The impact of these challenges and stigmas can pose a significant health risk (Almeida et al. 2009; Frost, Lehavot, and Meyer 2015; Meyer 2003; Rimes et al. 2019). They are disproportionately affected by negative health outcomes related to social discrimination, such as mental health disorders (e.g., lower self-esteem and psychological distress; see Stokes and Peterson 1998; Szymanski and Gupta 2009; Szymanski, Kashubeck-West, and Meyer 2008) and problems related to sexual health (e.g., elevated rates in sexually transmitted infections, and decreased sexual function and satisfaction; see Almeida et al. 2009; Li et al. 2019; Mays and Cochran 2001; Meyer 2003). Homo/bi-negativism or the internalization of negative social attitudes about oneself has been suggested to influence these health issues (Szymanski and Carretta 2019; Williamson 2000).

Canadian health surveillance data collected in 2016, the most current data available, show that 44.1 percent of reported cases of HIV were among adult men who have sex with men (MSM) (Bourgeois et al. 2017). Another Canadian study on sexual orientation and health found that, in addition to increased diagnoses of sexually transmitted diseases (STDs) and a higher prevalence of psychological distress (namely, anxiety and depression), gay and bisexual men reported a history of lifetime suicidality when compared to heterosexual men in the general population (Brennan et al. 2010).

While this chapter did not look at the underlying factors for the elevated levels of poor mental and sexual health status in this population, other studies have established a link between experiences of social discrimination and its negative impact on mental and sexual health outcomes (Diaz, Ayala, and Bein 2004; Meyer 1995; Nam et al. 2019). For example, Benibgui identified that LGB high school and college students in Montréal were fourteen times more likely to commit suicide compared to their non-LGB peers (Benibgui 2010). To understand these challenges, it is important to reflect on the intersecting and multiple social, individual, and structural factors that may explain elevated negative mental, physical, and sexual health outcomes among this group (Millett et al. 2012). Similarly, findings from a meta-analysis on the relationship between social prejudice and the health status of sexual and gender minorities revealed that the high prevalence of psychological distress in the group may be explained by experiences of social discrimination (Meyer 2003). Another study identified "a relatively robust association between experiences of discrimination and indicators of psychiatric [stress]" (Mays and Cochran 2001, 1876).

In addition, LGB community members are not homogenous. LGB people who are also members of racialized communities often face additional health risks (Millett, Gregorio, Jeffries et al. 2012; Millett, Gregorio, Peterson et al. 2012). In a meta-analysis looking at research on Black MSM in different parts of the world, the authors estimated that Black gay men "are 15 times more likely to be HIV positive compared with general populations and 8.5 times more likely compared with Black population" (Millett, Gregorio, Jeffries et al. 2012, 411). The same study noted that Black gay men in Québec "had a greater lifetime prevalence of syphilis or herpes diagnosis than did other MSM" (Millett, Gregorio, Jeffries et al. 2012, 419). This study suggests that the intersection of sexual minority status and racialized minority status leads to increased risk of negative mental and sexual health outcomes (Diaz, Ayala, and Bein 2004; Diaz, Bein, and Ayala 2006).

Finally, the mental health of racialized LGB people becomes even more compromised when one adds newcomer status to the mix. Settlement into a new country has been known to have impacts on the psychological health of newcomers because of stresses related to acculturation, economic uncertainty, and racial/ethnic discrimination (U. George et al. 2015). While immigrants coming into the country may self-report higher levels of health than Canadian-born persons, this advantage soon diminishes over time spent in the country (Elamoshy and Feng 2018; Fuller-Thomson, Noack, and George 2011). As a racialized LGB immigrant, an individual can face oppression and discrimination on account of race, newcomer status, and on being lesbian, gay, bisexual, transgender, or queer (LGBTQ) in complex ways not experienced by individuals who hold any one or two of these identity markers.

However, there is little research examining racism and homophobia and the impact of immigration on the health and well-being of racialized LGB immigrants in Canada.

This chapter examines the reported experiences of racism, homophobia, and immigration on the health and well-being of Black cisgender gay immigrants in Montréal, Canada. We begin with a literature review contextualizing the climate in which Black cisgender gay immigrants exist and the structural forces that shape their social conditions. Next, we delineate our theoretical framework: intersectionality theory, an appropriate paradigm for understanding the interconnections between multiple oppressed identity categories. Following that, we outline our methodology and data analysis process, before reporting and discussing the findings of our study and stating our conclusions.

LITERATURE REVIEW

In Canada, two seminal studies highlight same-sex prejudice in Black Canadian communities. The *MaBwana Black Men's Study: Community and Belonging in the Lives of African, Caribbean and Other Black Gay Men in Toronto* (C. George et al. 2012) and *Buller Men and Batty Bwoys: Hidden Men in Toronto and Halifax Black Communities* (Crichlow 2004). Both studies found that pervasive negative attitudes against same-sex sexual behavior ensure that Black MSM hid or lived in shame. Black cisgender gay men face ridicule as well as verbal and psychological abuse from Black community members (Crichlow 2004; C. George et al. 2012), with the effect that any sense of community and belonging can be elusive.

These accounts were corroborated in the *Montreal Community Contact* (Flegel 2001), an English-speaking newspaper for the Black and Caribbean communities in Québec. In an article entitled "Homophobia Rampant in the Community," two Black university students discussed their inability to disclose their sexual behavior to their immigrant relatives as a result of heterosexist prejudice. One stated: "I don't want to be the one to tear my family apart. My parents are from the Caribbean, and Caribbean people are very stone-aged with regards to sexuality and stuff" (Flegel 2001, 16).

Another anecdotal illustration of heterosexism in the Black community is the experience of Rudy Mudenge, a Black gay man who immigrated to Montréal from the Democratic Republic of Congo. Speaking to a local Montréal French newspaper, *Métro*, as part of a campaign to create awareness of homophobia in Québec, he said: "Ma mère m'a dit qu'elle préférait la guerre à un fils homosexuel [my mother preferred the civil war than having a homosexual son]" (Guthrie 2010). When Rudy came out, his mother gave him two options: accept a heterosexual lifestyle or face eviction from the family home;

he chose the latter. These first-hand accounts resonate with literature suggesting that homophobia within Black communities is an oppressive social force (Crichlow 2004; C. George et al. 2012; Giwa 2018).

Anti-Black racism in Canada, both within and outside of the LGB community, is another prominent theme in the literature. For the authors, anti-Black racism describes the nexus of intersecting oppressions of discrimination rooted in the history of subjugation of Black people, and their resistance to it so that they are disadvantaged at all levels and stages of life—social, economic, cultural, spiritual, and political. Some reports and studies shed light on racial inequalities experienced by Black people in Canada in the areas of access to social opportunity and social/health outcomes (Bourgeois et al. 2017; Government of Canada, Office of the Correctional Investigator 2014; Livingstone and Weinfeld 2018; Torczyner 2010). These reports have observed that Black communities in Canada do not fare well compared to other ethnic groups (Torczyner 2010). Blacks generally face disproportionate rates of unemployment, poverty, and incarceration, and negative health-related outcomes (Government of Canada, Office of the Correctional Investigator 2014; Livingstone and Weinfeld 2018; Torczyner 2010). A study by McGill University's School of Social Work (Torczyner 2010) found that although Blacks may have education comparable to non-Blacks, they index at the lowest percentile when accessing social opportunity structures, such as employment: "Black persons with a graduate degree had higher unemployment rates than non-Black high school dropouts (13.4% vs. 12.0%)" (Torczyner 2010, 34). When Blacks are employed, they tend to be paid less than non-Blacks in the same employment position. For example, the study noted: "Non-Black managers were three times more likely to earn more than $75,000 compared to Black managers (31.7% vs. 11.9%)" (Torczyner 2010, 33).

Similarly, a federal government report investigating racial differences in incarceration rates in Canada demonstrated that Blacks are disproportionately represented in the prison population (Government of Canada, Office of the Correctional Investigator 2014). According to this report, while 2.9 percent of Canada's population are people of African descent, they account for 9.3 percent of the entire federal prison inmate population. The two provinces with the highest Black populations, Ontario (4.3%) and Québec (3.2%), also have high Black incarceration rates: Ontario at 61 percent and Québec at 17 percent. Between 2002 and 2003, 767 Black Canadians were incarcerated in federal penitentiaries. However, when compared to rates in 2011 and 2012, the population of Black prison inmates surged to 1,340, representing an increase of 75 percent in almost 10 years (Government of Canada, Office of the Correctional Investigator 2014). These reports do not conclude that the differences in racial access to social opportunities and negative social outcomes are due to racism in and of itself. Rather, racism is one factor in understanding the realities of being Black in Canada.

In the context of the LGB community, Black MSM's experiences of racism and sexual objectification are well documented (Giwa 2018; Giwa and Greensmith 2012; Husbands et al. 2013; Roy 2012; Walcott 2006). For example, Roy investigated how queers of color are represented in Québec's three gay magazines. His study found that "the bodies of men of color are often fetishized and exoticized as objects of desire on the cover of Québec's gay magazines" (Roy 2012, 181). Corroborating this observation is an interview with a Black gay teacher featured in a local English-speaking newspaper, *The Montreal Gazette*, as part of activities marking the perennial LGBT Pride Week in Montréal (Burnett 1999). In the interview, the Black gay teacher underscored the experience of ethnic-based sexual objectification in Montréal's gay village. He indicated that when accosted by non-Black gays, they were more interested in the size and prowess of his genitalia:

> You're beautiful [a non-Black gay man said to him], explaining that he'd been to Spain, where he'd met a Black man with a 12-inch penis. He preferred making love with Black men because, [the non-Black gay man told the teacher], they were better lovers and had oversized penises. (Burnett 1999, C3)

Similar experiences have been reported in other Canadian cities. Warner, for example, described one Black gay man's experience in Ottawa's gay scene in the early 1990s: "Some gay men did not want to speak to [me] because of [my] color, while others tell me that they really like Black gays because we're great in bed and we have big dicks" (Warner 2002, 320). More recently, a participant in Giwa and Greensmith's study shared his apprehension about White gay men who introduced themselves to Black gay men as: "Damn you're hot, you must have a big dick" (Giwa and Greensmith 2012, 168).

Research confirms these accounts of Black gay men's encounters with sexual racism, and shows how racial exoticization is played out in inter/intraracial same-sex relationships. Husbands et al., for example, found that Black gay men are more likely to play a flexible sexual position (top and bottom) when in relationships involving individuals of the same racial and ethnic background. However, in sexual relations involving non-Black sexual partners, they adopt a more fixed sexual position (namely, aggressive, dominant top). Further, the research acknowledged, the expectation that Black gay men would play a single prescribed sexual role (i.e., aggressive, dominant top) in interracial relationships rendered Black gay men who did not live up to this rigid, fetishized role undesirable by non-Black sexual partners (Husbands et al. 2013).

In another study (C. George et al. 2012) exploring community and belonging among African, Caribbean, and other Black gay men in Toronto, the
researchers found that the idea of racial sexual objectification is not limited to
White gay men only; Black gay immigrants and sexual minorities from other
ethnic groups also fetishize White gay men, in a behavior known as "reverse
exoticisation" (C. George et al. 2012, 557; McKeown et al. 2010, 849–51).
Racial/ethnic-based sexual objectification thus "intersects and orders sexual
intimacy" (Husbands et al. 2013, 437) in interracial relationships in the LGB
community.

The theme of immigration and its intersection with sexual orientation in
shaping the experiences of racialized LGB people is an emerging research
area in Canadian literature. Immigrants in general have been known to face
many disadvantages in Canadian society, including difficulty finding work
(Chaze and George 2014; Li 2000), language-related barriers (Creese and
Kambere 2003), obstacles to accessing services (Guruge et al. 2009), and
racial/ethnic discrimination (Chaze and George 2014; Li 2001).

Racialized LGB immigrants experience unique vulnerabilities on account
of the interactions of their sexual orientation, race, and newcomer status
(Ghabrial 2017; Giwa 2018; Huang and Fang 2019; Patel 2019). They may
come from countries where same-sex relationships are stigmatized, criminalized, and/or even punishable by death (Carroll 2016). As well, they may
experience homophobia from within their own families and ethnic communities and racism within the LGB community (Nakamura, Chan, and
Fischer 2013). They may be reluctant to seek services, as they may find
service-providing agencies homophobic or not welcoming to LGB immigrants (Munro et al. 2013). Immigrant-serving agencies may inadvertently
portray a message of noninclusion toward LGB immigrants (Giwa and
Chaze 2018), which may further prevent newcomers from getting crucial
settlement-related help. Racialized LGB immigrants may be forced to hide
aspects of their identity to better fit in with their ethnic group or within the
LGB community (Giwa 2016).

THEORETICAL FRAMEWORK

This research is informed by the theoretical framework of intersectionality
(Crenshaw 1989), which recognizes that social categories of identity (e.g.,
race, sexual orientation, gender identity, class, and immigrant status) are
interconnected, mutually reinforcing, systems of social oppression (Nash
2008). This theory challenges the assumption of a single-story identity as a
sufficient lens through which societal oppression can be discerned; the single-
issue approach undermines any representation of a multidimensional reality

that coexists with other interlocking systems of oppression. Instead, intersectionality argues for a consideration of how multiple categories of identity operate interdependently to shape people's experiences of privilege and disadvantage. Focusing on a single-issue model of oppression (e.g., heterosexism) presents the LGB community as homogenous so that the discussion of homophobia, for example, is framed through the lens of White cisgender gay men. Using White cisgender gay men's experiences to account for the complexity of being Black cisgender gay immigrants in Canada gives the impression that these lives are interchangeable (Giwa 2018). In challenging this assumption, intersectionality echoes Lorde's (1984) position that single-category forms of oppression are not the lived experience of all members of the LGB community.

Intersectionality decentralizes the dominance of White cisgender gay men's narratives as the standard against which racialized others are measured (Bérubé 2001; Brotman and Lee 2011; Riggs 2008; Roy 2012). In decentralizing Whiteness, the current authors' work unsettles the idea of the LGB community as a model of inclusion, diversity, and tolerance (Ghabrial 2017; Giwa and Greensmith 2012; Hawkeswood 1997; Stephens 2014; Walcott 2006). An intersectional standpoint challenges the supremacy of Whiteness by examining the multifaceted experiences of marginalization that exist within the LGB community. As well, the theory permits an analysis of the ways in which immigration status and homophobia within the Black community combine with the social oppression of anti-Black racism in LGB and mainstream society to affect employment, health, and social status of Black cisgender gay immigrants in Montréal.

METHOD

The study employed a qualitative approach (Creswell 2013) to better understand the shared lived experiences of racism, homophobia, and immigration among Black cisgender gay immigrants in Montréal, Canada. Participants were recruited through word of mouth and snowball sampling. Eligibility for the study were based on the following criteria: (a) eighteen years of age or older; (b) immigrants from an African or Caribbean country; (c) understood and spoke English; (d) lived in the Greater Montréal Area; and (e) openly self-identified as gay. Six Black cisgender gay men meeting the eligibility criteria were recruited for the study. They ranged in age from 25 to 55, with a mean age of 36.5 years. Three participants were from the Caribbean countries of Jamaica, Barbados, and Grenada. The remaining three participants came from the African countries of Kenya, Sierra Leone, and Uganda. In terms of immigration status, three participants had Canadian citizenship, two were on student visa, and one was a permanent resident.

Semistructured interviews were conducted between April and December 2015, with the aid of an open-ended interview guide (Padgett 2008). Interviews lasted two hours. Individual interviews were digitally recorded and transcribed verbatim; personal information was redacted from the transcripts to protect the identity of research participants. All research activities followed the guidelines on ethical conduct for research involving humans, and the study received ethics approval from McGill University. Participation was voluntary, and participants provided written informed consent. No remuneration was offered for participating in the study.

Using thematic analysis (Braun and Clarke 2006), the authors read and reread the transcripts to immerse themselves in the data. Independent coding was done by the first and second authors; the results were then compared and discussed. Preliminary descriptive commentaries were written along the borders of the transcripts. Key phrases, sentences, and paragraphs were highlighted and assigned codes, making sure to keep close to participants' own language. The codes were listed in chronological order (i.e., in sequence of occurrence) and similar codes were grouped together into a category with overarching themes. The themes were reexamined to confirm their accuracy and support of the data. The final themes informed the analysis and interpretation of the data, which the third author reviewed to ensure the rigor of the findings.

FINDINGS

The following major themes arose from the data analysis of individual interviews: (a) anti-Black racism and homophobia outside of gay men's communities; (b) race-based sexual objectification and in-group tension among Black cisgender gay men; (c) intersectional impacts of the dual oppressions of immigration and poverty on health; and (d) coping with the stress of immigration, racism, and homophobia. These themes emerged across most or all individual interviews. The findings reflect how the experiences of migration, racism within and outside of the LGB community, and homophobia in the Black community can combine to negatively influence the health and social well-being of Black cisgender gay immigrants in Montréal. Pseudonyms have been used to protect the identities of research participants and, in some cases, textual data (i.e., verbatim quotations) have been edited lightly to improve readability or clarity of the point being made.

Anti-Black Racism and Homophobia
Outside of the Gay Men's Community

As racialized Black immigrants, the participants faced unique forms of oppression. Many of them reported that racial discrimination was a common and frequent form of social oppression in Montréal. Incidents of anti-Black racism they experienced affected almost every aspect of their lives. However, one particular setting in which they discussed experiencing anti-Black racism was in the labor market or at work, where their intelligence and competencies were repeatedly questioned by employers, colleagues, and/or clients. The perception of them as unintelligent, they surmised, reflected stereotypes about race that could have material consequences in the form of a lack of employment opportunity and limited or no chance for career advancement. Most, but not all, instances of anti-Black racism were subtle. The subtlety, however, did not erase the fact that they were being subjected to differential treatment:

> The thing is, [my job] is highly specialized. It is not something that, traditionally, a Black male would do. And so, when the clients come, if they are not warned by people before that I am Black, it kinda throws them off and you could clearly see that it throws them off. . . . Especially with my background and pedigree, it is a constant battle. A lot of the people who come to me, they grudgingly come to me because they have no choice because what I do is highly specialized and so they usually put up a lot of resistance. (Kojo, Sierra Leone, 37)[1]

Along with anti-Black racism in the general society and in the workplace specifically, most participants reported experiencing homophobia and anti-gay sentiment from within the Black community in Montréal. Often, the homophobic attitude was directed at them by their own immigrant families. These families originated from Africa and the Caribbean—regions of the world where stigmatization and criminalization of same-sex relationships exist. Their homophobic sentiments took the form of verbal assault, psychological put-down, and outright social and familial rejection. Being in Canada did not seem to shield them from this negative treatment. In this way, they continued to experience homophobia as if they were back home in their country of origin, and not in Canada where same-sex relationships are recognized by the law and are considered socially acceptable. One of the participants spoke about ways in which homophobia continued to be transmitted to children in immigrant families:

> I have nieces and nephews that were born here [in Canada], and they have been through a lot of problems, that got me thinking, what if one of them was gay? I am not surprised they are not accepting; they've been brought up homophobic because of me, mostly. Their father brought them up homophobic because he

didn't like me—why, I have no idea. He made his kids hate me because I am
gay. And so they associate gay with bad uncle, I don't know what he told them,
so surprisingly, for Canadian-born-kids, they are a little too homophobic than I
could ever imagined. (Kwebena, Kenya, 40)

When homophobia intersects with religion, the result can be undesirable.
Setting down roots in a place where Black religious people are seen to out-
number openly Black cisgender gay men makes coming out difficult, and
the internalization of homophobia more likely. Participants did not feel they
could come out because of the religious climate of their surroundings and the
real or perceived fear of rejection by religious Black people in their lives.
Yaw's words below suggest that the inability to freely express himself within
communal Black spaces had impacted negatively on his mental health—he
even contemplated taking his own life:

I really felt the social discrimination based on immigration status and poverty.
Before that when I was depressed and everything, I was having trouble coming
out, but I think that was discrimination based on sexuality, you know, I stayed in
[Ottawa] back then, few Blacks I knew were these really intense Christian Black
people. I just really didn't think I could really come out to anybody. I strongly
considered . . . I just wanted to end my whole life. (Yaw, Uganda, 25)

Race-Based Sexual Objectification and In-Group
Tension among Black Cisgender Gay Men

Most of the participants discussed their experiences with sexual objectification within and outside of Montréal's LGB community, where they were
repeatedly subjected to questions about their penis size at gay clubs. At
times, the questions turned into arguments where they felt the need to defend
their full humanity against attempts by White cisgender gay men to define
them solely on the size of their penis. Kweku's words below suggest that the
responsibility is put on Black cisgender gay men to demystify the mythology
about all Black men having big penises, in a strategic move to humanize them
and critique the centrality of racist thinking embedded in the line of questioning and interrogation:

If you go clubbing for instance and [White] people try to pick you up, they have
notions of what your anatomy should look like. If you are Black, they expect
you to have a big dick. In [Sherbrooke, Québec], that is the question I was frequently asked when I went into the clubs. You know, um, and people got into
huge arguments with me. Sometimes they were from Montréal. I'm like, come
on, we [Black MSM] are like all other human beings and [our penises] range
the gamut [of sizes]. You cannot convince [them], you know. Most of the guys

that I've slept with have been Black, and you know, I've encountered everything from almost nothing to monstrosities. So, [the] myth [that Black men all have large penises] is, in that sense, you know, a kind of discrimination. (Kweku, Jamaica, 55)

Many participants also felt that racialized sexual objectification can curtail the sexual freedom of Black cisgender gay men, by forcing them to perform rigid, predetermined, sexual roles. A Black man's White sexual partner may have false expectations or a fetishized idea about being with a Black cisgender gay man. For example, Black cisgender gay men are compared against each other in sexual positions, with Black bottoms seen as less desirable than Black tops:

> The Whites gays would be like, oh my God, you're a Black bottom? Well that sucks because you want a big dick when you're a bottom? I want my ass fucked; I'm a bottom and this doesn't work for me, right? The Black top have such an array of choices, of selections, that is like whatever, so the Black bottom is like damn it, I gotta compete with the few Blacks who're better looking than me. (Kwame, Grenada, 28)

In the same way that sexual objectification can limit the sexual opportunity of Black cisgender gay men who bottom, relegating them to a less desirable status, the potential for romantic relationship between White cisgender gay men and Black men who top can give rise to in-group animosity and arguments about interracial relationships. The idea of interracial dating seems perturbing for some Black cisgender gay men, while other Black cisgender gay men feel that they should not be limited in their relationship or dating choices to someone from their racial and ethnic group. Dating outside of one's racial and ethnic group, however, was enough to generate negative talk about someone in order to disparage them and possibly discourage them from dating outside of their race, according to this participant:

> They [other Black gay men] would create a gossip or story that never existed, [they] would invent stuff that never took place [just because] you're seeing someone who is non-Black. They will create . . . they created a problem [for me]. (Kwame, Grenada, 28)

Intersectional Oppressions of Immigration and Poverty on Health

For several participants, the intersection between immigration and poverty was acutely experienced in the context of daily living. Finding ways to survive as immigrants with a limited understanding of English, living in

Montréal presented a set of economic challenges, given the dominance of French as the preferred language. Participants who immigrated to Montréal and did not speak the language fluently faced chronic unemployment in which they had to consider employment opportunities outside of their normal frame of reference, such as sex work:

> At first, I was just gonna feel it out [sex work]. Kinda just go there. I guess I was almost hoping they would tell me that there is no way you can do it or something. I don't know. It was one of those things where I was looking for a job online and no money, I was looking for jobs, I could not get them because of the language thing and there was just this sex work. I strongly considered escorting; I came close. I mean it is almost like I did everything else, but actually have sex for money. I was now more open to any job opportunity. If I could not get the bare minimum, you know, I just felt like I could be more flexible. At that point, I abandoned any kind of social, any kind of cultural laws or restrictions or anything. I was much more open to it. Back when I was in that position, when I felt like I really needed the money, it was certainly, it shocked me how much open I was to doing it. The fact that I was even there, you know? (Yaw, Uganda, 25)

For some, the inability to exercise control over their lives due to the poverty created by their immigration status placed them in a compromised position. They felt obligated to pay back friends or someone whose house they were temporarily staying at with sex, to avoid living on the streets. Sometimes, at the risk of seeming ungrateful or resistive, this could mean conceding to unsafe sexual practices, putting their health at risk. As Kojo's comments below suggests, exchanging sex for housing or security can take a physical and psychological toll on the self:

> Here, it is that I am living with somebody. I have no choice; yes, you always have choice, but whatever. . . .This person has taken me in, and if this person wants to have sex with me, do I pass it up? If you put up a resistance how does it look on [you]? It's not necessary that the behavior was risk[y] per se, but I think it always affect you psychologically because you feel as though you are trashy and not worthy, especially for somebody like me with my educational background. It is like "are you kidding me"? This is what my life has deteriorated into and that can lead to uh, a lot of negative thoughts and I think it's more, not so much the physical, the depression and anxiety has physical ramifications. I guess I am lucky in the sense that I don't have too much of that. But little do I know, I don't know, it gonna manifest itself in time, but I have not had that burden. I have come close to it. (Kojo, Sierra Leone, 37)

The cost of not having a stable, well-paying job also meant that these participants were financially limited in their ability to take care of themselves medically. Not having money for healthy food and dental care, or being ineligible for access to health care because of their immigration status made it likely that they would look for high-risk, informal employment to meet their needs:

> Yes, not having the money, I can see in terms of health and not eating well. There was a period in time, when, I, you know, lived on five bucks. You say, ok, so the MacDonald's double cheeseburger is about one something. You can get that [and it will] keep you full for a while. I have been through that. So, from that standpoint, yes it [poverty] impacts your health. Do you have money to go to a Dentist? Do you have money to, you know, do basic things? I have experience that as well. (Kojo, Sierra Leone, 37).

Coping with the Stress of Immigration, Racism, and Homophobia

Participants alluded to the stressful nature of immigrating to another country. Regardless of the reason for immigrating, they experienced this process as taxing, and felt required to adopt varying coping strategies to deal with complications related to postmigration stress. At the time, the choice of coping strategy was seen as appropriate to the level of stress being experienced and its potential to provide immediate relief. The consumption of alcohol and drugs was not out of the question. Frequency of use increased with the complexity of immigration issue at hand:

> Every now and then, especially if I get stressed out with projects and immigration issue, I might increase drinking, or I might add something else or some other substance to it. Marijuana, that one, I have been smoking a little bit more consistently [in the] last few months. It helps me cope. Also, I do it because I feel like it helps me sleep better. I have problems sleeping and always worried about immigration issue, so I feel like doing weed or whatever helps me sleep better. (Kwesi, Barbados, 44)

Seeking out sex or getting "fucked up" was how another participant expressed coping with the stress and anxiety borne from social discriminatory experiences of racism and homophobia. The participant seemed to make a distinction between *sex*, in which protection is being used, and the so-called *real* experience of just having unadulterated sex where concern for safety might not be top of mind. The rawness of the sexual activity could be seen to match with the emotions and feelings being experienced:

> A friend of mine brought up a while ago that my frustrations sometimes manifest as [me] sexualizing my frustrations. How? I get "fucked up" and I wanna go out and see how getting fucked up is like. Like the real experience is a matter of language, right? Well, I deliberately use the word "fucked up." . . . It's a very

good use of language [giggling]. . . . Not a day goes by without me not thinking about getting fucked up. . . . It's a different experience getting fucked up in the sense that having sex is totally different from getting fucked up. If I am sexual-izing my frustration, that is exactly what happens. . . . It's a human experience, right? It is an easy thing to do. (Kwebena, Kenya, 40)

This same participant, like others interviewed, sought the support of health professionals, including a therapist. The therapist was seen as a neutral party in whom they could confide about anything they could not share with their immediate friends. Even when participants did open up to their friends, they were not convinced that the disclosure would be met with any supportive or well-thought-out response. A therapist, on the other hand, was seen as someone that could provide a reasoned point of view on the presenting issue, and help them think through their options in a safe and secure environment. Participants who used therapy found the experience positive and indicated that they would use it again:

It wasn't a joke. Seeing a psychologist is almost like being in a very meaningful marriage; I get a well-thought-out point of view from my therapist. I don't get this kind of audience with anybody; I don't know if it's the way I interact or the system that forces this kind of, this lack of interaction between members of the society. I am sure [that] I am not the exception, but I can't talk to my friends about most of the things [that] I talk to my therapist [about] because there is a lack of time. Even if I do talk to them about it, there is not going to be any feed-back or attention. Or [due to] lack of experience [there might be the response of] "I don't know [what] to tell you kinda of thing." So, it's very fulfilling to talk to a therapist, like a fantastic experience. It has given me that added security of having a person to talk to. (Kwebena, Kenya, 40)

DISCUSSION

Several limitations of the study should be kept in mind when interpreting the findings. Although the study was conducted in English, three out of the six participants were non-native English speakers. Having limited command of the English language could have inhibited the effective communication of concepts and sentiments aligned with their cultural codes and specificities. The term "gay" was used in the recruitment process and has some limitations as well. Those who do not identify in this way may have opted to not participate in the study, potentially limiting valuable sources of knowledge. Finally, the self-reported nature of the study may have resulted in social desirability bias, in which participants either exaggerated or underreported their experiences. These limitations notwithstanding, we were encouraged by the similarities of our findings with those of other extant research and the contributions to knowledge about factors contributing to vulnerability among this population.

This chapter explored the postmigration experiences of racism and homophobia among Black cisgender gay immigrants in Montréal. Our findings revealed how immigrant status, race, and being gay intersected to create unique experiences of discrimination for our participants. Echoing other studies (Adames et al. 2018; Ghabrial 2017; Huang and Fang 2019), the significance of the intersectionality framework for examining the lives of Black cisgender gay immigrants was underscored; this framework supports a holistic understanding of participants' experiences of social discrimination grounded in an integrative approach. Four salient themes were found in the study about Black cisgender gay immigrants' experiences of racism and homophobia in Montréal: (a) anti-Black racism and homophobia outside of gay men's communities; (b) race-based sexual objectification and in-group tension among Black cisgender gay men; (c) intersectional impacts of the dual oppressions of immigration and poverty on health; and (d) coping with the stress of immigration, racism, and homophobia.

Finding that Black cisgender gay immigrants in our study experienced anti-Black racism outside of the LGB community was important but not surprising. Anti-Black racism is deeply entrenched in the Canadian social fabric and represents a system of White supremacist logic, with its assertion of economic, political, cultural, and social power (Howard 2018; Maynard 2017; Mullings, Morgan, and Quelleng 2016). Beliefs in White superiority are institutionalized in the operations of society, and function to keep those who are not White at a disadvantage (Government of Ontario, Ministry of Children and Youth Services 2017). This has been the social order in Canada for Black people and other racialized immigrant groups (Howard 2018; Maynard 2017; Mullings, Morgan, and Quelleng 2016), who have had to endure the uncomfortable and painful experience of being discriminated against based on the color of their skin and other dimensions of social difference.

One major area in which participants in the current study experienced the injustice of anti-Black racism was in the employment domain. They noted that prospective employers, coworkers, and clients always questioned their intelligence and competencies. Employment barriers were most felt among participants who had been in the country for less than five years. For survival reasons, these participants either contemplated or engaged in sex work as a way to pay bills and maintain themselves. Other times, sex with friends or acquaintances was a transactional means for keeping a roof over one's head, but came with the complication of reduced self-agency. Specifically, participants felt that it was necessary to acquiesce to the needs of their friends or acquaintances so as not to jeopardize their living situation. Thus, when it came to sex, they were more likely to accommodate the sexual needs of their friends and acquaintances by not demanding that condoms be used during sexual intercourse, putting their own health at risk (Han et al. 2015). By contrast, participants who had lived in Canada for a longer time experienced blocked opportunities or were overlooked for career advancement due to the proverbial glass ceiling effect related to race and ethnicity (Kay 2018; Pendakur and Pendakur 1998).

Regardless of the length of time spent in Canada, the effect of institutionalized anti-Black racism was that participants were prevented from reaching their full potential. If one has no ability to work or progress in one's career, there is little to no opportunity for the economic growth and stability needed to promote self-determination and autonomy. This finding is significant in its reminder that the experience of anti-Black racism finds expression in the larger Canadian society as well as in the predominantly White LGB community (Greey 2018; Howard 2018; Maynard 2017; Mullings, Morgan, and Quelleng 2016). Anti-Black racism needs to be examined for its impact on Black and other racialized LGB immigrant populations. Moreover, the finding alerts us to the dangerous condition in which more recent Black cisgender gay immigrants find themselves, where they are pressured to compromise their health in order to meet their physiological/basic and safety needs. The sexual vulnerability and associated health risk of racialized immigrant MSM has been noted by past studies (Poon et al. 2013).

Participants in this study recounted experiences of homophobia in Montréal's Black community. These expressions of hatred mirrored sentiments of derision they may have encountered in their countries of origin. Religion was suggested as having a strong influence on the Black community's psyche in terms of what God is believed to have said about MSM or people who are in same-sex relationships, and how they should be treated. Previous studies have noted how religious environments perpetuate homophobia and discrimination against racialized LGB people (Jaspal and Cinnirella 2010; Lassiter, Brewer, and Wilton 2018; Miller 2007; Ryan 2003). Homophobic remarks and actions are felt from immediate family members and members of the Black community, and serve to uphold a noninclusive, nationalistic, Black cultural identity, from which Black cisgender gay men are excluded (Crichlow 2004).

Likewise, the image of Canada as a place of refuge from heterosexist discrimination was brought into disrepute by our findings, given the degree of heterosexist messages participants were exposed to. Canada has a global reputation as a progressive and safe country for LGB people (Giwa 2018; Lee 2018). However, despite legislative advancements at the provincial/territorial and federal levels, heterosexism remains a pervasive issue in the Black community as in other cultural communities (Hill 2013). Our data suggest that the inhospitable climate of these communities make it difficult for Black cisgender gay men to be themselves, free from any real or imagined violence that may be directed at them.

Similarly, there is no guarantee that one's family of origin will be supportive in times of need, and may even exacerbate the situation by banning the individual from the family home, as was the experience of one participant in our study. Thus, even if Black cisgender gay men wish to maintain a connection to the Black community or their family of origin, their ability to do so may be restricted due to heterosexist attitudes and bias that privilege opposite-sex sexuality and relationships (C. George et al. 2012). Consistent with other studies (Crichlow 2004; Grant 2018), one of the effects of homophobia that can be inferred from the data is that it can hinder the positive development of a collective Black identity, potentially getting in the way of the need for belonging and sense of connection.

Outside of the homophobia in the Black community, participants conveyed the feeling of being reduced to sexual stereotypes informed by Black sexual clichés, exposing racism inherent in the LGB community as reported in other research (Giwa 2018; Giwa and Greensmith 2012; Nakamura, Chan, and Fischer 2013; Patel 2019; Roy 2012). In the current study, the most enduring stereotype is that of Black cisgender gay men as virile, well-endowed, oversexed, and aggressive in bed. This narrow perception of Black sexuality impacted the social reality of our participants in one of two ways: Black men who fit or conformed to the dominant sexual trope were seen as desirable, whereas Black men who did not live up to that stereotype were rejected.

Interestingly, participants who identified as conforming to the Black dominant top did so for several reasons: poverty (in the case of transactional sex); racial identity power dynamics, in shunning sexual positions in which they were submissive to White cisgender gay men; and pragmatism, where being a top was seen to afford more opportunity and variety in choices of sexual partner. Rather than a state of preference devoid of any conscious reasoning, participants who acted in dominant sexual positions were motivated by the need for material security and/or desire to assert the agency of their selfhood. This finding underscores the intersections of class with race and sexuality while pointing to the fact that, even in the midst of personal struggles and challenges, participants were able to exercise some power in avoiding the pathology of victimhood. Also, although White cisgender gay men may feel like they hold all the power in deciding which Black man to favor with their social approbation and sexual intimacy (Smith, Morales, and Han 2018), performing the role of a dominant top is a conscious decision that some of our participants made early on for practical reasons that ensured their own position of power in the sexual encounter.

Beyond the Black/White paradigm of dominance and subservience, another consequence of the sexual clichés and stereotypes is that they reinforce in-group tension and discord among Black cisgender gay men. Our data point to economic differences and issues surrounding dating outside of the Black community as primary sources of this tension. Because White cisgender gay men's economic and cultural capital provides them with a higher social status (Bérubé 2001; Smith, Morales, and Han 2018), their Black partners can indirectly benefit from this status recognition, distancing themselves from other Black cisgender gay men.

In-group tension also manifests as interpersonal jealousy and resentment. For example, those who date outside of their racial and cultural group are resented by those who do not, perhaps because of the emotional and financial strain related to immigration, where some Black men (and not others) are seen to be "taken care of." This kind of behavior can further isolate Black cisgender gay men whose supportive social network might be weakened due to strain in family and community relationships. Instead of relying on each other for social and emotional support, especially at the critical time after immigrating to a new country, Black men who date outside of their social group may be left to deal with difficult life situations alone. This finding points to the importance of the provision of social support to help these men deal with social reactions to and stressors of interracial relationships. As well, the finding speaks to the need to address the socioeconomic and race-based inequalities that encourage a have-and-have-not mindset that can trigger jealousy and rivalries in the same social group.

The impact of the combined stresses of immigration, homophobia, and racism on our participants required them to adopt different coping strategies, mainly emotion-focused and problem-focused strategies (Lazarus and Folkman 1984). In emotion-focused strategies, the goal is to minimize the negative emotional response to the stressful situation, which is accomplished using avoidant-type responses. For example, having risky sex or consuming drugs and alcohol to relax and sleep were some of the ways that our participants dealt with homophobic, racist, and immigration-related stress.

In problem-focused strategies, the goal is to identify and remove the source of the stressor; in this way, these strategies are not concerned with emotional self-regulation. Avoiding social interactions and actively seeking out professional support in the form of a therapist typifies this kind of coping strategy (Niegocki and Ægisdóttir 2019); participants found the therapeutic process valuable.

It is worth mentioning that emotion-focused coping, in which the sources of stress are not addressed directly, may still serve a practical and expedient purpose (Giwa 2018). Our data highlighted how the use of marijuana, in particular, could be seen as an effective sleeping aid. However, its use intensified during periods of heightened stress, raising concern about the potential for abuse and dependence. Similarly, although engaging in unsafe sexual behaviors can help one to mentally escape from reality, there is the risk for acquiring sexually transmitted infections such as HIV/AIDS. Thus, while emotion-focused coping might offer temporary relief from stress, especially in situations where the problem is perceived to be outside of one's control, it may not promote resilience in the long run and might have the opposite effect of creating additional problems for an individual. For example, learning that one has acquired HIV/AIDS from having unsafe sex could add to an already onerous task of navigating the immigration system as well as dealing with homophobia and racial discrimination.

It might be tempting, then, to conclude that problem-focused coping is better than emotion-focused coping, but as our data suggest, this is not necessarily the case. The use of marijuana as sleep aid corroborates this point. However, we recognize that not all coping strategies are created equal. Facilitating Black cisgender gay immigrants' access to health and social service providers, similar to the therapeutic counseling that our participants found useful, can support them in identifying the source of the stress and effective methods to cope with it thereby promoting optimal health and well-being. This approach recognizes that emotion-focused coping, much like problem-focused coping, has an important role to play in the process of stress management.

Finally, this study joins others (C. George et al. 2012; Giwa and Greensmith 2012; Husbands et al. 2013; Nakamura, Chan, and Fischer 2013; Patel 2019; Roy 2012) in reporting on the pervasiveness of racism in the LGB community and homophobia in the Black community. In these contexts, the full humanity of Black cisgender gay men has yet to be fully recognized.

CONCLUSION

Our study focused on Black cisgender gay immigrants' experience of social discrimination in Montréal. The theory of intersectionality (Crenshaw 1989) was employed to challenge the single model of oppression, which does not always explain how different interlocking identities work together simultaneously to impact the lives of research participants. This framework allowed the authors to better contextualize their accounts in a nuanced way. Immigrating was revealed to create vulnerabilities for Black cisgender gay immigrants, opening them to a constellation of social and health risks. Addressing the economic inequality generated by immigration status can help to create a pathway out of poverty, to promote better health and well-being outcomes.

Despite Canada's progressive values, homophobia and anti-Black racism remain pervasive and can negatively affect the mental and physical health of Black cisgender gay immigrants, leaving them unsupported at an emotional and instrumental level. Combating homophobia and anti-Black racism remains important to creating a culture of acceptance and inclusion. The emotion- and problem-focused coping used by Black cisgender gay immigrants represents how they dealt with the intersectional experience of oppression. Recognizing that no two coping strategies are the same, health and social service providers can best work with this population by meeting them where they are. Treating emotion-focused coping as inferior to problem-focused coping may undermine self-determination and risk intervention to promote the identification of coping strategies most appropriate for a given stressor.

Ultimately, the hardship endured by our participants did not immobilize them; if anything, it strengthened their resolve to rise above their situations. Intervention and resources must focus in this context of overall strength.

NOTE

1. Pseudonyms have been used for all interviewees.

REFERENCES

Adames, Hector Y., Nayeli Y. Chavez-Dueñas, Shweta Sharma, and Martin J. La Roche. 2018. "Intersectionality in Psychotherapy: The Experiences of an Afrolatinx Queer Immigrant." *Psychotherapy* 55 (1): 73–79.

Almeida, Joanna, Renee M. Johnson, Heather L. Corliss, Beth E. Molnar, and Deborah Azrael. 2009. "Emotional Distress Among LGBT Youth: The Influence of Perceived Discrimination Based on Sexual Orientation." *Journal of Youth and Adolescence* 38 (7): 1001–14.

Benibgui, Michael. 2010. "Mental Health Challenges and Resilience in Lesbian, Gay, and Bisexual Young Adults: Biological and Psychological Internalization of Minority Stress and Victimization." PhD diss., Concordia University.

Bérubé, Allan. 2001. "How Gays Stay White and What Kind of White It Stays." In *The Making and Unmaking of Whiteness*, edited by Birgit Brander Rasmussen, Eric Klinenberg, Irene J. Nexica, and Matt Wray, 234–65. Durham: Duke University Press.

Bourgeois, Annie-Claude, Michael Edmunds, Amnah Awan, Leigh Jonah, Olivia Varsaneux, and Winnie Siu. 2017. "HIV in Canada—Surveillance Report, 2016." *Canada Communicable Disease Report* 43 (12): 248–56.

Braun, Virginia, and Victoria Clarke. 2006. "Using Thematic Analysis in Psychology." *Qualitative Research in Psychology* 3 (2): 77–101.

Brennan, David J., Lori E. Ross, Cheryl Dobinson, Scott Veldhuizen, and Leah S. Steele. 2010. "Men's Sexual Orientation and Health in Canada." *Canadian Journal of Public Health* 101 (3): 255–58.

Brotman, Shari, and Edward O. J. Lee. 2011. "Exploring Gender and Sexuality through the Lens of Intersectionality: Sexual Minority Refugees in Canada." *Canadian Social Work Review* 28 (1): 151–56.

Burnett, Richard. 1999. "Double the Demons: Gays and Lesbians from Minority Communities Face Double-Barreled Discrimination Because They Encounter Racism Even in the Gay Subculture Where They Seek Refuge from Homophobia," *Montreal Gazette,* August 1, 1999.

Carroll, Aengus. 2016. "State-Sponsored Homophobia: A World Survey of Sexual Orientation Laws—Criminalisation, Protection and Recognition." *Geneva: International Lesbian, Gay, Bisexual, Trans and Intersex Association.* Accessed August 18, 2018. https://ilga.org/downloads/02_ILGA_State_Sponsored_Homophobia_2016_ENG_WEB_150516.pdf.

Chaze, Ferzana, and Usha George. 2014. "Discrimination at Work: Comparing the Experiences of Foreign-Trained and Locally Trained Engineers in Canada." *Canadian Ethnic Studies* 46 (1): 1–21.

Creese, Gillian, and Edith Ngene Kambere. 2003. "What Colour Is Your English?" *The Canadian Review of Sociology and Anthropology* 40 (5): 565–73.

Crenshaw, Kimberle. 1989. "Demarginalizing the Intersection of Race and Sex: A Black Feminist Critique of Anti-Discrimination Doctrine, Feminist Theory and Anti-Racist Politics." *University of Chicago Legal Forum 1989* (1): 139–67.

Creswell, John W. 2013. *Qualitative Inquiry and Research Design: Choosing Among Five Approaches*, 3rd ed. Los Angeles: SAGE.

Crichlow, Wesley. 2004. *Buller Men and Batty Bwoys: Hidden Men in Toronto and Halifax Black Communities.* Toronto: University of Toronto Press.

Diaz, Rafael M., George Ayala, and Edward Bein. 2004. "Sexual Risk as an Outcome of Social Oppression: Data from a Probability Sample of Latino Gay Men in Three U.S. Cities." *Cultural Diversity and Ethnic Minority Psychology* 10 (3): 255–67.

Diaz, Rafael M., Edward Bein, and George Ayala. 2006. "Homophobia, Poverty and Racism: Triple Oppression and Mental Health Outcomes in Latino Gay Men." In *Sexual Orientation and Mental Health: Examining Identity and Development in Lesbian, Gay and Bisexual People*, edited by Allen Martin Omoto and Howard S. Kurtzman, 207–24. Washington, DC: American Psychological Association Books.

Elamoshy, Rasha, and Cindy Feng. 2018. "Suicidal Ideation and Healthy Immigrant Effect in the Canadian Population: A Cross-Sectional Population Based Study." *International Journal of Environmental Research and Public Health* 15 (5): 1–11.

Flegel, P. 2001. "Homophobia Rampant in the Community." *Montreal Community Contact*, May 31, 2001.

Frost, David M., Keren Lehavot, and Ilan H. Meyer. 2015. "Minority Stress and Physical Health Among Sexual Minority Individuals." *Journal of Behaviour Medicine* 38 (1): 1–8.

Fuller-Thomson, Esme, Andrea M. Noack, and Usha George. 2011. "Health Decline Among Recent Immigrants to Canada: Findings from a Nationally Representative Longitudinal Survey." *Canadian Journal of Public Health* 102 (4): 237–80.

George, Clemon, Barry D. Adam, Stanley E. Read, Winston C. Husbands, Robert S. Remis, Lydia Makoroka, and Sean B. Rourke. 2012. "The MaBwana Black Men's

Study: Community and Belonging in the Lives of African, Caribbean and Other Black Gay Men in Toronto." *Culture, Health & Sexuality: An International Journal for Research, Intervention and Care* 14 (5): 549–62.

George, Usha, Mary Susan Thomson, Ferzana Chaze, and Sepali Guruge. 2015. "Immigrant Mental Health, A Public Health Issue: Looking Back and Moving Forward." *International Journal of Environmental Research and Public Health* 12 (10): 13624–48.

Ghabrial, Monica A. 2017. "Trying to Figure Out Where We Belong: Narratives of Racialized Sexual Minorities on Community, Identity, Discrimination, and Health." *Sexuality Research and Social Policy* 14 (1):42–55.

Giwa, Sulaimon. 2016. "Surviving Racist Culture: Strategies of Managing Racism among Gay Men of Colour—An Interpretative Phenomenological Analysis." PhD diss., York University.

———. 2018. "Coping with Racism and Racial Trauma: An Interpretative Phenomenological Analysis of How Gay Men from the African Diaspora Experience and Negotiate Racist Encounters." In *The Psychic Life of Racism in Gay Men's Communities*, edited by Damien W. Riggs, 81–103. Lanham: Lexington Books.

Giwa, Sulaimon, and Ferzana Chaze. 2018. "Positive Enough? A Content Analysis of Settlement Service Organizations' Inclusivity of LGBTQ Immigrants." *Journal of Gay & Lesbian Social Services* 30 (3): 220–43.

Giwa, Sulaimon, and Cameron Greensmith. 2012. "Race Relations and Racism in the LGBTQ Community of Toronto: Perceptions of Gay and Queer Social Service Providers of Color." *Journal of Homosexuality* 59 (2): 149–85.

Government of Canada, Office of the Correctional Investigator. 2014. "A Case Study of Diversity in Corrections: The Black Inmate Experience in Federal Penitentiaries (Final Report)." Accessed August 18, 2018. https://oci-bec.gc.ca/cnt/rpt/oth-aut/oth-aut20131126-eng.aspx.

Government of Ontario, Ministry of Children and Youth Services. 2017. "A Better Way Forward: Ontario's 3-Year Anti-Racism Strategic Plan." Toronto: Queen's Printer for Ontario. Accessed August 18, 2018. https://files.ontario.ca/ar-2001_ard_report_tagged_final-s.pdf.

Grant, P. 2018. "Some 'Black Gay Fantasy': An Exploratory Study of Discrimination and Identity-Appraisal among Black Same Gender Loving Men." *Journal of Black Sexuality and Relationships* 4 (3): 49–72.

Greey, Ali. 2018. "Queer Inclusion Precludes (Black) Queer Disruption: Media Analysis of the Black Lives Matter Toronto Sit-in During Toronto Pride 2016." *Leisure Studies* 37 (6): 662–76.

Guruge, Sepali, Rachel Berman, Vappu Tyyskä, Kenise Murphy Kilbride, Isaac Woungang, Susanna Edwards, and Laurie Clune. 2009. "Implications of English Proficiency on Immigrant Women's Access to and Utilization of Health Services." *Women's Health and Urban Life* 8 (2): 21–41.

Guthrie, Jennifer. 2010. "La difficile lutte contre l'homophobia." *Journal Métro*, September 23, 2010.

Han, C. Winter, George Ayala, Jay P. Paul, Ross Boylan, Steven E. Gregorich, and Kyung-Hee Choi. 2015. "Stress and Coping with Racism and Their Role in Sexual

Risk for HIV Among African American, Asian/Pacific Islander, and Latino Men Who Have Sex with Men." *Archives of Sexual Behavior* 44 (2): 411–20.

Hawkeswood, William G. 1997. *One of the Children: Gay Black Men in Harlem.* Berkeley: University of California Press.

Hill, Marjorie J. 2013. "Is the Black Community More Homophobic? Reflections on the Intersectionality of Race, Class, Gender, Culture and Religiosity of the Perception of Homophobia in the Black Community." *Journal of Gay and Lesbian Mental Health* 17 (2): 208–14.

Howard, Philip S. S. 2018. "A Laugh for the National Project: Contemporary Canadian Blackface Humour and Its Constitution through Canadian Anti-Blackness." *Ethnicities* 18 (6): 843–68.

Huang, Yu-Te, and Lin Fang. 2019. "'Fewer but Not Weaker': Understanding the Intersectional Identities among Chinese Immigrant Young Gay Men in Toronto." *American Journal of Orthopsychiatry* 89 (1): 27–39.

Husbands, Winston C., Lydia Makoroka, Rinaldo Walcott, Barry D. Adam, Clemon George, Robert S. Remis, and Sean B. Rourke. 2013. "Black Gay Men as Sexual Subjects: Race, Racialisation and the Social Relations of Sex among Black Gay Men in Toronto." *Culture, Health and Sexuality: An International Journal for Research, Intervention and Care* 15 (4): 434–49.

Jaspal, Rusi, and Marco Cinnirella. 2010. "Coping with Potentially Incompatible Identities: Accounts of Religious, Ethnic, and Sexual Identities from British Pakistani Men Who Identify as Muslim and Gay." *British Journal of Social Psychology* 49 (4): 849–70.

Kay, Fiona M. 2019. "Social Capital, Relational Inequality Theory, and Earnings of Racial Minority Lawyers." In *Race, Identity and Work*, edited by Ethel L. Mickey and Adia Harvey Wingfield, 63–90. United Kingdom: Emerald Publishing.

Lassiter, Jonathan Mathias, Russell Brewer, and Leo Wilton. 2018. "Black Sexual Minority Men's Disclosure of Sexual Orientation is Associated with Exposure to Homonegative Religious Messages." *American Journal of Men's Health* 13 (1): 1–11.

Lazarus, Richard S., and Susan Folkman. 1984. *Stress, Appraisal, and Coping.* New York: Springer.

Lee, Edward O. J. 2018. "Tracing the Coloniality of Queer and Trans Migrations: Resituating Heterocisnormative Violence in the Global South and Encounters with Migrant Visa Ineligibility to Canada." *Refuge: Canada's Journal on Refugees* 34 (1): 60–74.

Li, Dennis H., Thomas A. Remble, Kathryn Macapagal, and Brian Mustanski. 2019. "Stigma on the Streets, Dissatisfaction in the Sheets: Is Minority Stress Associated with Decreased Sexual Functioning Among Young Men Who Have Sex with Men?" *The Journal of Sexual Medicine* 16 (2): 267–77.

Li, Peter S. 2000. "Earning Disparities between Immigrants and Native-Born Canadians." *Canadian Review of Sociology* 37 (3): 289–311.

———. 2001. "The Market Worth of Immigrants' Educational Credentials." *Canadian Public Policy/Analyse de Politiques* 27 (1): 23–38.

Livingstone, Anne-Marie, and Morton Weinfeld. 2018. "Black Families and Socio-Economic Inequalities in Canada." In *Immigration, Racial and Ethnic Studies in*

150 Years of Canada: Retrospects and Prospects, edited by Shibao Guo and Lloyd Wong, 129–51. Leiden: Brill Sense.

Lorde, Audre. 1984. *Sister Outsider: Essays and Speeches by Audre Lorde*. Freedom: The Crossing Press.

Maynard, Robyn. 2017. *Policing Black Lives: State Violence in Canada from Slavery to the Present*. Halifax, NS: Fernwood.

Mays, Vickie M., and Susan D. Cochran. 2001. "Mental Health Correlates of Perceived Discrimination among Lesbian, Gay and Bisexual Adults in the United States." *American Journal of Public Health* 91 (11): 1869–76.

McKeown, Eamonn, Simon Nelson, Jane Anderson, Nicola Low, and Jonathan Elford. 2010. "Disclosure, Discrimination and Desire: Experiences of Black and South Asian Gay Men in Britain." *Culture, Health and Sexuality: An International Journal for Research, Intervention and Care* 12 (7): 843–56.

Meyer, Ilan H. 1995. "Minority Stress and Mental Health in Gay Men." *Journal of Health and Social Behavior* 36 (1): 38–56.

———. 2003. "Prejudice, Social Stress, and Mental Health in Lesbian, Gay, and Bisexual Populations: Conceptual Issues and Research Evidence." *Psychological Bulletin* 129 (5): 674–97.

Miller, Robert L. Jr. 2007. "Legacy Denied: African American Gay Men, AIDS, and the Black Church." *Social Work* 52 (1): 51–61.

Millett, Gregorio A., William L. Jeffries IV, John L. Peterson, David J. Malebranche, Tim Lane, Stephen A. Flores, Kevin A. Fenton, Patrick A. Wilson, Riley Steiner, and Charles M. Heilig. 2012. "Common Roots: A Contextual Review of HIV Epidemics in Black Men Who Have Sex with Men Across the African Diaspora." *The Lancet* 380 (9839): 411–23.

Millett, Gregorio A., John L. Peterson, Stephen A. Flores, Trevor A. Hart, William L. Jeffries IV, Patrick A. Wilson, Sean B. Rourke, Charles M. Heilig, Jonathan Elford, Kevin A. Fenton, and Robert S. Remis. 2012. "Comparisons of Disparities and Risks of HIV Infections in Black and Other Men Who Have Sex with Men in Canada, UK, and USA: A Meta-Analysis." *The Lancet* 380 (9839): 341–48.

Mullings, Delores V., Anthony Morgan, and Heather Kere Quelleng. 2016. "Canada the Great White North Where Anti-Black Racism Thrives: Kicking Down the Doors and Exposing the Realities." *Phylon* 53 (1): 20–41.

Munro, Lauren, Robb Travers, Alex St. John, Kate Klein, Heather Hunter, David Brennan, and Chavisa Brett. 2013. "A Bed of Roses? Exploring the Experiences of LGBT Newcomer Youth Who Migrate to Toronto." *Ethnicity and Inequalities in Health and Social Care* 6 (4): 137–50.

Nakamura, Nadine, Elic Chan, and Benedikt Fischer. 2013. "'Hard to Crack': Experiences of Community Integration among First- and Second-Generation Asian MSM in Canada." *Cultural Diversity and Ethnic Minority Psychology* 19 (3): 248–56.

Nam, Boyoung, Hyun-Jin Jun, Lisa Fedina, Roma Shah, and Jordan E. DeVylder. 2019. "Sexual Orientation and Mental Health Among Adults in Four U.S. Cities." *Psychiatry Research* (273): 134–40.

Nash, Jennifer C. 2008. "Re-thinking Intersectionality." *Feminist Review* 89 (1): 1–15.

Niegocki, Kathleen L., and Stefania Ægisdóttir. 2019. "College Students' Coping and Psychological Help-Seeking Attitudes and Intentions." *Journal of Mental Health Counseling* 41 (2): 144–57.

Padgett, Deborah K. 2008. *Qualitative Methods in Social Work Research*, 2nd ed. Los Angeles: SAGE.

Patel, Sonali. 2019. "Brown Girls can't be Gay: Racism Experienced by Queer South Asian Women in the Toronto LGBTQ Community." *Journal of Lesbian Studies* 23 (3): 410–23.

Pendakur, Krishna, and Ravi Pendakur. 1998. "The Colour of Money: Earnings Differentials Across Ethnic Groups in Canada." *Canadian Journal of Economics* 31 (3): 518–48.

Poon, Maurice K.-L., Josephine P.-H. Wong, Noulmook Sutdhibhasilp, Peter T. T. Ho, and Bernard Wong. 2013. "Sexual Practices and Sex-Seeking Behaviours Among East and Southeast Asian Men Who Have Sex with Men in Toronto: Implications for HIV Prevention." *The Canadian Journal of Human Sexuality* 22 (2): 77–85.

Riggs, Marion. 2008. *Tongues Untied*. Motion Picture. Directed by Marion Riggs. USA: Strand Releasing.

Rimes, Katharine A., Sandhya Shivakumar, Greg Ussher, Dan Baker, Qazi Rahman, and Elizabeth West. 2019. "Psychosocial Factors Associated with Suicide Attempts, Ideation, and Future Risk in Lesbian, Gay, and Bisexual Youth: The Youth Chances Study." *Crisis: The Journal of Crisis Intervention and Suicide Prevention* 40 (2): 83–92.

Roy, Olivier. 2012. "The Colour of Gayness: Representation of Queers of Colour in Quebec's Gay Media." *Sexualities* 15 (2): 175–90.

Ryan, Bill. 2003. "A New Look at Homophobia and Heterosexism in Canada." Accessed August 18, 2018. https://www.rainbowhealthontario.ca/wp-content/upl oads/woocommerce_uploads/2014/08/NewLookHomophobia.pdf.

Smith, Jesús G., Maria Cristina Morales, and C. Winter, Han. 2018. "The Influence of Sexual Racism on Erotic Capital: A Systemic Racism Perspective." In *Handbook of the Sociology of Racial and Ethnic Relations,* edited by Pinar Batur and Joe R. Feagin, 389–99. New York: Springer.

Stephens, Kwame. 2014. *Dark Hard Chocolate*. Toronto: E. Ulzen/Kwame Stephens.

Stokes, Joseph P., and John L. Peterson. 1998. "Homophobia, Self-Esteem, and Risk for HIV among African American Men Who Have Sex with Men." *AIDS Education and Prevention* 10 (3): 278–92.

Szymanski, Dawn M., and Arpana Gupta. 2009. "Examining the Relationship between Multiple Internalized Oppressions and African American Lesbian, Gay, Bisexual, and Questioning Persons' Self-Esteem and Psychological Distress." *Journal of Counseling Psychology* 56 (1): 110–18.

Szymanski, Dawn M., and Rachel F. Carreta. 2019. "Religious-Based Sexual Stigma and Psychological Health: Roles of Internalization, Religious Struggle, and

Religiosity." *Journal of Homosexuality*. https://doi.org/10.1080/00918369.2019.16 01439.

Szymanski, Dawn M., Susan Kashubeck-West, and Jill Meyer 2008. "Internalized Heterosexism: Measurement, Psychosocial Correlates, and Research Directions." *The Counseling Psychologist* 36 (4): 525–74.

Torczyner, James L. 2010. "Demographic Challenges Facing the Black Community of Montréal in the 21st Century." *Montréal: McGill University School of Social Work*. Accessed August 18, 2018. https://www.mcgill.ca/mchrat/files/mchrat/Exe cutiveSummaryBlackDemograhic2010.pdf.

Walcott, Rinaldo. 2006. "Black Men in Frocks: Sexing Race in a Gay Ghetto (Toronto)." In *Claiming Space: Racialization in Canadian Cities*, edited by Cheryl Teelucksingh, 121–33. Waterloo, ON: Wilfrid Laurier University Press.

Warner, Tom. 2002. *Never Going Back: A History of Queer Activism in Canada*. Toronto: University of Toronto Press.

Williamson, Iain R. 2000. "Internalized Homophobia and Health Issues Affecting Lesbians and Gay Men." *Health Education Research* 15 (1): 97–107.

Chapter 8

The Crime of Black Male Sexuality

Tiger Mandingo and
Black Male Vulnerability

Jesús Gregorio Smith

WHEN THEIR SYSTEM WORKS AS PLANNED

In July of 2019, the doors opened to the Boonville Correctional Center and out stepped Michael "Tiger Mandingo" Johnson. He was originally set for parole on October 9, 2019, having served more than six years in prison (Johnson 2018), but then the unexpected happened, Johnson was set free twenty-five years earlier than expected (Rueb 2019). Johnson's sentence was longer than the state average for second-degree murder in Missouri (Rueb 2019). Given a thirty-year sentence, Johnson was charged and "convicted of 'recklessly infecting' one male sexual partner with HIV and exposing four others to the virus" (McCullum 2015), though this sentence was eventually reduced to ten years thanks to his public defender Samuel Buffaloe and a group of activists (Thrasher 2017). Still, the peculiarities of the case resulted in Johnson becoming the poster boy for unjust HIV criminalization laws in the United States.

Anti-Black misandry is "the cumulative assertions of Black male inferiority due to errant psychologies of lack, dispositions of deviance, or hyper-personality traits (e.g., hypersexuality, hypermasculinity) which rationalize the criminalization, phobics, and sanctioning of Black male life" (Curry 2018, 267). The case of Tiger Mandingo reveals how embedded racist anti-Black misandry is in the criminal justice system in the United States as well as the power behind Black male resistance and support for each other. Buffaloe, with help from the ACLU of Missouri and the HIV Law and Policy Center, won an appeal of the original thirty-year sentence. This was due in large part to what the Eastern District Court of Appeals of Missouri saw as a

149

"fundamentally unfair" trial because prosecutors waited until right before the end of the trial to submit a day worth of taped phone calls Johnson made from prison (Thrasher 2017). Also aiding in reducing the sentence for Johnson was a group of activists that formed The Committee for Michael Johnson's Defense (Thrasher 2017). They raised nearly $20,000 to offset legal fees. But possibly most significant to his release was the investigated journalism of gay Black male, Steven Thrasher. For BuzzFeed News, Thrasher made Johnson the subject of a three-year investigation, helping amplify his and the injustice he was served by the criminal justice system (Thrasher 2014). With the help of a major news investigation, activists, and a public defender, Johnson was able to reduce his extreme sentence and eventually walk free.

Johnson has been constructed as a unique case. A poor, Black, gay man, news stations, and media outlets have taken an interest in because of the sexual nature in the case and the ignorance of HIV from the public. Many argue that the extremity of the sentencing, and his inability to escape prison was due to a heterosexist justice system that resented Johnson's homosexuality. Evidence for this could be found in the fact that the jury selected for his case was entirely heterosexual with a majority finding homosexuality to be a choice. Others suggest it is a result of archaic and extreme HIV criminalization laws. These laws exist in most states and despite the changes in HIV treatment that render the disease as far less lethal then in the past, these laws target people with HIV as being largely responsible for the health of themselves and others (Hoppe 2015, 2013, 2014). In many ways, these arguments are true. Few, though, say that Johnson's case is the result of the criminal justice system working exactly the way it was intended to precisely *because* he is a Black male. From this perspective, Johnson's case is not an anomaly, but the direct result of a system embedded with racist anti-Black misandry. In this sense, Johnson's HIV status and sexuality all matter precisely because of how they are mapped onto a Black male body.

In this chapter, I argue that it was Johnson's Black *maleness* that was a danger and it was his Black maleness that had to be controlled, humiliated, and locked away. Society perceives Black male sexuality, whether straight or gay, as a peril to White patriarchy. Black men's bodies are understood as intimidations to White civility and control and are thus marked for imprisonment or death. In the end, Johnson's embrace of his Black maleness, as evident in his "Tiger Mandingo" persona, became his greatest risk. Johnson's story is *not* unique. It is part of a long line of salacious stories about Black men, of all sexual orientations, seen as too carless, too lustful and in the end, too dangerous to be in the outside world or even to live like Emmet Till and his supposed assault on a White woman that ended his life. Blackness became the thing in which White sexual fears and fantasies were, and still are, projected onto. The Black male body is twisted and morphed into the dichotomy racist misandry requires of it; the insatiable buck men and women desire for sexual fulfillment or the rapist and diseased pervert that harms others in his selfish pursuit of power. In essence, the Black man is not a man but a thing for the enjoyment and fears of Whites.

Over the last several years, Black Male Studies has emerged as a new paradigm through which to understand the particular genre vulnerability of Black men and boys in the United States. While there have been various feminist inspired accounts of Black masculinity, these accounts tend to claim that Black males are oppressed by racism but nonetheless privileged by their maleness (Hooks 2004; Crenshaw 2010). Because I am interested in the sexual vulnerability of the racialized maleness in the Tiger Mandingo persona, Curry's Man-Not thesis is the most appropriate. The Man-Not is a theoretical formulation that attempts to capture the reality of Black maleness in an anti-Black world (Curry 2017, 7). Accordingly, the Man-Not denies Black manhood and provides only the possibility of animality and savagery. In common with this comprehension of Black maleness is the fear of Black men, that influenced lynching's and institutionalized "police violence, ostracism, and incarceration" (Curry 2017, 7). It is here where the vulnerability of Black males exists. Scholar Tommy Curry coined the term "Black male vulnerability" (BMV) to reflect this precarious situation many Black boys and men find themselves in. BMV is meant to "capture the disadvantages Black males endure compared with other groups, the erasure of Black males actual lived experiences from theory, and the violence and death Black males suffer in society" (Curry 2017, 29).

Like the subordinate male target hypothesis introduced by Jim Sidanius and Felicia Pratto (2000), Curry's theorization of BMV suggests that because Black men *are* (alien-subordinate-racialized) males, they are targeted for imprisonment and extinction to protect the racial endogamy of White supremacist societies. I use this concept as an aid in analyzing the case of Michael Johnson. Reading Michael Johnson as a Man-Not, who is vulnerable not only to racism but specific misandric aggressions tied to his Black maleness allows us to more clearly see how previous theories, current laws, and people of all races reject the humanity of Black men. Said differently, BMV offers a conceptual coherence to the gratuitous violence that organizes and manages the lives of Black males in the United States. Rather than interpreting Black males as pathologically oriented toward violence against others or oppressed (by race) privileged (by gender) subjects, Curry's paradigm illuminates how it is Black maleness that puts their lives at risk every day.

Following in the footsteps of Brandon Andrew Robinson and his work on racial preferences as the new racism (Robinson 2015), I also apply what sociologist Roderick Ferguson calls a queer of color critique (QCC) to Johnson's story (Ferguson 2004). Defined as an interrogation of "social formations as the intersections of race, gender, sexuality, and class" (Ferguson 2004, 149), QCC sees categories of analysis as mutually informing cultural products. In this sense, how society comes to assume heterosexuality in all social relations or what from this point on shall be referred to as heteronormativity (Warner 2017) is not only by rejecting lesbian, gay, bisexual, and trans (LGBT) people, but also by seeing people of color's sexuality as anomalous and "queer" as well (Ferguson 2004).

In what follows, I lay out the historical and theoretical work that guides this chapter. Under the axioms of intersectionality, the historical impact that slavery and colonization had in shaping the lives of Black men have been relatively unexplored. Over the last several years, scholars from multiple fields (Curry 2017; Foster 2011; Woodard 2014) have shown that slavery and colonization involved various forms of sexual torture, rape, and erotic consumption. Black men were both penetrated by White men and made to penetrate by White women. Whereas previous intersectional and Black feminist interventions have highlighted the myth of the Black rapist, it has consistently missed the erotic logics intertwined with racialized maleness that have been active throughout the nineteenth and twentieth centuries concerning Black males. Despite the rich historiographical interventions made over the last decade, intersectionality has not incorporated these findings and in many ways remains blind to this aspect of Black male oppression. It is within this new historiography that takes seriously the history of Black men as raped and rapist that I explore the life of Johnson, from his humble beginnings, to his embrace of his sexuality, and his college wrestling days. Then, I follow this up by exploring some of the accusations against him by a gay White male. By examining his choice of language on the stand, I argue that the gay White man reinforced a heterosexual logic regarding sex roles and gender performance that further dehumanized Johnson and increased his BMV. After that, I examine the court case, from the jury selection, to the use of Johnson's penis in the court room, to give weight to the Man-Not thesis. I then end with a discussion of how gender theories and intersectionality have failed to understand the plight of Black males and the racist misandry that upholds systemic racism.

This chapter is indebted to the rigorous investigative work of journalist Steven Thrasher. Thrasher is a gay Black man who was named Journalist of the Year 2012 by the National Lesbian and Gay Journalists Association. His work has appeared in the *New York Times*, the *Village Voice*, *Rolling Stone*, and *Newsweek*. The courts refused to make the transcripts available to the public and did not allow Thrasher, who at the time, was covering the case for BuzzFeed News, to record the proceedings. He, none the less, took copious notes that he used for his investigative pieces, along with several interviews with numerous people, including jurors, teammates, lawyers, and Johnsons himself (Thrasher 2015). This chapter contributes to Black Male Studies by building off the laborious journalism of Thrasher's multiple pieces for BuzzFeed News and by adding a sociological analysis grounded in theory and history. It also highlights the role of homophobia and HIV within the criminalization of the Black male body. In this sense, I situate the life of Johnson and his trial in a larger context of anti-Black misandry.

Of note, I understand the complexities of identity. That is, I acknowledge that Black men are not a monolith, and that there is a plethora of masculinities encompassed in varying bodies, such as those of queer and transman. For the purposes of this analysis, I associate maleness with the perception of a group of people seeming to have a penis and testicles, among other physical attributes. This perception does not mean that these men in fact have such organs, but that the assumed "privileges" bestowed on these men is often associated with such crude biological distinctions. Along with this is also the perception of a hegemonic masculinity (Jewkes et al. 2015), one dominant over the others. As such, I use man and maleness interchangeably throughout the chapter and refer to hegemonic masculinity as the gendered performance associated with this maleness.

A BRIEF OVERVIEW OF RACE, GENDER, AND SEXUALITY FOR BLACK MEN

Colonization transformed gender dynamics in the United States. European settlers believed in the great chain of being, or a hierarchical structure that situated a male God (the Father) at the top, White people below that, different non-White people after that, and Black and Jewish people at the bottom of that chain (Feagin 2006). This belief system at the time associated masculinity not with gender but with race. The masculine races of man, who were the White European people because they were closest in the chain to God, were civilized, intelligent, and capable of gender division. Other races of man, such as Blacks, were understood to be feminine, that is, guided by emotion, less intelligent, and impulsive (Curry 2018). In this sense, the feminine race needed the masculine race to guide them, making way for their enslavement.

This understanding was further legitimized by ethnologist of the day, who believed the Black race was incapable of gender differentials because they could not evolve beyond savagery to need gender distinctions (Curry 2018). Evidence of Black inferiority was said to be found in the size of the Black penis. Its largeness was evidence that Blacks reasoned through impulsiveness, and that Black men were, by design, rapists who needed slavery and White men to control them (Curry 2017, 2018). Slavery then was a natural offshoot of the great chain of being, providing a natural order to the races. Slavery also helped White colonizers develop modern ideas about gender.

As Whites occupied the lands of Indigenous and Black populations, they "imposed sexual homogeneity" on these groups by means of "sexually specific segregationist logics" (Curry 2018, 243). In this sense, this helped to create distance between Black men so as to protect the womanhood of White women while allowing White men access to native women (Curry 2018).

For Black males, they were understood as being unable to control their sexual impulse and thought to desire White women and whiteness above all else (Curry 2017; Hill Collins 2004). Frazier, in a study of Black men in the South, argued that White desire for Black males was akin to incest and forbidden. The repression of this desire instead resulted in a projection of White sexual inhibitions onto Black bodies (Frazier 1927). Thus, the buck stereotype was created to rationalize Black male sexuality. As Curry points out, the buck has been "the American trope of Black male sexuality since slavery" (Curry 2017, 331). The stereotype allowed for White male fears of Black males to be inscribed onto the Black male body. By contrasting themselves against the buck, White men could characterize themselves as the noble protectors of White womanhood and motivated lynching groups to rise and attack Black communities (Daniels 1997). Therefore, the film *Birth of Nation* was so powerful because it tapped into White fears of Black male sexuality by depicting a White actor in Black face pretending to be a Black slave and pursuing a White woman with the desire to rape her. The film was so popular that it birthed the modern-day Klu Klux Klan and empowered other Whites to rise up, organize and terrorize Black communities (Feagin 2006). By using White womanhood as a symbol of innocence and vulnerability, White men were able to unite the White race against the threat of Black people and their Black men (Daniels 1997).

At the time Black sexuality was being mischaracterized and manipulated by Whites, queer sexuality was also being created. Black sexual behavior was understood as out of the norm or queer precisely because it diverged from the Puritanical way. Similarly, controlling images like the Welfare Queen or Black woman who is husbandless and relies on the government for assistance and the Black male buck who sleeps with numerous women were used to uphold heterosexual, monogamous, and discreet sexuality as the norm (Ferguson 2004). Simultaneously, "homosexuality" was the term used by scientist to describe sexual behaviors that were also dubbed abnormal, in these cases same-sex desire. Given the work of Sommerville as she analyzed the historical development of race and sexuality against the color-line, it is clear how the scientific racism of the time arose alongside the development of the medicalizing and institutionalizing of homosexuality (Sommerville 2000). This coincidence was not an accident, but purposeful, as the science at the time aimed to keep Blacks and Whites from engaging in sex that could result in mixed race infants, children viewed as the epitome of queer. In both scenarios, Black sexuality is by virtue queer and homosexuality is raced, making the two very much intertwined.

THE MAN-NOT THESIS VERSUS INTERSECTIONALITY

Largely, intersectionality has become the dominant theory used to investigate the connections between gender, race, and sexuality (Parent, DeBlaere, and Moradi 2013; Haile et al. 2014; Brennan et al. 2013). Kimberley Crenshaw coined intersectionality as a means to illuminate the lived experiences of Black women, thus the intersection of sex and race being both sexed as a woman and raced as Black (Crenshaw 1989). Since the coining of the term, the theory has been added to, enabling a multilevel analysis along lines of race, class, gender, and sexuality. It is especially noted for centering the voices of Black women predominantly, allowing Black women to self-define and provide self-valuation, examining the interlocking nature of oppression and highlight the importance of Black women's culture (Hill Collins 1986). Nonetheless, the theory is limited in the way it understands Black men.

Typically, intersectionality sees Black men as privileged based on their gender as males in a patriarchal society. When Black men do suffer inequality, it is along lines of race or sexual orientation (C. Han 2007; Loiacano 1989). For instance, Black men are thought to have male privilege when Black women don't in employment, housing, and education (Butler 2013). Similarly, Black straight men are privileged over Black gay men because of their heterosexuality. In tracing the uses of intersectionality theory, Crenshaw highlighted the work of Butler, who argued that Black male exceptionalism assumed Black men did worse than Black women and as such responded with programs aimed at correcting this disparity (Carbado et al. 2013; Butler 2013). Arguing that "empirical data does not support the claim that Black males are burdened more than Black females," the paper went on to suggest that programs with the aim of supporting Black men did so at the expense of Black women (Butler 2013, 485). This called for a decentering of Black maleness so as to not perpetuate patriarchy. As such, intersectionality did not, in and of itself, provide the theoretical space for Black men to be valued and understood as men. Nonetheless, intersectionality exploded in popularity and has become the main theoretical framework for analyzing race, gender, and sexuality.

To fill in the gap left by intersectionality regarding Black men's lived experiences, Curry conceptualized the Man-Not and BMV. Where intersectionality saw Black men privileged by gender and marginalized by race, Curry argues that this understanding of gender is ahistorical (Curry 2017). Because of the history of colonization and slavery that Africans have been subjected to, he argues that gender dynamics in the Black community developed differently than that of Whites. As previously mentioned, Black men and women were characterized under colonial control and racist logic, as closer to Apes and savages, incapable of achieving a civility that demanded gender distinction. Thus, Black slave women and men toiled in the fields and both Black men and women were raped by slave masters (Curry 2017). The social order of the White male patriarch could only be maintained if Black men were not seen as men. Therefore, Black men needed to be controlled, raped, abused, imprisoned, and murdered at higher rates than Black women, to maintain that social order (Woodard 2014). By affirming this history, Curry explains how Black men are actually vulnerable to White patriarchy and not privileged within it (Curry 2017). By using White womanhood as a symbol of susceptibility, White men could inspire all White people to unite against the Black man. This symbol becomes important on the stand during Johnson's trial.

Research shows that the appearance of being a cisgender, heterosexual Black male falls in line with traditional White racist stereotypes about Black criminality. This stereotype seems to be captured in a mesomorphic body type and cis-hetero gender performance (Trautner, Kwan, and Savage 2013). Studies looking at body type and orientation imply that perceived obesity and homosexuality result in a softening of the image of the scary, angry, and violent Black man (Trautner, Kwan, and Savage 2013; Pedulla 2014). Research examining obesity and gender suggests that obesity in men results in them being perceived as less masculine (Hebl and Turchin 2005). This explains why "the overweight Black man challenges, even neutralizes, our association of Black men with thugs, rapists, gangsters, and criminals" which in turn suggest that "overweight Black men are no longer seen as a threat to the social order" (Trautner, Kwan, and Savage 2013, 443). A physically fit Black man, in contrast, would embody the sort of masculinity associated with negative stereotypes about Black males. In fact, Johnson's physicality arguably played an important role in how he was later perceived on the stand and by other White men as images of his body were shown to the jury.

While heterosexuality is privileged in a heteronormative society, this is complicated in the context of Black men of all sexual orientations. The stereotype of the threatening Black man can be challenged in the work place, for instance, by the appearance of homosexuality. Sociologist Pedulla conducted experimental research using a national probability sample of 231 White individuals. He asked them questions about an imaginary potential employee regarding starting salaries and likelihood to break workplace rules, steal from work, and make female coworkers feel uncomfortable (Pedulla 2014). Straight Black men were more likely to be perceived as threatening while gay Black men were not. Gay Black men were also seen as more feminine than gay White men, given the highest salaries and considered the most valuable employees overall (Pedulla 2014). In essence, the stereotype of the effeminate gay man countered the Black heterosexual stereotype of being dangerous and threatening. This adds to the understanding of why Johnson's embrace of the Tiger Mandingo identity, the muscular Black slave fighter, was so threatening. By embracing the Black sexual stereotype and taking on a straight appearing persona, Johnson became the Black threat to White patriarchy all Black men are always assumed to be.

NEW DIRECTIONS FOR RESEARCHING BLACK MALES

Historically, Black people were not conceptualized as fully human. Slavery resulted in Black people being more egalitarian than Whites, a factor that continues to this day. This is important because theoretical analysis applied to the gender dynamics among Blacks must keep this in mind. Intersectionality, which posits that Black men have privilege based on their maleness, distorts this history. Currently, intersectionality is the most commonly used theoretical orientation in analyzing race, gender, and sexuality. The Man-Not thesis is a stronger theoretical grounding for analyzing the experiences of Black males. According to this theory, Black men are the greatest physical threats to White patriarchy. As such, the goal is to control, incarcerate, and murder Black men. With the Man-Not thesis, Black men are understood as savages and beasts of burden. Being a male makes Blacks particularly vulnerable because of the racist beliefs projected onto Black men and their bodies. Thus, BMV illuminates the pathway for investigating Black men. By using BMV, it becomes clearer how Black men are seen by Whites not based only on their race and sexuality but also on their gender.

In the case of Michael Johnson, he was stripped off of his humanity, seen as nothing more than a large Black penis with HIV. While he was valuable to his college as a college athlete and wrestler and his sexual partners as "Tiger Mandingo," his embrace of his Blackness robbed him of his humanity. Blackness is seen as diseased and animal-like. Therefore, HIV status was precisely more threatening because it is exactly what is understood about Black maleness in general. He was vulnerable to state-sanctioned imprisonment precisely because he was a HIV-positive Black gay male.

THE CASE OF THE TIGER MANDINGO

Michael "Tiger Mandingo" Johnson is a Black gay male. Johnson, who suffers from dyslexia, used sports to propel him to success. Like many young Black boys and men, sports are viewed as way out of poverty and

an opportunity for success (May 2008). Wrestling was especially important for Johnson because his dyslexia wouldn't hinder his opportunities
through the sport (Thrasher 2014). He took on the name "Tiger" because of
his "lucky Tiger shirt" (Thrasher 2014). His skill in wrestling was so great
that he was recruited to compete in college. Johnson wrestled for Lindenwood University in Missouri. Johnson was also a gay man who embraced
his sexuality privately but did not center it in his public identity. This was
because of his Christian background and because his single mother asked
for it out of fear of him being harmed. Also, because of the close contact
and aggression in wrestling, Johnson feared he would not be accepted in
wrestling if he was open about his sexuality. As a result, he took on a
more "straight acting" performance that protected him in wrestling while
making him appear more desirable to gay men (Eguchi 2009; Sánchez and
Vilain 2012).

Nonetheless, Johnson explored his sexuality in Indianapolis. There he
made friends with other Black men, joined the House of Mizrahi, and com-
peted in "ballroom drag house ball competitions" (Thrasher 2014). For Johnson, being in a house meant having a home with other Black gay men who
understood what it meant to be gay. In an interview for Buzzfeed, Johnson,
who never knew his father, stated, "Being in a house, you got a mother and a
father" (Thrasher 2014). Balls are pageants in which LGBT people compete
for local fame and trophies. These Balls have a long history in Black communities, where many working-class, Black and Latinx people compete in
different categories as both a mockery of upper-class White society and a
celebration of their own identities. In video footage from YouTube, Johnson
can be seen competing in the "butch queen" category. This category is for
gay men whose demeanor is "butch" or hypermasculine and whose bodies
resemble those of body builders (Thrasher 2014).

During these times, a friend of Johnson suggested he take on the moniker
"Mandingo" to go along with his nickname Tiger. Thus, "Tiger Mandingo"
was born. Johnson took on the name "Tiger Mandingo" because he believed it
came from "a brave black slave fighter" who "got the title of Mandingo" and
because he "'heard about the definition of Mandingo,' which he said, 'came
from Africa, and in Africa, big dick, Mandingo!'" In actuality, Mandingo
comes from the violent 1975 blaxploitation film *Mandingo*, where a West
African Mandingo slave named Mede fights other slaves to the death for his
slave master. He is rewarded for his successful matches by being allowed
to impregnate the other female slaves. In the film, the slave master's wife,
Blanche, sexually desired Mede. When Mede resisted her come-ons, she
threatened to cry rape. She in turn rapes Mede, forcing him to comply or lose
his life. In the end, she becomes impregnated by Mede, resulting in her, the
baby's and Mede's violent end. Nonetheless, Johnson took on the person of

"Tiger Mandingo," the Black, African slave fighter with the large endowment and he was very popular in gay dating sites as a result. Here again, Johnson, while being a gay man, embraces a gender performance more in line with straight Black men, inadvertently increasing his BMV.

Johnson's masculine or "butch" performance allowed him to fit in with his other straight, White peers in wrestling in the 91 percent White suburb of St. Charles. In an interview with Thrasher for Buzzfeed in 2014, a fellow wrestling student who remained anonymous stated that everyone thought he was straight because "he was easily approachable to girls and stuff—and some of the guys were like, 'What the fuck? This guy is taking all the girls!'" Clearly, Johnson's masculine gender performance read as a straight Black male on campus. Once it was discovered that Johnson was gay and HIV positive, he was scapegoated as the sole person to bring the threat of HIV to the campus (Thrasher 2014). In another interview with Thrasher, another student, Marvin Bird III, likened Johnson to Hitler but "worse" for putting people on their death bead because of HIV. The student also said that he feared "get(ting) with a girl" because he was afraid that she could have been with Johnson and, as a result, could be putting him at risk for HIV (Thrasher 2014).

The case of Tiger Mandingo is complex and compelling because of what it reveals not only about race and sexuality, but also about gender performance, class, and disability. While in a White patriarchal family, the home is headed by a straight man with a wife and kids, Johnson's case ruptures this notion with a single Black mother and his chosen gay house with a gay Black "mother and father." Johnson also chose to take on the name "Mandingo" despite its racist history in the United States. "Tiger Mandingo" for Johnson was about a Black African slave fighter who won titles and whose "big dick" was a testament to the manhood denied him in a slave society. This pro-Black male persona also increased his vulnerability in an anti-Black world. While Johnson's real, single Black mother and gay Black family provide protection, love, and respect for him, his embrace of a butch and "straight presenting" persona made him the type of gay man White men desired for sex, but the type of Black man White society feared, increasing his BMV. Even as a gay man, Johnson's Black maleness was seen as a threat to heterosexual White male patriarchy. Like the film *Mandingo*, Johnson's perceived Black masculinity meant straight White women might desire him the way Blanche desired Mede. This could result in queer sexuality, mixed race children, and the degenerating of the White race. Where HIV was understood as a "poor" thing, mostly impacting Blacks, Johnson was now seen as the person who brought the threat of infection to Lindenwood and made straight White men fear hooking up with the woman who might be defiled from being with "Tiger Mandingo."

THE CASE OF THE ACCUSER DYLAN KING-LEMONS

According to the Man-Not thesis, it is a society that only sees Black men and boys as dangerous and savage that renders them vulnerable to imprisonment and death. While Black men are devalued by all people, regardless of race, they are especially at risk at the hands of Whites. This is amplified by White men who find Black men a threat to patriarchy and a risk to White women. Where intersectionality envisions White women as being vulnerable to patriarchy because they are women (Crenshaw 2010), it does not extend that analysis of gender and sex to White women's roles in the harming of Black men. Instead, it sees White women's threat over Black men as a race issue. Conversely, the Man-Not thesis illuminates how gender plays a role in the subjugation of Black men and boys. The case of Johnson and his accusers makes this abundantly clear. The accusers and the prosecution, seeing Johnson's erotic worth, engage willingly in sex with him but once one of the White males became infected with HIV, they reduced him to the sexually racist stereotypes assigned to all Black men. Johnson was no longer the desirable Black "Mandingo," but a threat, a diseased man, and a danger to all, thus representing the contradictions signified in the Black phallus.

Phallicism, according to Curry, refers to "the condition by which males of a subordinated racialized or ethnicized group are simultaneously imagined to be a sexual threat" and "sexually desirous by the fantasies or fetishes of the dominant racial group" (Curry 2018). We see this consistently in the case of Johnson who is desired for his body, a body epitomized with his large, Black "Mandingo" penis. Yet, the same body became the cause of the spread of disease and the embodiment of recklessness and danger to Whites. Through the concept of phallicism, we can better understand the "contradiction between the description of racialized males" under oppressive governments and ruling classes and "their hyper-sexualization as objects of desire, possession, and want" (Curry 2018, 265).

While six people took the stand, four were White and two were Black (Thrasher 2013, 2015). The testimony that sealed Johnson's fate came from one White male. According to Thrasher's investigative report, a "young blonde man" named Dylan King-Lemons first pressed charges against Johnson (Thrasher 2015). This resulted in the persecution seeking other alleged victims and resulted in the six men who would eventually stand trial. King-Lemons testimony proved to be the most powerful because he was infected with HIV. King-Lemons, also a student at the same university as Johnson, took the stand and described his relationship with Johnson. King-Lemons testified that Johnson told him several lies, including that the condoms were too small for his large penis and that he was HIV negative. King-Lemon also stated that he only had sex with Johnson that year and as such, knew it was

Johnson who infected him. Of note is the way King-Lemons described his sex role with Johnson. He said on the stand that he agreed to condom-less sex with Johnson in the "traditional female role" (Thrasher 2015). King-Lemons stated that because of not having health insurance, he was unable to cover his medical bills, resulting in him declaring bankruptcy. Still, King-Lemons was able to move on after his time with Johnson and that he was currently "engaged to marry a man who is HIV-negative and that they have never had sex—not even with condoms—out of fear of transmission" (Thrasher 2015).

King-Lemons testimony on the stand contradicted his and his best friend's statements to the police (Thrasher 2015). In the police report, King-Lemons could "'narrow it down between two people,' Johnson and another sexual partner, a woman" (Thrasher 2015). King-Lemons best friend stated that there was possibly a third person and that all his partners were "very promiscuous" (Thrasher 2015). Further investigation by BuzzFeed News could not find evidence supporting the claim that King-Lemons filed for bankruptcy. While Johnson was made out to be a liar on the stand, King-Lemons discrepancies were never under scrutiny. He very much was left unscathed despite the falsehoods presented in his narrative. Like Emmet Till and his White accusers who later admitted to lying and getting away with it, Johnson's accuser walked away without being held to bear for his dishonesty.

Several points are of importance here. BMV makes clear that Johnson is particularly vulnerable because Black males are distrustful, dangerous, and diseased. The history that erases the manhood of Black males and essentializes them into the rapist and savage still resonates here. King-Lemon painted a picture of a deceptive Black man who seduced him with his large Black penis, infected him with HIV and stole money from him, in the form of $100,000 of medical debt, and now is slowly stealing his life through HIV as well. This description on the stand tapped into all the fears White people have of Blacks. Johnson is the Black male that must be enslaved (via prison), or he will rape White women or White men in the "female position." He is the Black man that, like the film *Birth of a Nation*, will seduce Whites, pillage them of their resources like he pillaged King-Lemons of his funds, and then slowly but surely kill them like he is slowly killing King-Lemons with HIV.

With his reference to Johnson's large penis, it played into the fears Whites have of Blacks using their penises to spread their Blackness. This fear harkens back to White men's worry of Black men impregnating White women and tainting the White race with mongrel blood, of which the littlest amount can make a civilized man become bestial. Again, this highlights the Man-Not thesis by pointing out how the terror around Black male sexuality resonated in the minds and fears of Whites. White women were the carriers of the White race, through their traditional sex role on bottom. If Black men impregnated White women, this risked infecting the entire White race with more than mixed-race children, this would degenerate the race into savagery. In King-Lemons choice to use this language, he implicitly tapped into this history for the majority White women and White men who made up the jury. The White man is supposed to protect the White women from such infection and even though King-Lemons himself is a man, his "traditional female role" elicits the sympathy and understanding of heterosexual White men and women, reifying heteronormativity and the heterosexist structure (Ferguson 2004). This demonstrates that even in the case of men who have sex with men, Black men of all orientations are a threat. This is because the same logic that undergirds the hatred of straight Black men also threatens gay Black men. Similarly, King-Lemons reference to being engaged to marry and abstinence from sex reify heteronormative sexuality as monogamous, White and chase while his "traditional female role" reinforces the idea of sex being between one man and one woman. In this sense, the way that gay sexual communities can reinforce heterosexist practices are rooted in White patriarchal notions of gender roles for men and women, further supporting Ferguson's argument that racism is a heterosexist enterprise (Ferguson 2004).

THE CASE OF THE JURY, THE
PROSECUTION, AND THE TRIAL

According to Thrasher, there was a pool of fifty-one potential jurors. Most of the potential jurors were older, heterosexual, and White. Several of them believed homosexuality was a preference and not an orientation while a small fraction supposed that homosexuality was not sinful (Thrasher 2015). In describing homosexuality, some potential jurors used the words "sick," "wrong," and "immoral" (Thrasher 2015). None of the jurors revealed being HIV positive themselves though they did have a trust in police and a persecution system. For example, they all "believed HIV-positive people who do not tell their sexual partners that they have the virus should be prosecuted" (Thrasher 2015). The final jury was composed of entirely HIV negative and straight people. Four older White men, seven older White women, and one Black retired nurse made up the racial composition of the jury.

Taken together, these points reveal several significant factors. By having an almost exclusively White potential jury pool and final jury, the language that the accusers would later use would resonate in an anti-Black misandry way. For instance, with seven White women on the jury, using ideas of Black masculinity, Black physical endowments, and disease taps subconsciously into the fear Whites have of Black sexuality, especially White women. Similarly, with several White men on the jury and the history of White men using the criminal justice system to police Black communities and Black men, this increased Johnson's BMV. As Curry points out, Black women are not immune to ideas about Black male savagery either (Curry 2017). An example of this comes from the down-low phenomenon. Aside from gay Black men, Black women disproportionately held the burden of HIV infections in the Black community (Fenton 2009). The reason for this was long believed to be because seemingly straight Black men with Black wives and girlfriends would sleep with gay men "on the down low" so as not to be discovered. This behavior resulted in HIV infections that rapidly spread to Black women. While some bisexual White men also conducted themselves in similar fashion, the behavior became associated with Black men (Robinson and Vidal-Ortiz 2013). The spread of HIV in the Black community was then laid at the feet of Black men who were accused of being deceptive in their behavior and homophobic for failing to embrace their gay identities and instead engaging in risky, dangerous behavior that harmed the Black community (Fenton 2009). The reality though is that drug injections and promiscuous unprotected sex among heterosexuals accounted for HIV infections in a vastly larger rate than bisexual activity among Black men. That is, the Center for Disease Control and Prevention found that the "down low" was a myth. Nonetheless, Black men were blamed. Thus, having an older Black woman on the jury did not assure Johnson a jury of peers because many anti-Black misandry beliefs permeate the very communities that should be protective of Black men.

Using a QCC (Ferguson 2014), it becomes apparent how Whiteness reifies heteronormative society. No peers on the jury were Black men, none were gay, and all were HIV negative (Thrasher 2015). This is important because in White gay communities, access to HIV treatment and advancements in HIV medication are well documented (Calabrese and Underhill 2015). In fact, so many men are on Pre-exposure Prophylaxis (PrEP) in general that the Trump Administration announced a plan to eradicate HIV by 2025 (Johnson 2019). This plan was made because of how far society has come in being able to treat HIV, rendering a once lethal infection to something so manageable that people infected with it can live basically normal lifespans. Pre-exposure Prophylaxis or (PrEP), a-one-a-day pill that HIV negative people can take to protect against HIV, is so successful, that once on the pill, chances of infection are nearly nonexistent (Bone 2017). Similarly, evidence suggests that HIV-positive men with undetectable HIV viral loads cannot pass HIV to their partners through unprotected anal sex (Rodger et al. 2016). In essence, HIV is no longer a threat to life as it once was and access to medications is more readily available depending on the community.

Still, gay Black men are less likely to have access to and be on PrEP and less likely to know their HIV status (C. S. Han et al. 2014). They are also more likely to be targeted by HIV laws for recklessly infecting partners (Lawless 2017). Thus, spreading HIV comes to be understood as a low-income

Black defect and a reflection of Black pathologies. Take, for instance, a comment from one of Johnson's fellow wrestlers, where he asks, "Why do 'people around the poverty line . . . continually choose to infect one another [with HIV]? It's because they get selfish pleasure.'" In this comment and in the way the jury trusts the criminal justice system, we see how race and sexuality mutually reinforce each other. Straight, White sexuality is seen as normal, healthy, and legal, while gay, Black sexuality in seen as queer, sick, illegal, and irresponsible. Wrapped up in a Black male body, Black sexuality is now lethal and must be kept away from society.

Philip Groenweghe, the White, male prosecutor on the case, effectively utilized sexually racist stereotypes of Black men during the trial (Thrasher 2015). In the police reports, several of the other accusers described Johnson's penis as "'very large,' 'too tight' for condoms, and too big to fit in a mouth 'due to his large size'" (Thrasher 2015). Groenweghe pounced on these statements and weaponized them in court, reducing Johnson to nothing more than a large, Black phallus (Curry 2018). He showed jurors images of it on the stand, taking stills from erotic tapes Johnson and a consenting partner made. During sentencing, Groenweghe mentioned that there were more videos similar to the film stills, from several men who came forward but didn't press charges (Thrasher 2015). One such person was a man who didn't press charges out of fear his wife would find out. Despite not pressing charges and not being on the stand, Groenweghe made sure to highlight the case of the man who could have been exposed to HIV from Johnson and then exposed his wife, infecting someone who didn't even know Johnson and wasn't even gay. Thus, by locking Johnson up for a long time, Groenweghe argued the jury was in fact protecting the health of the public (Thrasher 2015). This was an effective strategy as it resulted in Johnson receiving a thirty-year sentence. Many of the months Johnson would unfortunately spend in solitary confinement, with no contact with other human beings.

Groenweghe accentuated the fears people of all races have of Black males: that they are dangerous, diseased, and sexually reckless. His performance in the court room best exemplified the Man-Not thesis and phallicism, transforming Johnson from a college athlete into an HIV-positive Black phallus. The emphasis on public health also demonstrates the need to contain Black sexuality, so as not to let it harm, infect, or impregnate others. Johnson's humanity as a person was divorced from him not only because of his race and sexuality but explicitly because he was and is male. The Man-Not thesis suggests that this is the reality for Black males in an anti-Black world. It is this reality that makes Black men vulnerable to the criminal justice system and state sanctioned death. Johnson had no previous criminal record, had a college degree, and was described as gentle and kind by friends and family. Still, this could not go against the tide of racist anti-Black misandry that is perpetuated against Black men.

Using a QCC reveals how once again, even in the context of same-sex encounters, heteronormativity is reified. Groenweghe's choice to end his stand by emphasizing how a straight wife might become infected with HIV because of Johnson demonstrates how heterosexuality becomes privileged at the expense of blackness and gayness. Thanks in part to the "down-low," the myth has been used to cast Black men as the sexual boogeyman to hetero-sexual relationships. The Black penis symbolizes the power to spread via sex, blackness, and gayness, infecting the White patriarchal design. The White woman consistently represents the body that carries the Black seed, either via mixed-race children or HIV-riddled bodies. By tapping into these beliefs, Johnson was made vulnerable to a racist system, devalued as less of a man but more of a threat, and his threat was handled through a heterosexist criminal justice system that viewed race and sexuality as a danger to the well-being of society at large.

TIGER MANDINGO AND THE NEED
FOR BLACK MALE STUDIES

Michael "Tiger Mandingo" Johnson is the personification of the Man-Not and BMV. Seen not as a human being but a buck, a phallus, and threat, Johnson had to be controlled and thus locked away in prison where even there he was further hid away from society via solitary confinement. The very same system that saw Johnson as a danger to the White male patriarchy also reified heteronormativity via the judicial system. That is, heterosexism was reproduced in the jury selection, in the way the accusers described their sexual infection at the hands of Johnsons and in the way the prosecution described Johnson as not just a threat to other men who have sex with men, but as a threat to straight White women and in connection, their men. The same system designed to protect White womanhood functioned precisely as it should by locking away Johnson for much of his young life. Never once were the accuser, whom themselves were described as having "promiscuous" life-styles, held accountable for their own health. That is because Johnson was the perfect threat, a mixture of race, sexuality, and health rolled into one male.

Many factors increased Johnson's vulnerability, including his sexual orien-tation which simultaneously was constructed as pathological alongside race, and his HIV status which has been understood as a gay related disease, and the result of working-class sexual proclivities. This chapter focused primarily on gender and sex as wielding significant explanatory power in the case of Johnson. That is, I argued that Johnson being a Black male was enough to be envisioned as a threat to White male patriarchy. Where varying forms of research might suggest that a more effeminate performance and noticeably queer presentation might have, in the eyes of Whites, lessened this view of the Black man as a threat, Johnson embraced his blackness and incorporated Black masculinity in his persona as exemplified with his persona, *Tiger Mandingo*. Johnson's Black maleness provided him family in the form of his drag ball, protection in the form of his mother, and success in competitions as a butch male. It simultaneously increased his risk of imprisonment and social death at the hands of White men and women. To Whites, Johnson was already a diseased nonman. He was nothing more than a phallus, therefore the pleasure of Whites and the fear of Whites

Research is starting to highlight the disparities in racial sentencing for HIV. HIV criminalization laws in Michigan and Tennessee, for example, have been found to disproportionately target working-class Black communities (Hoppe 2015; Bone 2017). This should not be a surprise. This is the way the criminal justice system was devised, to target those bodies seen as dangers to the health and well-being of society. Black people and Black men specifically have always embodied that danger. The Man-Not thesis helps us to understand how Black people have come to be constructed as such, and how this construction leaves Black males vulnerable precisely because they are males. Past gender theories have left Black men out of the equation. Intersectionality often only understands Black men's oppression in terms of race. In this narrow view, the humanity of Black male life is diminished. The trial of Michael Johnson demonstrates why we need theory that centers Black male narratives and their vulnerabilities.

Mused Magazine published an open letter signed by 115 gay Black men. These men, including "thought leaders, academics, HIV policy experts, writers and more" (McCullum 2015), stated:

> HIV criminalization laws unfairly impact Black people and stigmatize people living with HIV. HIV criminalization laws push people living with HIV further and further away from HIV treatment and care and make HIV prevention efforts more difficult. As Black gay men, we are deeply impacted by HIV; and these laws harm us and damage our relationships and communities.
>
> HIV should be treated as a public health issue not as a criminal one. Legally requiring disclosure privileges the lives of White people not living with HIV over Black people who are living with HIV.
>
> These laws feed into stereotypes that assume Black gay men are irresponsible and hypersexual. For you, your accusers saw your Black and masculine body as a site of ultimate sexual pleasure, until they had to deal with you as a whole

person. At that moment you became a problem and were disposable to them. . . . We care about you—your life matters. HIV is not a crime and you should not be in prison.

One of the signatures on the letter was from Atlanta-based activist Charles Stephens. In an interview for *The Nation* focused on Johnson, Stephens said the "dominant media narrative presented him as a Monster. . . . Part of the desire was to humanize Michael Johnson" (McCullum 2015). Much like Sam Buffaloe, the ACLU of Missouri, the HIV Law and Policy Center and The Committee for Michael Johnson's Defense before them, this group of Black men came to the aid of Johnson. Yet, their support was something entirely different. It was a validation of Johnson's Black humanity. Therefore, a Black Male Studies is so imperative. It is a field that can begin to more fully theorize not just the death and imprisonment of Black men, which is so often done, but the love, support, and life Black men provide each other.

Michael Johnson walked out of prison in the summer of 2019. He was welcomed by the few loved ones who stood by his side. Thrasher himself, who worked tirelessly to tell Johnson's story and get his truth out to the public, was there to support him, gay Black man to gay Black man. Black Male Studies provides scholars and activists a new opportunity to understand the powerful and positive ways Black males support each other, care for each other, and fight for each other in a way that hasn't been available prior. From this perspective, Black men understand the plight they face from a racist society, regardless of orientation, that targets them precisely because they are men. They understand how society deems them dangerous based on their gender, how society sees them as diseased and violent, and they support each other in ways that other theories failed to comprehend. From this perspective, Black men write letters of support to each other, see each other as fully realized men, and like Thrasher, dedicate themselves to fighting to free each other.

Johnson was locked away from society, often thrown in solitary confinement, and closed off from humanity. Now, Johnson is free. Johnson, and the many Black men of all orientations like him, deserves a community that can encompass him entirely, that can allow him to embrace his gayness, his Blackness, and just as importantly, his maleness. He deserves respect and love. He deserves a home, like the one he had before, the House of Mizrahi. Yet, this time, a larger house where all people see him entirely. While several people did many things to get Johnson liberated, in the end, it was his own bravery in telling his story to Thrasher, that fundamentally set him free. Johnson chose the name "Mandingo" because he thought Mandingo was "a brave black slave fighter." In the end, it was Michael Johnson who was the brave, Black fighter.

REFERENCES

Bone, Brigid. 2017. "Whose Responsibility Is It to PrEP for Safe Sex? Archaic HIV Criminalization and Modern Medicine." *Washington University Journal of Law & Policy* 53: 319–40.

Brennan, David J., Kenta Asakura, Clemon George, Peter A. Newman, Sulaimon Giwa, Trevor A. Hart, Rusty Souleymanov, and Gerardo Betancourt. 2013. "'Never Reflected Anywhere': Body Image among Ethnoracialized Gay and Bisexual Men." *Body Image* 10 (3): 389–98. https://doi.org/10.1016/j.bodyim.2013.03.006.

Butler, Paul D. 2013. "Black Male Exceptionalism? The Problems and Potential of Black Male-Focused Interventions." *Du Bois Review* 10 (2): 485–511. http://scholarship.law.georgetown.edu/facpub/1314%5Cnhttp://ssrn.com/abstract=2388981%5Cnhttp://scholarship.law.georgetown.edu/facpub.

Calabrese, Sarah K., and Kristen Underhill. 2015. "How Stigma Surrounding the Use of HIV Preexposure Prophylaxis Undermines Prevention and Pleasure: A Call to Destigmatize 'Truvada Whores.'" *American Journal of Public Health* 105 (10): 1960–64. https://doi.org/10.2105/AJPH.2015.302816.

Carbado, Devon W., Kimberlé Williams Crenshaw, Vickie M. Mays, and Barbara Tomlinson. 2013. "Intersectionality: Mapping the Movements of a Theory." *Du Bois Review: Social Science Research on Race* 10 (02): 303–12. https://doi.org/10.1017/S1742058X13000349.

Crenshaw, Kimberle W. 2010. "Close Encounters of Three Kinds: O Teaching Dominance Feminism and Intersectionality." *Tulsa Law Review* 46 (1): 151–89.

Crenshaw, Kimberlé Williams. 1989. "Demarginalizing the Intersection of Race and Sex: A Black Feminist Critique of Antidiscrimination Doctrine, Feminist Theory and Antiracist Politics." *University of Chicago Legal Forum* 1 (1): 139–68. https://doi.org/10.3868/s050-004-015-0003-8.

Curry, Tommy J. 2017. *The Man-Not: Race, Class, Genre, and the Dilemmas of Black Manhood*. Philadelphia: Temple University Press.

Curry, Tommy J. 2017. "This Nigger's Broken: Hyper-Masculinity, the Buck, and the Role of Physical Disability in White Anxiety Toward the Black Male Body." *Journal of Social Philosophy* 48 (3): 321–43. https://doi.org/10.1111/josp.12193.

Curry, Thomas. 2018. "Killing Boogeymen: Phallicism and the Misandric Mischaracterizations of Black Males in Theory." *Res Philosophica* 95 (2): 235–72. https://doi.org/10.11612/resphil.1612.

Daniels, Jessie. 1997. *White Lies: Race, Class, Gender and Sexuality in White Supremacist Discourse*. New York: Routledge.

Eguchi, Shinsuke. 2009. "Negotiating Hegemonic Masculinity: The Rhetorical Strategy of 'Straight-Acting' among Gay Men." *Journal of Intercultural Communication Research* 38 (3): 193–209. https://doi.org/10.1080/17475759.2009.508892.

Feagin, Joe R. 2006. *Systemic Racism: A Theory of Oppression*. New York: Routledge.

Fenton, Kevin. 2009. "Myth: HIV/AIDS Rate Among Black Women Traced To 'Down Low' Black Men." By Michael Martin. NPR Tell Me More. October 28. https://www.npr.org/templates/story/story.php?storyId=114237523.

Ferguson, Roderick A. 2004. *Aberrations in Black: Toward a Queer of Color Critique*. Minneapolis: University of Minnesota Press.

Frazier, Edward Franklin. 1927. "The Pathology of Race Prejudice." *The Forum* 77 (6): 856–62.

Haile, Rahwa, Tawandra L. Rowell-Cunsolo, Edith A. Parker, Mark B. Padilla, and Nathan B. Hansen. 2014. "An Empirical Test of Racial/Ethnic Differences in Perceived Racism and Affiliation with the Gay Community: Implications for HIV Risk." *Journal of Social Issues* 70 (2): 342–59. https://doi.org/10.1111/josi.12063.

Han, Chong-suk. 2007. "They Don't Want To Cruise Your Type: Gay Men of Color and the Racial Politics of Exclusion." *Social Identities* 13 (1): 51–67. https://doi.org/10.1080/13504630601163379.

Han, Chong Suk, George Ayala, Jay P. Paul, Ross Boylan, Steven E. Gregorich, and Kyung Hee Choi. 2014. "Stress and Coping with Racism and Their Role in Sexual Risk for HIV Among African American, Asian/Pacific Islander, and Latino Men Who Have Sex with Men." *Archives of Sexual Behavior* 44 (2): 411–20. https://doi.org/10.1007/s10508-014-0331-1.

Hebl, Michelle R, and Julie M Turchin. 2005. "The Stigma of Obesity: What About Men?" *Basic and Applied Social Psychology* 27 (3): 267–75. https://doi.org/10.1207/s15324834basp2703.

Hill Collins, Patricia. 1986. "Learning from the Outsider Within: The Sociological Significance of Black Feminist Thought." *Social Problems* 33 (6): S14–32. https://doi.org/10.3868/s050-004-015-0003-8.

Hill Collins, Patricia. 2004. *Black Sexual Politics: African Americans, Gender, and the New Racism*. New York: Routledge.

Hooks, Bell. 2004. *The Will to Change: Men, Masculinity, and Love*. New York: Atria Books.

Hoppe, Trevor. 2013. "Controlling Sex in the Name of 'Public Health.'" *Social Problems* 60 (1): 27–49. https://doi.org/10.1525/sp.2013.60.1.27.

Hoppe, Trevor. 2014. "From Sickness to Badness: The Criminalization of HIV in Michigan." *Social Science and Medicine* 101: 139–47. https://doi.org/10.1016/j.socscimed.2013.11.007.

Hoppe, Trevor Alexander. 2015. "Disparate Risks of Conviction under Michigan's Felony HIV Disclosure Law: An Observational Analysis of Convictions and HIV Diagnoses, 1992–2010." *Punishment and Society* 17 (1): 73–93. https://doi.org/10.1177/1462474514561711.

Jewkes, Rachel, Robert Morrell, Jeff Hearn, Emma Lundqvist, David Blackbeard, Graham Lindegger, Michael Quayle, Yandisa Sikweyiya, and Lucas Gottzén. 2015. "Hegemonic Masculinity: Combining Theory and Practice in Gender Interventions." *Culture, Health and Sexuality* 17: 96–111. https://doi.org/10.1080/13691058.2015.1085094.

Johnson, George M. "Will the Parole of Tiger Mandingo Shift Views on HIV Criminalization?" *The HIV Equal Online Magazine*, April 20, 2018. http://www.hive

qual.org/homepage/will-the-parole-of-tiger-mandingo-shift-views-on-hiv-crim
inalization.

Johnson, Steven Ross. "Trump's Call to End HIV Epidemic Hindered By His Administration's Policies." *Modern HealthCare*, February 9th, 2019. https://www.mod
ernhealthcare.com/article/20190209/NEWS/190209931/trump-s-call-to-end-hiv-e
pidemic-hindered-by-his-administration-s-policies.

Lawless, Joseph F. 2017. "The Deceptive Fermata of HIV-Criminalization Law:
Rereading the Case of 'Tiger Mandingo' Through the Juridico-Affective." *Colum-
bia Journal of Gender and Law* 35 (1): 117–59.

Loiacano, Darryl K. 1989. "Gay Identity Issues among Black Americans: Racism,
Homophobia, and the Need for Validation." *Journal of Counseling Psychology* 68
(1): 21–24.

May, Reuben Buford. 2008. *Living through the Hoop: High School Basketball, Race,
and the American Dream*. New York: New York University Press.

McCullom, Rod. "The Reckless Prosecution of "Tiger Mandingo."" *The Nation*, May
29, 2015. https://www.thenation.com/article/reckless-prosecution-tiger-mandingo/.

Parent, Mike C., Cirleen DeBlaere, and Bonnie Moradi. 2013. "Approaches to
Research on Intersectionality: Perspectives on Gender, LGBT, and Racial/Ethnic
Identities." *Sex Roles* 68 (11–12). https://doi.org/10.1007/s11199-013-0283-2.

Pedulla, David S. 2014. "The Positive Consequences of Negative Stereotypes." *Social
Psychology Quarterly* 77 (1): 75–94. https://doi.org/10.1177/0190272513506229.

Pratto, Felicia, James H. Liu, Shana Levin, Jim Sidanius, Margaret Shih, Hagit
Bachrach, and Peter Hegarty. 2000. "Social Dominance Orientation and the Legiti-
mization of Inequality Across Cultures." *Journal of Cross-Cultural Psychology* 31
(3): 369–409. doi:10.1177/0022022100031003005.

Robinson, Brandon Andrew. 2015. "'Personal Preference' as the New Racism: Gay
Desire and Racial Cleansing in Cyberspace." *Sociology of Race and Ethnicity* 1 (2):
317–30. https://doi.org/10.1177/2332649214546870.

Robinson, Brandon Andrew, and Salvador Vidal-Ortiz. 2013. "Displacing the Dominant 'Down Low' Discourse: Deviance, Same-Sex Desire, and Craigslist.Org."
Deviant Behavior 34 (3): 224–41. https://doi.org/10.1080/01639625.2012.726174.

Rodger, Alison J, Valentina Cambiano, Tina Bruun, Pietro Vernazza, Simon Collins, Jan van Lunzen, Giulio Maria Corbelli, et al. 2016. "Sexual Activity Without
Condoms and Risk of HIV Transmission in Serodifferent Couples When the
HIV-Positive Partner Is Using Suppressive Antiretroviral Therapy." *Jama* 316 (2):
171–81. https://doi.org/10.1001/jama.2016.5148.

Rueb, Emily S. "He Emerged From Prison a Potent Symbol of H.I.V. Criminalization." *The New York Times*, July 14, 2019. https://www.nytimes.com/2019/07/14/
us/michael-johnson-hiv-prison.html?fbclid=IwAR3FSzShJfVDfCocfuKes0Nk2F
KHzcBFdZqN0kA7U8yf3Qo89ZpWnRajfYU.

Sánchez, Francisco J., and Eric Vilain. 2012. "'Straight-Acting Gays': The Relationship between Masculine Consciousness, Anti-Effeminacy, and Negative Gay
Identity." *Archives of Sexual Behavior* 41 (1): 111–19. https://doi.org/10.1007/s
10508-012-9912-z.

Somerville, Siobhan B. 2000. *Queering the Color Line: Race and the Invention of Homosexuality in American Culture*. Durham, NC: Duke University Press.

Thomas A. Foster. 2011. "The Sexual Abuse of Black Men under American Slavery." *Journal of the History of Sexuality* 20 (3): 445–64. https://doi.org/15353605.

Thrasher, Stephen. "How College Wrestling Star 'Tiger Mandingo' Became An HIV Scapegoat." *Buzzfeed News*, July 7, 2014. https://www.buzzfeed.com/steventhrasher/how-college-wrestling-star-tiger-mandingo-became-an-hiv-scap?utm_term=.sbmb5bn1L#.lka3q3Lm0.

Thrasher, Stephen. "A Black Body on Trial: The Conviction of HIV Positive 'Tiger Mandingo.'" *Buzzfeed News*, November 30, 2015. https://www.buzzfeednews.com/article/steventhrasher/a-black-body-on-trial-the-conviction-of-hiv-positive-tiger-m#.pw5XjXbL1.

Thrasher, Stephen. "'Tiger Mandingo,' Convicted of Spreading HIV, Wins A Major Victory." *Buzzfeed News*, April 5, 2017. https://www.buzzfeednews.com/article/steventhrasher/tiger-mandingo-convicted-of-spreading-hiv-wins-a-major#.buDzlzGJd.

Trautner, Mary Nell, Samantha Kwan, and Scott V. Savage. 2013. "Masculinity, Competence, and Health: The Influence of Weight and Race on Social Perceptions of Men." *Men and Masculinities* 16 (4): 432–51. https://doi.org/10.1177/1097184X13502667.

Warner, Michael. 2017. "Fear of a Queer Plant?" *GLQ: A Journal of Lesbian and Gay Studies* 23 (3): 419–29. https://doi.org/10.1215/10642684-3818477.

Woodard, Vincent. 2014. *The Delectable Negro: Human Consumption and Homoeroticism with U.S. Slave Culture*. New York: New York University Press.

Chapter 9

Experiencing Queer Spaces as a Transgender Man of Color

Mario I. Suárez

I was born and raised in a small town on the Texas-México border known as Eagle Pass, Texas. I was also assigned sex of female at birth. I say this for several reasons. Up until the end of my undergraduate studies at the University of Texas at Austin, my best friends were always gay men of color. When I first came out to my family, three of my best friends who were gay cisgender men of color drove the almost four-hour trip with me to Eagle Pass for a couple of hours, only to come back to Austin that same night. As I began exploring my sexuality and gender identity, I found that I felt safe in queer spaces. Living in Austin, Texas, at that time meant that most of these queer spaces were predominantly white[1], cis, and homonormative. Before transitioning to male, I was perceived as a cisgender lesbian, and therefore, gay men would not bother me much when we would go out to gay nightclubs in Austin. I remember dancing all night at clubs like Rain, Oilcan Harry's, and Rainbow Cattle Company on 4th and 5th Street, often by myself or with my friends. All that changed once I started my transition and began "passing" as a cisgender male for many different reasons.

This chapter explores not only how my particular experience with transitioning as a transgender man of color has shaped the way I navigate queer spaces, but also how I feel am perceived in predominantly queer spaces. I am informed partially by Gloria Anzaldúa's notion of shape-shifting as a means to better explain the spaces I come in and out of as a means of survival (Anzaldúa 2015). How is it that I am perceived now as co-opting the very space that made me feel safe as a young adult? Why is it that I do not feel welcome anymore in the community I am a part of?

GENDER, SEX, AND SEXUALITY

There seems to be a conflation of the terms "gender" and "sex" and how those intersect (or not) with sexuality. While the call for chapters for this very anthology focused specifically on experiences of "how gay men of color come to make sense of race and sexuality and how their experiences reflect what it means to be raced and sexed in America" (Smith and Han 2016), I am not a gay man. Depending on the chronological timestamp of my life, at one point I identified as a lesbian. I now identify as a transgender heterosexual man. I am certainly not the first to mention how society conflates sex and gender, nor the inherent problems with the sex and gender binary (Butler 2006; Fausto-Sterling 2000, 2016, 2017).

Definitions of gender and sex vary, so I will operationalize it as I understand it. Sex is assigned to us at birth. At the time this chapter was written, in most countries and states up until a while ago, there have mainly been two options for sex that the doctor assigns: male or female. Recently, several states have adopted the option to add a third marker to a child's certificate (Grinberg 2018; Newman 2018; Parks 2017; Sopelsa 2018). Genitalia is often the "go-to" for a doctor to determine the sex of the baby, which makes it challenging to identify for intersex children born with ambiguous genitalia or chromosomal abnormalities (Money and Ehrhardt 1972; Suarez, Lai Hing, and Slattery 2018). That being said, there are many who still use the term "gender," when they mean sex. Gender, or more specifically, gender identity, requires a certain level of consciousness or complex understanding from an individual, as well as the vocabulary and awareness of one's own identity. For example, while we have categories of male and female for sex, for young ones, they may identify their gender as boy or girl, and later on as man or woman, and all other identities in between. In 0.6 percent of the cases, according to the University of California at Los Angeles Williams Institute, sex assigned at birth and gender do not align, as about 1.4 million people in the United States identify as transgender (Flores et al. 2016). This in it of itself is an impressive amount of people, not counting those who do not identify within the binary or those who identify as both genders. For instance, as a child, my understanding and vocabulary of anyone outside of the binary was very limited due to non-exposure to other trans people. I knew deep inside that I did not meet the "standards" for what it meant to be a girl, but also, society told me I was not a boy because I did not have the genitalia to be recognized as such. I want to make it very clear that I am not trying to oversimplify the definitions between gender and sex merely to vocabulary and exposure, because then that could make it seem like I somehow became influenced by someone or something. I was not. I already knew who I was. I just did not have the vocabulary to express who I knew I was, in large part due to the standards set by society.

An added challenge is that sexual orientation complicates the topic further. Sexual orientation refers to a set of behaviors (or lack thereof) that include attraction, arousal, desire, and self-identification, among others (Bogaert 2012; Durso and Gates 2013; Laumann et al. 1994), and who an individual performs (or not) those behaviors with. The conflation between gender, sex, and sexual orientation happens when someone may think they know a person simply for the sex assigned at birth and who they were attracted to. For example, those who knew me before I transitioned and "claim" that I am a lesbian because I was born in a female body and am married to a cisgender woman have found it difficult to see me now as a transgender heterosexual male. To me, that shows a lack of awareness and/or information regarding the differences already mentioned, as small as they may be. The organization known as Trans Student Educational Resources (www.transstudent.org) has an excellent graphic organizer that visually represents all of these much better than I can likely explain. When called upon to give presentations about gender and sexuality around the university, I often use "The Gender Unicorn" shown on figure 9.1 as a way to have the audience capture the small differences between each. While there is another graphic that others use, I find that this one is different as it more explicitly captures nonbinary and intersex individuals, apart from other controversial reasons for not using the other graphic.

Anzaldúa's (2015) Epistemology

My understanding of gender and sexuality has been greatly expanded thanks to Anzaldúa's theories of *autohistoria-teoría*, *nos/otrxs*[2] *(*Anzaldúa 2015), and Nepantla (Keating 2006), along with her seminal book *Borderlands/La Frontera* (Anzaldúa 1997). Therefore, a short discussion of her theories in relation to my experiences as a transgender man with regards to queer spaces merits mentioning.

Anzaldúa's (2015) notion of *autohistoria-teoría* and the theory of *nos/otrxs* shift our perspective from the individual (*autohistoria-teoría*) to the collective and intersections that connect us with one another (*nos/otrxs*). Anzaldúa alludes to the importance of using our individual his/her/they/stories to relate to each other and be able to find connections between us. Until we can break out of these metaphorical cages that exist between us, we cannot become *nosotrxs* (without the slash). Anzaldúa theorizes that *nepantlerxs*[3], or intermediaries who are able to live in different worlds simultaneously will ultimately serve as social justice warriors that will help decolonize power structures and help create bridges between seemingly different worlds (Anzaldúa 2015). Anzaldúa (2015) writes:

The Gender Unicorn

Gender Identity
- Female/Woman/Girl
- Male/Man/Boy
- Other Gender(s)

Gender Expression
- Feminine
- Masculine
- Other

Sex Assigned at Birth
Female   Male   Other/Intersex

Physically Attracted to
- Women
- Men
- Other Gender(s)

Emotionally Attracted to
- Women
- Men
- Other Gender(s)

To learn more, go to:
www.transstudent.org/gender

Design by Landyn Pan and Anna Moore

Figure 9.1 The Gender Unicorn. *Source*: Trans Student Educational Resources. 2014. The Gender Unicorn. http://www.transstudent.org/gender/.

The imagination's power to shift (what I call la naguala) enables la *nepantlerx* (emphasis and change mine) to flow from one identity or theoretical position to another. When we shift geographical or social positions, another identity may spring into being. Roots grow and ground us in a particular moment or reality if we're available to the emotional currents among those present. In a particular situation you become a person with particular identifiable features; in another situation, you metamorphose into another type with other distinguishing characteristics. Like train way stations, our "self" stops for a few minutes or a few years on el viaje de la vida; each way station expands the self or creates another self. Nepantleras constantly articulate and redefine identity positions to include what has previously been excluded or has not been part of consensual reality. (Anzaldúa 2015, 83–84)

In defining *nos/otrxs* and *nosotrxs,* Anzaldúa writes:

We all of us find ourselves in the position of being simultaneously both insider and outsider. The Spanish word "nosotrxs" means "us." I see this word with a slash (rajadura) between "nos" (us) and "otrxs" (others), and use it to theorize my identity narrative of "nos/otrxs." La rajadura gives us a third point of view, a perspective from the cracks and a way to reconfigure ourselves as subjects outside binary oppositions, outside existing dominant relations. By disrupting binary oppositions that reinforce relations of subordination and dominance, nos/otras suggests a position of being simultaneously insider/outside, internal/external exile. (Anzaldúa 2015, 79)

For Anzaldúa, it is this disruption caused not being able to be packaged in a neat little box or fitting in either world that helps create this third perspective, what I refer to as a *callo*, or a callus in Spanish. Like a *callo*, this third perspective that Nepantlerxs have to be inside and outside of different worlds is only created from past injuries or scars. In my particular experience, that involves the insider/outsider perspective as a member of the LGBTQ community before transition, but being perceived as a cisgender outsider post-transition, especially when occupying that space with my partner, a cisgender woman. My hope is that being able to communicate my experience contributes to an awareness of situations that may not be previously thought of by cisgender folks.

As Anzaldúa wrote in reference to this awareness, "When we adapt to cambio (change), we develop a new set of terms to identify with, new definitions of our academic disciplines, and la facultad (the ability) to accommodate mutually exclusive, discontinuous, and inconsistent worlds" (Anzaldúa 2015, 79–81). In my opinion, though not all of us have the same exact experiences, we all experience situations that expand our ability to understand the epistemological and ontological. In doing so, our "facultad" leads us toward being *nosotrxs* without the slash.

CISGENDER PERCEPTION

I have been in transition for the last greater part of a decade. By transition, I really mean the process of transforming my body, both hormonally and externally in appearance. I started doing more research about the process of obtaining hormones from a medical doctor around my sophomore year of college. I tried to keep it a secret, mostly because I did not want family to find out, or friends of family. Aside from the fact that I knew I did not have the money to pay for all the medical and therapy expenses out-of-pocket, social transition was extremely difficult for me as a Mexican American who was socialized as a female. I started therapy right after obtaining my first salaried job as a high-school mathematics teacher. My employer's medical insurance did not cover "elective" procedures, which included therapy or other medically necessary treatments for transgender people. There are many sources that estimate hormonal and medical transition in the hundreds of thousands of dollars (Bradford 2015; Jackson 2015; Yang 2018). I was lucky enough to know folks in Austin, Texas, who told me where to find a sliding-scale center. That place and my therapist quite literally saved my life. Even then, it took about six or seven years before I legally transitioned through court, and I just had a mastectomy two summers ago. In it of itself, top surgery is expensive in the United States, so I opted to go to Ciudad Juárez, Chihuahua, México, with a world-class surgeon with whom I paid considerably less than what I would have paid in the United States. I try to be as honest about the process as I can be without disclosing so much that it leaves no privacy for trans people like me. However, I do want to disclose enough so that those who are not familiar with the process catch a glimpse into how tremendously difficult and challenging it is. Not only have I lost people whom I thought were friends, I have also spent almost a decade researching medical doctors, therapists, lawyers, and other folks who can help me become the person on the outside who I know I am, especially in the eyes of the law. It is draining, and at times, I thought about giving up in every sense of the word. I write this, precisely because I vehemently push back on anyone who considers the decisions to transition (or not) for a transgender person a "choice." As I have told peers, if it was a choice for me, I would choose to spend the tens of thousands of dollars that I have spent thus far on other things. Moreover, though I am a person of color, in spite of not having the funds readily available as others that I know who have transitioned, I am still privileged because I have been lucky enough to have access to resources and information that is not common for people of color. The National Center for Transgender Equality (James et al. 2016) estimates that my trans siblings who are people of color are three times more likely to live in poverty, four times more likely to be unemployed, and five times more likely to have health challenges than the national average. In addition, transgender people of color are statistically more disadvantaged with regards to health care, such as being denied medical coverage for medically necessary procedures and medicines, being misgendered by health care professionals (James et al. 2016). Personally, I do not know anyone who would *choose* to be a transgender person if it was not a life-or-death decision, myself included, especially knowing those statistics. Fast forward to over a decade later, my bare face is now occupied by a short beard. My voice has deepened. While I remain the same height (I am 5 feet 1 inch tall), the androgynous pieces of clothing I wore back in college have been replaced with ties, slacks, blazers, and button-down long-sleeve shirts. Unless I *out*[4] myself, I am pretty much read as a cisgender male, even in queer spaces and among trans people. This is not meant as a bragging right. Instead, it is meant as a way to show how society often only thinks in binaries. However, this paints a challenge for me, as I am tasked with negotiating my passing as a means of survival, or outing myself as a way to "validate" my ability to belong or be in a queer space. When I go to a queer space, for example, though folks do not always mention it, I have an internal voice that tells me that I am taking up space as a cisgender-perceived man. Walking into a gay club now may sometimes mean it is assumed I am a gay cisgender man if I go by myself with friends. That is further complicated when I am in queer spaces with my partner. The understanding is that we are perceived as a cisgender, heterosexual couple, and again, though people do not say anything, I am conscious of the space we take up. This is an interesting conundrum, because early on in my transition, queer spaces shaped my understanding of my gender and sexuality and I sought refuge in these spaces because I felt safe. I find it difficult now to go into a gay bar with my partner, because if we show to much public displays of attention, we get looks that show attendees' hesitation with having us occupy that space. I am very much aware that queer spaces are places where many LGBTQ folks seek refuge and as a perceived cis guy, I want to respect that space. However, I am left not belonging in a fully cisgender space anymore because of how I was socialized, and not fully queer space because of my "passing" privilege.

TOWARD A PRO-AMBIGUITY CONSCIOUSNESS

I want to ponder for a little bit about the structures that society has set in place regarding dichotomies. It seems that either an individual can safely be male or female, gay or straight, transgender or cisgender. Rarely are there opportunities to engage in discussion about all the identities that lie in that in-between space—Nepantla, as Anzaldúa would call it (Anzaldúa 2015), or even the borderlands at an earlier time (Anzaldúa 1997). In reference to *nepantlerxs* Anzaldúa:

> As intermediaries between varios mundos, las *nepantlerxs* "speak in tongues"— grasp the thoughts, emotions, languages, and perspectives associated with varying individual and cultural positions. By living on the slash between "us" and "others," la *nepantlerxs* cut through isolated selfhood's barbed-wire fence. They trouble the *nos/otrxs* division, questioning the subject's privilege, confronting our own personal desconocimentos, and challenging the other's marginal status. Las *nepantlerxs* recognize that we're all complicit in the existing power structures, that we must deal with conflictive as well as connectionist relations within and among various groups. Ensuring that our acts not mirror or replicate the oppression and dominant power structures we seek to dismantle, las nepantleras upset our cultures' foundations and disturb the concepts structuring their realities. (Anzaldúa 2015, 83)

Additionally, others have called for us to move past the gender and sexuality binary in society (Fausto-Sterling 2000). Fausto-Sterling writes, "It is possible to envision a new ethic of medical treatment, one that permits ambiguity to thrive, rooted in a culture that has moved beyond gender hierarchies" (Fausto-Sterling 2000, 101). However, I strongly believe that this societal shift cannot happen with the amount of division that comes from within our communities, whether it is the gay/lesbian/trans split, the Black/white split, or any other division that exists. Our society is in need of more shapeshifters, or *nepantlerxs*, who can help bridge these communities. We exist everywhere, though we are not always visible, often for very valid reasons mentioned before, namely, the murders of trans women of color at disproportionately high rates, fear of losing our jobs, fear of losing the little legal rights we have—the list goes on. Anzaldúa spoke to this: "Today, the division between the majority of "us" and "them" is still intact. We are *nos/otrxs*. This country does not want to acknowledge its walls—its limits, the places some people are stopped or stop themselves, the lines they're not allowed to cross. Hopefully, sometime in the future we may become nosotras without the slash (Anzaldúa 2015, 81)." My belief is that as a society, we need to embrace ambiguity in order to become *nostrxs* without the slash.

CONCLUSION

This chapter sets out to provide an insight into my specific experience as a transgender man of color and how challenging it has been to navigate queer spaces after being perceived as a cisgender heterosexual man. I used several of Gloria Anzaldúa's theories (1997, 2015) to conceptualize those experiences. Additionally, I tried to clarify minute differences between the terms "sex" and "gender," which tend to be conflated.

NOTES

1. I use the term "white" without capitalizing it as a way to decenter whiteness throughout the chapter.
2. Though Anzaldúa (2015) uses the term "nos/otras," I use the term "nos/otrxs" throughout the chapter to decenter the hetero- and cis-normative nature of the Spanish language.
3. Similarly with *nos/otrxs,* Anzaldúa (2015) uses the term "nepantlera," which I change to *nepantlerx* throughout the chapter to decenter the hetero- and cis-normative nature of the Spanish language.

4. The act of being *out* refers to what is known, colloquially, as being "out of the closet." Specifically, it often entails disclosing either sexuality or gender identity to friends, family, coworkers, supervisors, and so on and can be a very traumatic and dangerous experience for many of us. Particularly for transgender women of color, that anxiety may increase as a result of the disproportionately high number of trans women of color who are violently murdered every year (Allen 2018; Pitofsky 2018).

REFERENCES

Allen, Samantha. 2018. "2018 is Shaping Up to Be Another Terrible Year for Trans Murders." *The Daily Beast*, July 8, 2018. https://www.thedailybeast.com/2018-is-shaping-up-to-be-another-terrible-year-for-trans-murders.

Anzaldúa, Gloria. 1997. *Borderlands/La Frontera: The New Mestiza*, 2nd ed. San Francisco, CA: Aunt Lute Books.

———. 2015. *Light in the Dark/Luz en lo Oscuro: Rewriting Identity, Spirituality, Reality*. Durham, NC: Duke University Press.

Bogaert, Anthony F. 2012. *Understanding Asexuality*. Lanham, MD: Rowman & Littlefield Publishers.

Bradford, Elle. 2015. "You Won't Believe How Much It Costs to Be Transgender in America." *Teen Vogue*, November 25, 2015. https://www.teenvogue.com/story/transgender-operations-hormone-therapy-costs.

Butler, Judith. 2006. *Gender Trouble: Feminism and the Subversion of Identity*, 2nd ed. New York: Routledge.

Durso, Laura E., and Gary J. Gates. 2013. "Best Practices: Collecting and Analyzing Data on Sexual Minorities." In *International Handbook on the Demography of Sexuality*, edited by Amanda K. Baumle, 21–42. New York: Springer.

Fausto-Sterling, Anne. 2000. *Sexing the Body: Gender Politics and the Construction of Sexuality*. New York: Basic Books.

———. 2016. "Pink and Blue." Boston Review: A Political and Literary Forum, August 9, 2016. http://bostonreview.net/wonders/anne-fausto-sterling-trans-kids.

———. 2017. "Against Dichotomy". *Evolutionary Studies in Imaginative Culture* 1 (1): 63–66.

Flores, Andrew R., Jody L. Herman, Gary Gates, and Taylor N. T. Brown. 2016. *How Many Adults Identify as Transgender in the United States*. Los Angeles, California: The Williams Institute.

Grinberg, Emanuella. 2018. "Washington State Offers Third Gender Option on Birth Certificates." *CNN*, January 4, 2018. https://www.cnn.com/2018/01/04/health/washington-state-gender-neutral-birth-certificate/index.html.

Jackson, Alyssa. 2015. "The High Cost of Being Transgender." *CNN*, July 31, 2015. https://www.cnn.com/2015/07/31/health/transgender-costs-irpt/index.html.

James, Sandy E., Jody L. Herman, Susan Rankin, Mara Keisling, Lisa Mottet, and Ma'ayan Anafi. 2016. *The Report of the 2015 U. S. Transgender Survey*. Washington, DC: National Center for Transgender Equality.

Keating, AnaLouise. 2006. "From Borderlands and New Mestizos to Nepantlas and Nepantleras: Anzaldúan Theories for Social Change." *Human Architecture: Journal of the Sociology of Self-Knowledge* 4 (3): 5–16.

Laumann, Edward O., John H. Gagnon, Robert T. Michael, and Stuart Michaels. 1994. *The Social Organization of Sexuality: Sexual Practices in the United States.* Chicago: University of Chicago Press.

Luna, Taryn. 2017. "California Legally Recognizes Third Gender Option." *The Sacramento Bee,* October 16, 2017. https://www.sacbee.com/news/politics-governme nt/capitol-alert/article179062891.html.

Money, John, and Anke A. Ehrhardt. 1972. *Man & Woman, Boy & Girl: The Differentiation and Dimorphism of Gender Identity from Conception to Maturity.* Baltimore, MD: Johns Hopkins University Press.

Newman, Andy. 2018. "Male, Female or 'X': The Push for a Third Choice on Official Forms." *New York Times,* September 27, 2018. https://www.nytimes.com/2018/0 9/27/nyregion/gender-neutral-birth-certificate.html.

Parks, Casey. 2017. "Oregon Becomes First State to Allow Nonbinary on Driver's License." *The Oregonian,* June 15, 2017. https://www.oregonlive.com/portland /index.ssf/2017/06/oregon_becomes_first_state_to.html#incart_river_home_pop.

Pitofsky, Marina. 2018. "'Epidemic of violence': 2018 is Worst for Deadly Assaults Against Transgender Americans." *USA Today*, September 26, 2018. https://ww w.usatoday.com/story/news/2018/09/26/2018-deadliest-year-transgender-deaths -violence/1378001002/.

Smith, Jesús Gregorio, and C. Winter Han. 2016. *Explorations on the Intersection of Race and Sexuality (Call for Chapters).*

Sopelsa, Brooke. 2018. "Gender 'X': New York City to Add Third Gender Option to Birth Certificates." *NBC News,* September 12, 2018. https://www.nbcnews.com/ feature/nbc-out/gender-x-new-york-city-add-third-gender-option-birth-n909021.

Suárez, Mario. I., Ebony Lai Hing, and Patrick Slattery. 2018. "A Brief Exercise in Currere and Bathroom Bills." *Journal of Curriculum and Pedagogy* 15 (3): 1–6. doi: 10.1080/15505170.2018.1525449.

Trans Student Educational Resources. 2014. "The Gender Unicorn." http://www. transstudent.org/gender/.

Yang, Linda. 2018. "The True Cost of Transitioning Without Health Insurance." *Broadly Vice,* April 23, 2018. https://broadly.vice.com/en_us/article/7xdaax/cost -transitioning-without-health-insurance-trump-trans-healthcare-rollback.

Conclusion

C. Winter Han

In June, rainbow flags dot the landscape of gay America like happy poppies seeking sunlight. Once relegated to dark corners of urban gay enclaves, the flag has now come to adorn bumper stickers, window dressings, T-shirts, and even government buildings. Given this proliferation, it is all too easy to imagine tourists wandering the storefronts of San Francisco's Castro district and buying rainbow imprinted mugs or key fobs as souvenirs to share with their friends back home, wherever that home might be. Some read the widespread acceptance of the flag, the quintessential symbol of gay pride, as a testament to the rising acceptance of gay men and women in mainstream America. Like gayness itself, the flag not only has come to have a place in strictly defined gay spaces, but has found a level of prominence in the public arena. As the protest chant goes, "We're Queer, We're Here," and now "here" is everywhere.

Taking a cue from Jesse Jackson, contemporary gay leaders like to promote the rainbow flag as being representative of the diversity that is allegedly found in the gay community. For example, in an article titled "The Rainbow Flag" by Steven W. Anderson which appeared in *GAZE Magazine* in 1993, the author wrote that "the most colorful of our symbols is the Rainbow Flag, and its rainbow of colors—red, orange, yellow, green, blue, and purple—represents the diversity of our community." This line, now repeated in a number of websites and pamphlets, has come to be taken as gospel among gay rights leaders who want to paint gay history with a politically correct brush of inclusion. Yet, the origins of the flag betray a much less racially inclusive history.

Rather than a symbol of diversity, the flag is widely reputed to have been inspired by the Judy Garland song "Somewhere Over the Rainbow," an homage to Kansas, one of the whitest places in America. Rather than an ode to diversity, the song represents Dorothy's deeply held desire to return "home," far away from OZ, which she finds not so wonderful after all given all of the multiformity of characters she encounters there who are starkly different from those found in her white bread world. Rather than embrace the diversity that she finds in Oz, Dorothy desperately seeks to escape it. In fact, none of the meaning assigned to the original colors of the flag by creator Gilbert Baker remotely suggested racial diversity in any form. In Baker's imagining, the original eight colors stood for sex (pink), life (red), healing (orange), sun (yellow), nature (green), art (turquoise), harmony (indigo), and spirit (violet). Revisionist history aside, the fact that the flag was never meant to be a symbol of racial diversity would not be surprising to many gay men and women of color, particularly given the history of the gay rights movement that is publicly promoted or the social organization of contemporary gay life. In fact, when activist in Philadelphia added a brown and black stripe to the original flag in 2017, the backlash from (mostly) gay white men was notable. The colors, added following a number of racist incidents at some of Philadelphia's largest "gay" businesses, was originally intended to "make big strides toward a truly inclusive community," according to the website "More Color, More Pride." Instead, many gay white men were nearly outraged at what they saw as a sacrilege despite the dozens of variations to the flag that already existed that were met with no such resistance. More importantly, their argument that "the" flag represents "all" gay people was never scrutinized that businesses and organizations that routinely fly the flag were, in fact, not for "all" people. As Allen has noted in his highly influential essay, "How Gay Stays White and What Kind of White It Stays," contemporary gay life, in all of its forms, is extremely white (Bérubé 2001).

In many ways, the whitening of, and whiteness within, the gay "community" can be traced to a gay movement that attempts to position gays and lesbians, and by extension the gay and lesbian community, as being similar to heterosexuals and having values and norms parallel to those found in the mainstream culture by pushing for inclusion in mainstream organizations and social institutions. While the push for marriage equality and the right to serve in the military clearly benefits gays and lesbians of color, the singular focus on these two issues by "national" gay rights organizations such as the Human Rights Campaign spotlights gay white men and white lesbians and helps to maintain the illusion of a gay community that is monolithically white. As Allan Bérubé noted, the fight for social justice by gay men which focused on achieving visibility and individual equality within existing social and political institutions led to the emergence of "an exclusively gay rights agenda isolated from supposedly non-gay issues, such as homelessness, unemployment, welfare, universal health care, union organizing, affirmative action, and abortion rights" (Bérubé 2002, 235). Thus, gay acceptance came at the cost of presenting the "gay community" as upscale, mostly male, and a mostly white consumer market. As Bérubé notes, "such a strategy derives its power from an unexamined investment in whiteness and middle-class identification" (Bérubé 2002, 235). Achieving acceptability for the "gay community" meant "reinforcing a racialized class divide." In essence, gays became heteronormalized and racialized as white and middle class. As whiteness has become the currency by which the gay movement attempts to win mainstream approval, whiteness, and the desire for whiteness, has come to be the central organizing principal of gay social life. Given the centrality of whiteness in the gay community, gay white men not only come to occupy a higher social status than gay men of color, the experiences and expectations of gay white men are accepted as the "gay norm" by which all other gay experiences are measured and judged. For gay men of color, this measuring stick leaves them short of being a "good gay" (Ward 2008). In fact, in many situations, people of color are simply and blatantly unwelcome and even criminalized (Rosenberg 2016).

Also, as David Bell and Jon Binnie have noted, "debates about sexual citizenship were, and continue to be, marked by questions of geography" (Bell and Binnie 2006, 869). In fact, a key debate has been about how spaces, both private and public, get defined as "sexual," and how those definitions influence the ability of sexual citizens to make citizenship claims. When certain segments of a population are excluded from public spaces, their ability to negotiate the rights to citizenship are seriously hampered. As Joseph Bristow noted, there are only a limited number of spaces where it is possible to be gay (Bristow 1989). Limited as they may be, it is clear that those spaces where one can engage with the physical environment and others found within that environment as gay men and lesbian women have important connotations for who gets to be a "good gay." Questions of who gets to enter those spaces, who is prevented from entering those spaces, and which spaces where sexuality is enacted is counted as "being gay," can help us understand who gets to be gay.

Examining the positioning of gay men and women of color, we find they are excluded from many of those already limited geographic spaces that are labeled gay. For example, Han discussed the ways that gay men of color are excluded from mainstream gay bars through various tactics by bar owners specifically in order to maintain a white clientele (Han 2007). From Boston to San Francisco, gay men of color are actively discouraged from entering "gay identified" spaces and patronizing spaces marked more by their race than their sexuality. A gay bar frequented by white men is a "gay bar," but one frequented by black men is a "black gay bar." Much like residential neighborhoods that "turn" once they reach a certain percentage of nonwhite residents, gay social spaces also turn with white clients quickly abandoning clubs and bars that come to be seen as being too popular with blacks, Latinos, or Asians. Not only are these spaces abandoned by gay white men, they come to be marked as racialized spaces rather than gay spaces. Rather than come to be known by the sexuality of their clientele, they come to be known by the race of their clientele instead. Even when gay spaces are racially integrated, that integration is at best surface level (Orne 2017).

In a similar vein, racialized spaces are not considered gay spaces by gay commentators or by gay white men. For example, in an op-ed that appeared in Slate, Lance Richardson noted the racial tone-deafness of *The Advocate*, the larger of the two national gay publications. In his op-ed, Richardson takes issue with a column that appeared in *The Advocate* about the "thriving" gay nightlife evidenced by such clubs like VIVA which appeared in the same week as a *New York Daily News* article announcing the closing of No Parking, a bar frequented almost exclusively by gay black and Latino men, to make room for a Planet Fitness, a national chain of fitness centers that offers a gym with "no judgments" (Richardson 2014). As the author notes, the drive to declare that gay nightlife is alive and well makes no mention of who frequents these bars and how the demise of smaller venues that cater to men and women of color does, in fact, mean the end of gay nightlife for many men of color. Yet these racialized spaces, because they are racialized rather than (homo)sexualized is not a loss worth mourning in the pages of *The Advocate*. Because gay nightlife is alive and well for gay white men, it is simply alive and well.

Media images, too, help construct the borders of belonging. Not surprisingly, the resistance to visible exclusion and confrontation of negative media images has long been an important component of the gay rights movement. A part of the strategy of gaining visibility has been efforts to have positive gay representations in various media products as well as promoting gay-owned media outlets. Yet ensuring a fair racial representation of the gay community has clearly not been a strategy deployed by national gay and lesbian media advocates. In fact, invisibility in gay media is part and parcel of the exclusion of gay men and women from gay spaces as evidenced by the trending hashtag #GayMediaSoWhite in response to the whiteness of "gay" media.

As if invisibility is not enough, gay media advocates sometimes use non-white gays and lesbians specifically for the purpose of normalizing gay white citizens. This is done in a number of ways. For example, gay Asian men are often used to present gay white men as being "just like" straight men by using gay Asian men as the feminized "other" to the masculine gay white man (Han 2008). The use of black men in gay publications is no less nefarious. While black men are virtually invisible in gay publications, they are nonetheless prominently displayed in countless ads for HIV medications. Even the most perfunctory glimpse through the pages of a gay magazine makes it clear that the majority of the few black faces that one sees are intimately tied to a "diseased" body. Using black bodies to embody HIV/AIDS allows gay white men to escape the stigma of the "gay plague," and embody a normative, healthy body.

The language of "coming out," also constructs a "good gay." The tendency to make white gay experiences the only legitimate gay experience is evident in one of the few stories to feature gay men of color in *The Advocate*, discussed in this volume by Han and Rutledge. Published online on May 17, 2013, the article titled "Rising Above the Down Low" by Sunnivie Brydum traces the "coming out" process of two black men that, unsurprisingly, sensationalizes the down-low "phenomenon" popular in media discourse and blames black culture as the source of the phenomenon. Rather than make any attempt to discuss the social context of a "down low" which has been discussed by gay scholars and activist of color as both an "activity" and an "identity," or to explore the role that racism plays in the down low phenomenon and the adaptation of a down low identity, the article celebrates the two men for finally coming out of the closet and living an "openly" gay life endorsed by mainstream gay social norms (Brydum 2013). As if the endorsement of mainstream gay social norms was not enough, any attempt to create a gay existence or subjectivity outside of that norm, such as through developing a down low identity, is demonized as not being true to one's "authentic" self and being "trapped" by society. So in Brydum's reckoning, the only way to be a "good gay" is to be a white gay, or at least to be gay in the white way.

Taken together, these multiple tendencies in the gay "community" centers not only gay white men but also the gay white experience. If we imagine the sexual citizen as an individual who has the right to make claims on membership in a sexually identified group, and that sexually identified groups are the basis of citizenship rights granted to the individual through group membership, we can argue that to be denied membership in a sexual group is equatable to the denial of the ability to make claims of being a citizen.

The chapters in this book are an attempt to re-center what it means to be gay by moving the discussion away from gay white men and collectively challenging what it means to be a gay citizen. Through their work, the authors have examined the experiences of gay men of color, but more importantly, have presented these experiences as central gay experiences, not marginal ones. In this way, the authors have centered race in sexuality scholarship and centered sexuality in race scholarship. Yet clearly, this volume is far from the only scholarly collection to attempt such feats. Rather it should be viewed as another step in a growing and lively turn in both race and sexuality scholarship. The collection, of course, does not address all the myriad of ways that gay men of color experience their lives. So hopefully, it is just another step in that direction rather than the last step.

REFERENCES

Bell, David and Jon Binnie. 2006. "Geographies of Sexual Citizenship." *Political Geography* 25: 869–73.

Bérubé, Allan. 2001. "How Gay Stays White and What Kind of White it Stays." In *Making and Unmaking of Whiteness*: 234–65. Durham, NC: Duke University Press.

Bristow, Joseph. 1989. "Being Gay: Politics, Identity, Pleasure." *New Formations* 9: 61–81.

Brydum, Sunnivie. 2013. "Rising Above the Down Low." *The Advocate*. Last edited May 17, 2013. https://www.advocate.com/arts-entertainment/television/2013/05/17/two-stories-rising-above-down-low.

Han, C. Winter. 2007. "They Don't Want to Cruise Your Type: Gay Men of Color and the Racial Politics of Exclusion." *Social Identities* 13: 51–67.

———. 2008. "A Qualitative Exploration of the Relationship Between Racism and Unsafe Sex Among Asian Pacific Islander Gay Men." *Archives of Sexual Behavior* 37: 827–37.

Orne, Jason. 2017. *Boystown: Sex and Community in Chicago*. Chicago: University of Chicago Press.

Rosenberg, Rae. 2017. "The Whiteness of Gay Urban Belonging: Criminalizing LGBTQ Youth of Color in Queer Spaces of Care." *Urban Geography* 38: 137–48.

Ward, Jane. 2008. "White Normativity: The Cultural Dimensions of Whiteness in a Racially Diverse LGBT Organization." *Sociological Perspectives* 51: 563–86.

Index

Note: *Italic* page numbers refer to figures and tables and page numbers followed by "n" denote endnotes.

Douchebags of Grindr website, 41
down low (DL), 72n1
Dylan King-Lemons case, 160–62

early-stage gentrification, 92
educative lessons, about intersecting
identities, 69–71
educators: educative lessons
about intersecting identities,
69–71; implications for, 68–71;
supporting Black gay males,
69
Effex, 107, 108, 114
Eguchi, Shinsuke, xii
Elia, John P., 110
emotion-focused coping, 140–42
emotion-focused strategies, 140
enclaves, 88–90
Eng, David L., 110
ethnic, ix
"ethnically straight," 86–88
ethnic groups, 92
Evans, Nancy J., 75
exclusion, gay racism, 36–39
"Exotic Becomes Erotic" (EBE) theory
of sexuality, 6, 20, 22
exoticism, 4, 6, 20
experiential evolution, 49, 58, 62, 63,
65, 68

face-to-face interviews, 12
Fausto-Sterling, Anne, 180
Ferguson, Roderick, 151
fetishism, 21
formal interviews, 90
Frazier, Edward Franklin, 154
Freeman, Linton, 2
Fryer, Roland G., 91

Garland, Judy, 183
gay African American men, 31
gay Asian/American male identities,
108–9, 119
gay black man, 33, 34
Gay Black men, 156
gayborhoods, 88–90

gay community, 21, 33, 34, 36, 37,
45, 46, 183, 184; Black community
versus, 88; sexual rejection in, 39–40
gay dating sites, rampant racism on,
41–42
"gay Disneyland," 94, 97, 99–101
gay enclaves, 92, 94, 183
The Gay Lesbian Straight Education
Network's (GLSEN) 2015 Climate
Survey, 51–52
gay lifestyle, 93
gay male subculture, 4–5, *5*
#GayMediaSoWhite, 186
gay men, 31, 95, 96, 98; in Boystown,
assimilation of, 103; of color use
racism, 32; fight for social justice
by, 36; intersectionality of, 108,
110, 117; sexual assimilation of,
99; sexual attitudes of, 102; sexual
networks of, 89; U.S. American
nationalist and patriotic agents, 118
gay men of color, ix–xi, 31–34, 36–38,
42–46, 86, 101, 173, 174, 185, 187
gay men's community, anti-black
racism and homophobia of, 131–32
gay nightclub, 107
gay racism, 33–36, 38; invisibility and
exclusion, 36–39; objectification,
43–45; sexual rejection, 39–43
gay sexual cultures, Asian/American in,
116
gay sexual networks, 91
Gaysian American, 109, 114–17, 119,
120
gay slang terms, for racial preferences,
4, *5*
gay website, 34
gay white men, 31, 32, 40; blatant
racism of, 35
gender: for Black male, 153–55; sex and
sexuality, 174–77, *176*
gendered attractions, for bisexuals and
pansexuals, 23
gendered sexual orientation, 22, 24;
narratives of, 5–6; *vs.* racial, 13–19
gender inequalities, 2

The Gender Unicorn, 175, *176*
gentrification, *93*, 88, 89, 91–94;
    intertwined character, assimilation,
    94–96; sexual field restructuring,
    96–101
Giwa, Sulaimon, xii
GLBTQ groups, 35
"good gay," 185
Grindr, 90
Groenweghe, Philip, 164, 165
Guardia, Juan R., 75

Han, C. Winter, xi, 44, 108, 109, 115,
    116
Handler, Chelsea, viii
Harding, 54
Hart, Kevin, viii, ix, xiii
Hatch, J. Amos, 54
health, poverty on, 133–35
heteronormativity, 71, 118
heterosexism, xi; racism and, 69
heterosexuality, 53, 156
heterosexual male, viii
Hirschfeld, Magnus, 33
HIV/AIDS, 141
HIV criminalization laws, 166
HIV Law and Policy Center, 149, 167
Holt, Martin, 40
homonormativity, 87
homophobia, 135–36, 140, 142, 153; in
    Black community, 139; of gay men's
    community, 131–32; postmigration
    experiences of, 137
homosexuality, 87, 88, 92, 150, 154
hooks, bell, 45
hopefulness, 109, 119
Horowitz, Janna L., 7, 8, 10
Huang, Yu-ping, 72n2
Human Rights Campaign, 184

identity, Black gay youth and, 50–52
immigrant-serving agencies, 128
immigration, 140; intersectional
    oppressions of, 133–35; theme of,
    128

individual interviews, 130; data analysis
    of, 130
inequalities, racial and gender, 2
informal interviews, 90
in-group tension, 140; among Black
    cisgender gay men, 132–33
institutionalized racial system, 53
integrative narrative approach, 7
interracial relationships, 2–4
intersectionality, 85, 90; of gay and
    Asian/American, 108, 110, 117;
    Man-Not thesis *versus,* 155–57;
    theoretical framework of, 128–29
intersectional knot, 85, 86, 88, 90
intertwined character, assimilation,
    94–96
invisibility, gay racism, 36–39
Irvine, Jacqueline, 69

Jackson, Jesse, 183
Jackson, Peter, 39
Johnson, E. Patrick, 53, 119
Johnson, Michael, xiii, 149–50; case of,
    157–59; and need for Black Male
    Studies, 165–67
"jungle fever," 24n1

Kaiser, Cheryl R., 32
Kaplan, Adam M., 2
Kappa Sigma fraternity, 80
Kaufman, Gayle, 4, 40
Kim, Claire Jean, 116
Klu Klux Klan, 154

late-stage gentrification, 92, 94, 97
Latino/a fraternities and sororities, 75–
    76, 81–83; analysis, 78; challenges,
    80–81; familia finding, 78–79;
    methodology and participants,
    77–78; queer familia finding, 79–80;
    theoretical framework, 76–77
Laumann, Edward O., 89
Leong, Russell, x
lesbian, gay, and bisexual (LGB)
    community, 124, 126–30, 132

About the Contributors

Michael D. Bartone, PhD, is assistant professor of elementary education in the Department of Literacy, Elementary, and Early Childhood Education at Central Connecticut State University. He focuses on the intersections of race and sexuality and youth come to know and understand these intersecting identities through schooling experience. Further, he examines what teachers know about these intersecting identities and how their instruction includes/excludes these identities.

Ferzana Chaze, PhD, is professor at the Faculty of Applied Health and Community Studies at Sheridan College. Her research interests include issues related to diversity and inclusion of marginalized populations. Her scholarship focuses on immigrants and their settlement into Canadian society.

Jason Crockett joined the Department of Anthropology and Sociology at Kutztown University in the fall of 2010 after completing his PhD at the University of Arizona and received tenure in the fall of 2015. His teaching and research interests are in areas of sexualities and gender, social movements, communities, culture and religion, knowledge/science, methods, and race/ethnicity. His research examines the phenomenon of racial sexual orientation and sexual and dating preferences based on race.

Manuel Del Real has been a member of a Latino fraternity for eleven years and an active alumnus serving as an advisor for a local chapter and chairmen of the Rocky Mountain Alumni Network. He is the assistant director for Student Life at Front Range Community College and an Adjunct Faculty in the Ethnic Studies Department at Colorado State University. His dissertation was an exploratory case study of five chapters of a Latino fraternity in the

Midwest region of the United States, using critical race theory to illustrate how they contribute to civic engagement.

Shinsuke Eguchi is associate professor of intercultural communication in the Department of Communication & Journalism at the University of New Mexico. Their research interests focus on global and transcultural studies, queer of color critique, race, gender and intersectionality, Asian/Pacific/American studies, and performance studies. Their work has appeared for publication in various outlets such as *Communication Theory*, *Communication, Culture, & Critique*, *Critical Studies in Media Communication*, *Text and Performance Quarterly*, *Journal of International and Intercultural Communication*, *Journal of Communication Inquiry*, and *Popular Communication*.

Sulaimon Giwa is assistant professor of social work at Memorial University of Newfoundland, with over a decade of experience in research, policy, and direct practice experience at the community and federal level, in youth health promotions, community, and organizational practice in diverse communities, forensic social work, and policing. His research examines LGBTQ+ and racialized groups experiences; migration and resettlement; social justice and human rights; critical social work pedagogy; antiracism and anti-Black racism; and the criminal justice system. His applied research program and professional activities centralize critical race transformative pedagogies and theories as frameworks and analytic tools for social justice and equity.

C. Winter Han is associate professor of sociology at Middlebury College. Prior to becoming an academic, he was an award-winning journalist and served as the editor-in-chief of the *International Examiner,* the oldest continuously publishing pan-Asian Pacific American newspaper in the United States. He is the author of *Geisha of a Different Kind: Race and Sexuality in Gaysian America*, published by New York University Press.

Born in Ghana and raised in Canada, **Kofi Norsah** worked as a board-certified high-school teacher before graduating with a master's degree in social work from McGill University in 2016. He is an avid runner, having completed seven full marathons and ten half-marathons over the course of a decade, and an ardent devotee and aspiring critic of the visual and performing arts. Norsah currently resides in Albany, New York State, where he works for a non-profit human service agency.

Jason Orne, PhD, is assistant professor in the Department of Sociology. He received his PhD from the University of Wisconsin-Madison. He teaches courses related to urban sociology, as well as the department's introductory course. His book *Boystown: Sex and Community in Chicago* examines the importance of sex to queer male communities and the transformation of gay enclave neighborhoods, "gayborhoods."

Scott E. Rutledge is associate dean for Faculty Affairs in the College of Public Health and associate professor in its School of Social Work at Temple University. His research focuses on the HIV/AIDS prevention and care continuum, particularly for African American men and transgender persons, as well as stigma in health services.

Jesús Gregorio Smith is a tenure track, assistant professor of ethnic studies at Lawrence University and an Associated Colleges of the Midwest (ACM) Andrew W. Mellon Fellow. His expertise centers on the intersections of race, gender, and sexuality online and how they contribute to health behaviors such as condom use and sexual-risk activity. He has published in the areas of race and pornography, Latino LGBT issues, sex in the digital age, and race and racism online.

Mario I. Suárez (he/him/his) is assistant professor in the School of Teacher Education and Leadership in the Emma Eccles Jones College of Education and Human Services at Utah State University. He was a high-school mathematics teacher for eight years in Austin, Texas, before pursuing his doctoral work. His physical transition from female to male as a teacher has been documented by nprEdand Univision Austin. His research interests sit at the intersection of queer issues, teacher education, STEM education, and critical quantitative research methods.

\26
)B/1088